Liberal Leadership

Great Powers and Their Challengers
in Peace and War

Mark R. Brawley

Cornell University Press | *Ithaca and London*

First published 1993 by Cornell University Press.

International Standard Book Number 0-8014-2808-4
Library of Congress Catalog Card Number 93-4844
Printed in the United States of America
Librarians: Library of Congress cataloging information
appears on the last page of the book.

⊗ The paper in this book meets the minimum requirements
of the American National Standard for Information Sciences—
Permanence of Paper for Printed Library Materials, ANSI Z39.48-1984.

For my family

Contents

Acknowledgments

My interest in international relations, and international political economy in particular, was sparked at the University of California by the reading of Robert Gilpin's *U.S. Power and the Multinational Corporation.* As I read more of the literature, and became more familiar with the history, I saw many possible points of comparison in the relations between states and societies. I was fortunate to take courses with Vinod Aggarwal, John Zysman, and Robin Gaster, in which I familiarized myself with theories of hegemony.

As I began to discern patterns in history, I also felt uncomfortable with most of the models constructed to identify and explain them. Existing models of hegemony or long cycles made me uneasy, for they tended to smooth over the history to fit the model. When I scanned world history over the past four centuries, I saw a vast, rich set of international relations, full of details that were being brushed aside or forgotten in a quest to pull together similarities between periods. The most appropriate approach, I came to believe, is to create a deductive model that incorporates more of the specifics—one that does not shy away from evidence but instead uses as much as possible, to explain similarities between periods and also to explain why some periods are unique.

This sort of work is possible only in reaction to the works of other scholars. Portions of this book seem critical of earlier models and theories, but in fact I follow in the steps of earlier scholars, trying to refine their concepts and improve their arguments. My criticisms may at times be sharp, but I appreciate how these earlier works shaped my own ideas and interests.

I learned much about hegemony, and international political economy more generally, at UCLA. I specifically thank Arthur Stein and David Lake for all their assistance. Both made time to read drafts promptly and gave me positive criticism and support. Jeffry Frieden, Ronald Rogowski, and Richard Rosecrance also helped me formulate my ideas and make sense of the overall project. Every time I step into a classroom, I realize just how much I learned from these teachers; I hope my own teaching reaches the standards they set. Thanks, too, to my classmates in the international political economy (IPE) and strategy workshops at UCLA, for all their help and advice. I only hope they will be willing to suffer through the first rough versions of my next project. I thank David Dollar, Sule Osler, and Kenneth Sokoloff of the UCLA Department of Economics for teaching me about their discipline. I also owe thanks to people at McGill University who read part or all of the manuscript and gave me comments, especially Ruth Abbey, Michael Lusztig, Mary McKinnon, and Hudson Meadwell. My students in the honors international relations seminar in the winter of 1991 also deserve a note of thanks for helpful comments on the manuscript.

People at Cornell University Press have been helpful, especially Roger Haydon, who gave me critical editorial advice from which I have benefited greatly. Kal Holsti, Hilton Root, and a third reviewer also made suggestions concerning concepts, approaches, and historical material.

Last but not least, I thank Lawrence Broz, who kept me sane through graduate school, and my family, whose love and support are always behind me. Their strength made the effort much easier.

MARK R. BRAWLEY

Montreal, Quebec

ONE

Leadership of Liberal Subsystems:
A Model

Over the past four centuries, the most powerful nation-states have fought global wars four times. These conflicts have occurred at approximately 80- to 100-year intervals. In the periods between the major wars, well-ordered liberal economic subsystems have emerged, only to collapse as a major war approaches. Realists have explained this dramatic fluctuation between international order and the chaos of war as the result of the concentration and diffusion of power in the international system. Liberal international subsystems emerge from periods of widespread warfare because the victor of global war can use its power to organize and then maintain a stable international community. Over time, as the organizer or leader weakens relative to other nation-states, cohesion and order in the subsystem decline. With this decline, international trade is disrupted, military and political rivalries increase, and eventually another major war erupts.

With the erosion of America's premier position in the postwar international system over the past two decades, the policy implications are obvious. Yet proper responses to the current situation are difficult to ascertain because of weaknesses or imprecision in existing models that seek to explain this pattern using the concept of hegemonic leadership. Theorists of hegemonic leadership argue that stability in the international political economy requires the existence of a single dominant actor capable of creating and maintaining the international regimes or relationships that characterize the system and also willing to use its power to attain those ends.

Why hegemonic powers accept the costs of leadership, why they construct economic subsystems around liberal principles, as well as why some but not all other states oppose hegemonic leaders are but a few of the central questions existing models have difficulty explaining. The model I construct here is designed to resolve some of these theoretical puzzles within the cycles of hegemony. After outlining the model in this chapter, I apply it to various historical cases (Chapters 2–5) to demonstrate its ability to interpret these periods with convincing accuracy and precision. In the final chapter, after evaluating the model's performance, I speculate on the future of the international system and emphasize some wider theoretical implications of the argument.

Puzzling Aspects of Cyclical International Leadership

Although arguments about international cycles of dominance come in several different styles (the most prominent being hegemonic stability theory, long cycle theory, and core-periphery models), each explains the creation of liberal international subsystems as the result of the actions of a particular state. International order emerges only when a powerful state is willing to support or enforce order. These approaches also place importance on the same set of examples of international subsystems organized around liberal economic principles, most notably those bringing markets together, guaranteeing the right to private property, and giving market forces free play. To capture the sense of this state's organizing activities, I use the term *liberal leadership* (or occasionally *liberal hegemony*) rather than simply *hegemony*. These more specific terms encompass the two key facets of this state's role: not only does the state act as a leader creating and then maintaining an international political economic subsystem, but this subsystem can be described as having a liberal character.[1] Using the term *hegemony* without a modifying adjective is inadequate, since it implies that these states are capable of dictating international rules all other states must follow, a situation of which we have no evidence; instead, these states are capable of using their power to coerce or cajole some (but certainly not all) other states into participating in an international political economic subsystem with liberal rules. In peacetime, these states take the lead in providing the political underpinnings necessary for liberal international economic relations to function smoothly; during major wars, they lead the alliance defending the open economic subsystem. The con-

---

1. I have deliberately separated out the issue of power in this definition; I am more interested in understanding why different states wield their international power to establish different sorts of international subsystems. Power is merely a means to an end, and these ends of the state are determined by other factors, not power. One might also object to using the term *liberal*, since it has specific historical connotations.

cept of leadership is therefore more appropriate for exploring the sorts of political and economic interactions we are interested in.

A desire to explain the occurrence of liberal international economic systems sparked the study of hegemony more broadly.[2] By focusing on the stabilizing role the United States played after World War II but failed to play in the interwar period, early hegemonic stability theorists linked the international economy's characteristics to the actions of a leading state. Yet an obvious question is why a state would accept the burdens of leadership. Clearly the task is to show that the leader gains from having a liberal trading system; otherwise, it would not provide leadership, or would construct a subsystem organized on other principles.[3]

Not only must the logic behind a state's liberal leadership be explicated, but that logic must be confirmed by evidence from the domestic and international levels concerning the process in which state policies are formed and executed. As Scott James and David Lake pose the question, "what do hegemonic leaders do when they are being hegemonic?"[4] Although it is possible to correlate concentration of power in the international system with the emergence of liberal subsystems, to be convincing the argument must show how that power is used to create the open economic subsystem.[5] To satisfy a definition of leadership, we would also expect the liberal leader to act in ways clearly different from other states in the subsystem.

Creating a *dynamic* explanation of liberal hegemony presents further problems. For one thing, the liberal rules the leading state creates seem to diffuse economic power out of that country and into others, undermining the leader's own position.[6] A fuller explanation should provide not only testable

2. Charles Kindleberger's arguments concerning America's part in the breakdown and closure of the international economy during the interwar period are most often cited; see *The World in Depression, 1929–1939* (Berkeley: University of California Press, 1973).

3. Two early explanations of the hegemon's willingness to organize a free trade system argued that the hegemon receives benefits disproportionately higher than other states in the system because of its relative size and economic efficiency; see Stephen D. Krasner, "State Power and the Structure of International Trade," *World Politics* 28 (April 1976): 317–347, and Robert Gilpin, *U.S. Power and the Multinational Corporation: The Political Economy of Foreign Direct Investment* (New York: Basic Books, 1975). These arguments have been criticized on theoretical and historical grounds, most saliently by John A. C. Conybeare in "Public Goods, Prisoners' Dilemmas, and the International Political Economy," *International Studies Quarterly* 28 (1984): 11, and Timothy McKeown in "Hegemonic Stability Theory and Nineteenth-Century Tariff Levels in Europe," *International Organization* 37 (Winter 1983): 88.

4. Scott James and David Lake, "The Second Face of Hegemony: Britain's Repeal of the Corn Laws and the American Walker Tariff of 1846," *International Organization* 43 (Winter 1989): 3.

5. McKeown, "Hegemonic Stability Theory," p. 79.

6. Robert O. Keohane, "Theory of World Politics: Structural Realism and Beyond," in *Political*

propositions of how the liberal leader's interests change over time but also propositions of how other countries' interests change, too, in order to explain acceptance of or resistance to the liberal hegemon's leadership.[7] This dynamic capability must be compatible with the other tasks of explaining the liberal hegemon's interest in trade liberalization, the domestic and international processes of liberal leadership, and the liberal hegemon's relative decline.

Attempts to construct such a dynamic explanation of leadership have created an image of hegemonic cycles. As was noted earlier, these cycles are punctuated by major wars. This connection to major wars also marks a convergence between hegemonic stability theories and work on long cycles and world-systems.[8] Scholars such as Robert Gilpin, George Modelski, A. F. K. Organski, and Immanuel Wallerstein, drawing on varied traditions, argue that hegemonic decline causes major war.[9] Unfortunately, few authors distinguish economic from political or military decline. Treating the possibility of political decline apart from economic decline calls for a rereading of the evidence these authors bring to bear on the relationship between economic decline and major war.[10] In addition, the process linking hegemonic decline to major war has never been satisfactorily presented.

Part of the difficulty in explaining how hegemonic decline might lead to major war involves the inability to single out which countries will oppose the hegemon. Gilpin states that differential growth of power between countries is the driving force behind major wars; but, if this is so, why do only some countries rising in power challenge the hegemon?[11] The causal relationship between

---

Science: The State of the Discipline, ed. Ada W. Finifter (Washington, D.C.: APSA, 1983), p. 517. Earlier, Gilpin had argued against further unquestioned American support for a liberal international economic system, in the final chapters of *U.S. Power and the Multinational Corporation.*

7. Duncan Snidal, "The Limits of Hegemonic Stability Theory," *International Organization* 39 (Autumn 1985): 584. Some of David Lake's work on hegemony has been to formulate just such a model.

8. Joshua Goldstein, *Long Cycles* (New Haven: Yale University Press, 1988), shows how deep the convergence runs.

9. Ibid., p. 169. This point of view is tested and accepted by Goldstein. His work provides a valuable review of these other authors' works.

10. Such a distinction is required to prevent this question from always producing tautological answers: if decline is only thought of in terms of military power, arms races leading up to major war become a cause of war rather than a symptom closely associated with the impending conflict.

11. Robert Gilpin, "The Theory of Hegemonic War," in *The Origin and Prevention of Major Wars,* ed. Robert I. Rotberg and Theodore K. Rabb (New York: Cambridge University Press, 1989), p. 15. This question is especially pertinent given that several countries are usually rising together, yet some do not challenge; see Richard Rosecrance, *The Rise of the Trading State: Commerce and Conquest in the Modern World* (New York: Basic Books, 1986), p. 51. In making this same distinction, A. F. K. Organski invokes "satisfied" and "dissatisfied" rising powers, in "The Power Transition," in *World Politics* (New York: Knopf, 1968), chap. 14.

hegemony and major war has also been reversed, with the argument that major war creates hegemony.[12] Does this mean that major war is the only source of new leaders? Do all major wars create new *liberal* leaders? It may appear that major war leads to a new cycle of liberal hegemony simply because the challengers always seem to lose. Almost all writers argue that challengers are bound to lose, but little attention is given to explaining why.[13] This raises questions about how major wars are fought and won, another subject often left unexplored or disconnected from other issues.[14]

These cyclical models characterize the evolution of the modern international system as a series of very similar patterns of international relations. Each cycle starts with stability under liberal hegemonic leadership. Hegemonic decline leads to challenge and major war, the challenge by a rising power fails to defeat the declining hegemon, but out of the major war a new leader emerges. Since most observers agree that the United States no longer has the concentration of power it once held, and the overall pattern suggests that another major war will break out, the most pressing question concerns why (and when) major wars occur; a comprehensive argument would answer the other questions posed above, too.

In this chapter, I address the motivations and interests driving certain states to undertake the leadership of liberal subsystems. In doing so, I also provide the logic for other states' reactions to this liberal leadership (including challenge), thereby allowing for the construction of systemwide models. My argument's persuasiveness lies not only in its performance in these tasks but also in its ability to resolve the various puzzles mentioned above. I begin with an examination of the domestic gains and losses from trade, then add domestic political institutions to the picture to clarify domestic actors' preferences concerning trade liberalization and related foreign policies.

The argument is rooted in the combination of broad theoretical conjectures which are generally applicable to the interstate system; if the patterns we are interested in explaining fall over several centuries, the factors behind the ex-

---

12. Goldstein, *Long Cycles*, p. 169.

13. Modelski and Thompson do spend time on this matter, arguing that hegemonic leaders are island or continental naval powers, able to defend themselves against and eventually overpower land-based challengers. Although this may appear to be true of the last two hegemonic powers (the United States and Britain), it could hardly be said of the two prior leaders Modelski and Thompson identify (the Netherlands and Portugal), which were naval powers forced to defend extensive land borders. Nor would this approach deal with Imperial Japan as a challenger.

14. Several explanations are possible: Paul Kennedy, for instance, suggests that wars between major powers are primarily decided by economic means but that strategies and technological innovation may also be significant; see *The Rise and Fall of the Great Powers: Economic Change and Military Conflict from 1500 to 2000* (New York: Random House, 1987), p. 439.

planation must be not only generalizable but salient in each of these historical epochs. Conversely, factors specific to one historical era (and therefore relevant to the understanding of a single period) I relegate to the background; while this method may do some injustice to the historical episodes I describe later, I must follow it in order to establish a model relevant to the present and the future.[15] After elaborating how combinations of institutional structure, economic interests, and international power affect state policies with systemic consequences, I illustrate the model's ability to resolve the puzzles described above.

Trade Liberalization as a Catalyst

Liberal leadership and its challenge are behaviors that hinge on international economic liberalization: the liberal leader desires freer economic relations so strongly that it is willing to bear the high costs of creating and then maintaining a liberal international subsystem, whereas any challenger is rejecting participation in that same subsystem.[16] Other countries may gain from the existence of a liberal subsystem and will choose to participate in it, particularly if the liberal leader is willing to bear most of the associated financial and political obligations. This is the source of the often cited "free rider" problem, a situation in which others participate in the liberal subsystem to garner some of the benefits from freer trade but also do their best to shirk any related costs.

Any country willing to challenge the liberal leader in major war must not be satisfied with participation in the subsystem: it must prefer something else (achieved through major war) over free riding on liberal leadership. The explanation below begins by analyzing countries' interests in participating in liberal international economic systems. Those with the strongest interest in participation have the greatest incentive to become liberal leaders; other countries may also desire participation, though perhaps not as strongly, so that, although they are unlikely to take the initiative to lead such a system, they

15. This also means that the sources of major wars involve other issues tied up with economic and political competition as modeled in this book. For an innovative and systematic discussion of the sources of international war and how they have changed over time, see K. J. Holsti, *Peace and War: Armed Conflicts and International Order, 1648–1989* (New York: Cambridge University Press, 1991).

16. Many hegemonic stability theorists consider freer trade a public good; I clearly do not treat liberalized trade as a public good, for I wish to explain why some countries reject participation in a free trade system.

gladly accept the leadership of another country; some countries are ambivalent toward membership in a liberal subsystem, and others find even free riding less desirable than other alternatives.

We begin with a purely economic investigation into the gains and the losses from liberalizing trade. In one of the earliest analyses of international trade, David Ricardo argued that free trade was mutually beneficial for countries under normal conditions, or at worst neutral in its effects.[17] Ricardo's great contribution was establishing that international trade takes place through comparative rather than absolute advantage. By trading the goods each country has a comparative advantage in producing, the total quantity of goods produced could be raised, allowing total consumption to increase.

Ricardo suggested that free trade is mutually beneficial, and therefore that all countries would be wise to open up trade. Since all countries do not support free trade at all times (and in fact periods when more than a handful of countries simultaneously pursue policies of free trade are short and somewhat rare), the utility of Ricardo's model for our concerns can be questioned. Specifically, the wide variety of trade policies employed by the major powers over the past few centuries clearly shows that within countries there are both supporters and opponents of free trade. To determine when the supporters of free trade dominate foreign economic policy, it is necessary to identify them and the conditions in which they can influence state policy.

By placing Ricardo's ideas into more sophisticated forms, modern trade theory is able to establish the distribution of gains and losses from trade within countries. In particular, the Heckscher-Ohlin model and its variants locate the incentives for international trade in differences in countries' relative endowments of the factors of production. Gains in international trade are possible because countries with different attributes can specialize in complementary areas. According to the Heckscher-Ohlin theorem, with different endowments of the factors of production, identical demand, and the same ratio of inputs in each industry, each country exports those goods made intensively with its more abundant factor of production.[18]

When exporting goods made intensively with the factor a country has most abundantly and importing goods made intensively with the scarce factor, production is reorganized, which alters the relative returns to factors. According to the Stolper-Samuelson theorem, trade causes the scarce factor's relative re-

---

17. See David Ricardo, *The Principles of Political Economy and Taxation* (London: John Murray, 1817).

18. See Jagdish N. Bhagwati and T. N. Srinivasan, *Lectures on International Trade* (Cambridge: MIT Press, 1983), chaps. 5–7.

turns to fall and the abundant factor's relative returns to rise. Wolfgang Stolper and P. A. Samuelson argued that in a country such as the United States in the 1940s, when labor was relatively scarce compared to capital, trade gave consumers the opportunity to purchase labor-intensive goods made in countries where labor was relatively more abundant (and hence cheaper to hire). Since trade has the effect of substituting for flows of the actual factors of production themselves, labor-intensive imports in effect bid down the price of labor-intensive goods, which in turn reduces the demand for labor, and labor's wages fall. Stolper and Samuelson generalize this analysis to argue that sectors that intensively use the abundant factor of production gain, whereas those intensively using the scarce factor lose from trade expansion.[19]

Having recognized that different sectors of the economy have different interests in liberalizing trade, we can now introduce politics. Stolper and Samuelson developed their theorem to explain which sectors oppose free trade. Since trade lowers the relative returns to the scarce factor of production by making the scarce factor appear more plentiful through the importation of goods and services made intensively with this factor, the sectors that use the scarce factor intensively have incentives to restrict such imports through protectionism. Eliminating these imports restores the scarce factor's appearance to the previous level and drives the relative returns back toward those achieved before free trade.

We can conclude that any country willing to participate in a liberal international economic subsystem, let alone lead it, is necessarily a country in which the abundant-factor-intensive sectors strongly influence the formation of for-

---

19. P. A. Samuelson and Wolfgang Stolper, "Protection and Real Wages," *Review of Economic Studies* 9 (1941): 58–73. For a description of the links between the returns to factors and the interests of the sectors that use those factors intensively, see Ronald Rogowski, *Commerce and Coalitions: How Trade Affects Domestic Political Alignments* (Princeton: Princeton University Press, 1989), pp. 19–20. The point is that sectoral models assume that a worker in a capital-intensive industry draws income from the prices commanded by capital-intensive goods. Similarly, the capitalist who owns a factory producing a labor-intensive good is interested in the returns to that labor-intensive good.

One might also challenge the use of the simple two-factor model, and the Stolper-Samuelson version, since more accurate specific-factor models are now available. In fact, though, since I am concerned with developing a model that looks at the long-run and must be able to deal with a variety of cases drawn from several different periods, the simpler version of these models is probably more appropriate than a specific-factors model. Moreover, a true specific-factors model might be even less useful, since it predicts little change over time; theoretically, it would be possible to create a model that would capture the degree of specificity in each set of the factors of production within each sector. To apply such a model across a broad set of cases over several centuries would be impossible because of the lack of accurate data, so I use a more direct, simpler approach.

eign economic policy. Only in countries in which foreign economic policy is controlled by the scarce-factor-intensive sectors is free trade rejected and the country's normal imports reduced via protectionism, and even in these situations the country still has an interest in raising exports (of the abundant-factor-intensive goods). From this information alone, it is not clear why any country would reject participation in a liberal subsystem so strongly as to desire its destruction rather than simply try to exploit the situation by controlling or limiting its participation.

For a country to reject liberal subsystems so strongly as to engage in a war, it must prefer military victory over the possible benefits of exploitation. Either the scarce- or the abundant-factor-intensive sectors of the economy must have preferences above engaging in free trade, if major war is preferred over free riding and partial participation. Since the scarce-factor-intensive sectors' preferences can be served through protection or nonparticipation, they also have no interests in attacking the subsystem. We can explain why countries might want to assault a liberal subsystem politically only by focusing on the abundant-factor-intensive sectors' interests. These sectors normally earn higher returns internationally than domestically; if these sectors are willing to turn their backs on free riding on the liberal leader (policies that enhanced their exports), they must be earning more than normal rates of return domestically. For domestic returns to the abundant-factor-intensive sectors to be higher than international returns, normal market outcomes must be manipulated. Just as returns are open to manipulation through protection from foreign competition, other forms of political interference with markets are possible, which may mitigate these sectors' desire to engage in liberalized trade.

How the Sanctioning of Rents Distorts Trade Preferences

The domestic returns of the abundant-factor-intensive sectors can be higher than international returns only if there is political intervention in the domestic market.[20] Only the granting of rents can push domestic prices significantly above normal rates. Economists have used the term rent to distinguish income gained through actions which do not improve or which in fact reduce productivity. Although rents have been defined in a variety of ways, all definitions center on the notion of economic gain via nonproductive activity; the specific

---

20. Of course, other naturally occurring domestic market distortions are possible; but if such existed, free trade could be pursued as a policy *to end* them. For these distortions to remain when there is the option to trade, the distortions must be supported by state policy.

sort of rents focused on in this book are those monopoly profits deliberately created by government policies.[21] If such policies are established to favor the abundant-factor-intensive sectors, then neither the abundant- nor the scarce-factor-intensive sectors have an interest in pursuing free trade. In this instance only would destruction of the liberal subsystem yield benefits and therefore be preferred over limited participation in liberal trade, since destruction of the subsystem could give the state a larger domain in which to sanction rents.

To see why policies granting rents can become so deeply entrenched that normal market returns are distorted, we should examine the domestic political system. As the sole domestic actor legitimately able to use force, the state must play a central role in sanctioning rents. I use a neoclassical model of the state similar to that developed by Douglass North.[22] The state provides internal order and protection from external threats to other social actors in return for revenues. The state seeks to maximize revenues and attain a level of domestic support high enough to remain in power. This amount of support required to stay in power varies according to domestic political institutions; specifically, decision makers in autocratic states can remain in power with less support than decision makers in states with representative (or republican) institutions.[23] Accordingly, there are weaker constraints on autocratic state decision makers to pursue revenues, for they are able to ignore the interests of some sectors in order to benefit themselves and bestow privileges on other sectors. Decision

21. Much of the work on rents focuses on rent-*seeking*. This literature emphasizes not only the degree of society's loss in the transfer of monopoly profits from consumers to producers but also how the political pursuit for such monopoly profits uses up resources in nonproductive activities. I stress, instead, the distorting impact such political arrangements have on sectoral preferences once they are granted; changes in sectoral preferences lead to changes in trade policy, which in turn affects foreign policy decisions more broadly. For some specific definitions, see the pieces by James A. Buchanan and by Gordon Tullock in *Toward a Theory of the Rent-Seeking Society*, ed. Buchanan, Robert D. Tollison, and Tullock (College Station: Texas A&M University Press, 1980).

22. Douglass North, *Structure and Change in Economic History* (New York: Norton, 1981), pp. 23–24. One of the aims in using this approach is to see the state as acting simultaneously at the domestic and international levels, thereby attempting to cope with the problems that plague purely systemic theories of hegemony. For a discussion of some of those criticisms, see John Vincent Nye, "Revisionist Tariff History and the Theory of Hegemonic Stability," *Politics and Society* 19 (June 1991): 209–232.

23. I define republican states as those in which decision makers are either directly responsible to the electorate or indirectly responsible to elected representatives. It is important for the model to work that all sectors of the economy are represented, but not that all individuals are. Autocratic governments are those in which decision makers are not accountable to the public in regular elections. These definitions are fleshed out in more detail below.

Lake has recently made similar points about the greater ability of the public to place constraints on state activities in republics, in his article "Powerful Pacifists: Democratic States and War," *American Political Science Review* 86 (March 1992): 24–37.

makers in republican states are in constant electoral competition and must therefore build a wider base of domestic support, which more greatly constrains their ability to pursue revenues.

A combination of these statements about the economic sectors and their interests with the argument about state interests and rents produces a broad model of the likely state policies vis-à-vis the international economy. The Stolper-Samuelson theorem gives us the abundant- and scarce-factor-intensive sectors' rankings concerning trade openness and mere protection, but to these must be added preferences on domestic rents. For all sectors (assuming they produce normal goods), the privilege of rents is preferred over other policies.[24] The abundant-factor-intensive sectors rank their policy preferences as domestic rents in their favor first (which obviously entails a high level of protection from foreign competition), open trade second, and mere protection third.[25] The scarce-factor-intensive sectors also rank their preferences as rents in their favor first, with mere protection second and open trade third.[26]

Since republican states are trying to increase revenues within the constraint that they must maintain a high level of political support, they choose to mix free trade in the sectors that intensively use the abundant factor with protec-

24. There are examples of industries that might not prefer rents, such as those that may not make higher profits when prices rise due to demand or supply elasticities; but since sanctioned rents almost always include limits to competition, the producers even of these goods are often able to adjust production to levels with the highest profit. Mancur Olson gives a brief argument as to why rents are preferred over simple profits in *The Rise and Decline of Nations: Economic Growth, Stagflation, and Social Rigidities* (New Haven: Yale University Press, 1982), 42–43. As George Stigler hypothesized in *The Citizen and the State: Essays on Regulation* (Chicago: University of Chicago Press, 1975), p. 118, "every industry or occupation that has enough political power to utilize the state will seek to control entry."

25. I make a distinction here between purely domestic rents and mere protection. Domestic rents drive returns beyond those achieved in the absence of trade, whereas mere protection drives returns back to those achieved without trade. Domestic rents may also show favoritism of one domestic producer over others within the same sector, whereas mere protection only separates the domestic producers as a group from foreign competition.

26. If this argument is portrayed more specifically, trade theory suggests that the world price of the abundant-factor-intensive good (WP_a) is greater than the domestic price of those goods (DP_a), whereas the reverse is true for the prices of the scarce-factor-intensive good. Expressed as rankings, these are $WP_a > DP_a$ and $WP_s < DP_s$. In the case of scarce-factor-intensive goods, monopoly rents sanctioned by the state push prices higher than the domestic price (MP_s), so the new ranking is $WP_s < DP_s < MP_s$. Monopoly rents sanctioned by the state in favor of the abundant-factor-intensive goods push the price up above the domestic level, and perhaps above the international level. The latter is of most interest to us here, for it changes those sectors' interests in trade: $MP_a > WP_a > DP_a$. Where monopoly rents are sanctioned but prices are not pushed above the international level, there are no ramifications on trade policy. Also, trade liberalization is a cheaper, more effective way to raise the returns to the abundant-factor-intensive sectors, so monopoly rents below world prices are unattractive.

tion of the sectors using the scarce factor intensively. This approach allows for gains from trade to be made by some sectors while restraining the negative impact of trade on others. In any other combination of policies, the state is either making the gains from trade unnecessarily difficult to achieve (as when both sectors are protected) or punishing some sectors for the benefit of others (as when total free trade is selected or when domestic rents are sanctioned). By mixing free trade in some sectors with protection of others, the republican state maintains domestic political support and increases the economic tax base for the state's revenues.[27]

In autocracies, the constraint on raising revenues is not to satisfy as many domestic groups as possible but to satisfy some important domestic groups fully, regardless of the impact on other sectors. The autocratic state's disregard for broader interests frees it to increase revenues at many sectors' expense. This makes the sanctioning of rents particularly attractive. The real distinction in policy is whether the state grants rents to the abundant- or to the scarce-factor-intensive sectors.

Rather than assume that the autocratic state selects the sectors it grants rents to based on the abundance or scarcity of the factor of production they use intensively, I assume that autocracies make this choice according to sectors' ability to reach arrangements enforcing the collection of rents in partnership. Instead of choosing between abundant- and scarce-factor-intensive sectors, an

27. On first glance, the argument that distorting rents are not sanctioned as often in republics as in other types of states appears to fly in the face of much of the literature on American politics, in which the United States is often portrayed as rife with rent-seeking. The point I am making is that all economic sectors in republics seek rents, but that the state is unlikely to grant significantly distorting rents for extended periods of time. Unfortunately, cross-country comparisons of levels of rent-seeking, or of the costs associated with the rents actually sanctioned, are few—undoubtedly because of problems associated with measuring these phenomena. For an elaboration of these problems, see Hilton Root, "The Redistributive Role of Government: Economic Regulation in Old Regime France and England," *Comparative Studies in Society and History* 33 (April 1991): 338–369.

Actual levels of rent-seeking may be lower when compared to autocracies for several reasons: as Robert Ekelund and Robert Tollison argue in *Mercantilism as a Rent-Seeking Society* (College Station: Texas A&M Press, 1981), democratic settings create diffuse political authority, which makes lobbying uncertain; authority that is not centralized is also less able to formulate and enforce rent-seeking; democratic legislatures have practices (such as logrolling) that mask voting positions in such a way that uncertainties in monitoring the results of lobbying are produced; and finally, in democracies countervailing pressures build to eliminate successful rent-seeking. This last point is significant and has been borne out by several later studies, most notably by Helen Milner in *Resisting Protectionism: Global Industries and the Politics of International Trade* (Princeton: Princeton University Press, 1988). As Vinod K. Aggarwal, Robert O. Keohane, and David B. Yoffie describe political backlash against rent-seeking in the United States, in "The Dynamics of Negotiated Protectionism," *American Political Science Review* 81 (June 1987): 364, "protectionism's economic failures are often its political successes and vice versa."

autocratic state chooses between capital-intensive and labor-intensive sectors. If the state wishes to increase its revenues by granting rents to economic sectors (collect the more revenues at the lesser cost), partnerships with capital-intensive sectors are more attractive than arrangements with labor-intensive sectors. Rents are easier and cheaper to monitor and enforce when the members of the arrangement are fewer in number. Since capital tends to be concentrated in the hands of fewer actors than does labor regardless of capital's relative abundance or scarcity, the argument here assumes that sanctions delivering rents to the capital-intensive sectors are easier to create, monitor, and maintain than similar arrangements with labor.[28]

Conjoining the economic and political arguments produces four combinations of variables, with each combination expected to pursue different policy mixes. Republics have relatively open domestic markets and greater interests in participating in liberal trading subsystems: capital-abundant republics follow policies of free trade in capital-intensive goods and services while protecting the domestic market for labor-intensive goods and services; labor-abundant republics follow policies of free trade in labor-intensive goods and services while protecting the domestic market for capital-intensive goods and services. Autocracies promote domestic rents in favor of capital-intensive sectors: capital-abundant autocracies follow policies giving rents to the capital-intensive sectors while protecting the domestic market for goods and services produced by the labor-intensive sectors; labor-abundant autocracies follow similar policies, with rents given to the capital-intensive sectors but more open trade in labor-intensive sectors.

Identifying the liberal leaders and their enemies requires a further specification of interests. It is possible to introduce further gradations of the interests among states that desire trade liberalization in some sectors by examining the impact of the expansion of trade. Although the model I introduce here suggests that countries' sectors that use the abundant factor intensively have an interest in expanding trade if the sanctioning of rents is not an option, and the Heckscher-Ohlin model does not draw any distinction between labor-intensive and capital-intensive sectors, both are missing a significant form of reward to the capital-intensive sectors when trade levels rise. The Heckscher-Ohlin model and its variants measure the gains to sectors based on the *content*

28. This position is consistent with the literature on collective action and rent-seeking, specifically as explored in Olson, *Rise and Decline of Nations.* Although it is possible for labor to be highly concentrated in organizations, situations in which labor is *more* concentrated than capital are few—and not significant for the cases developed in the later chapters. Perhaps the autocratic state in major powers has a particular affinity with the capital-intensive sectors because of its need to compete internationally.

Expected mix of trade policies

	Policy	
Political-economic type	Capital-intensive sector	Labor-intensive sector
Republic		
Capital-abundant	free trade	protection
Labor-abundant	protection	free trade
Autocracy		
Capital-abundant	rent	protection
Labor-abundant	rent	free trade

of that trade. This method does not capture gains to capital-intensive services which grow whenever trade expands, regardless of its content. Even if the increased trade consists of labor-intensive goods only, this adds to the demand for capital-intensive services such as transportation, finance, marketing, and insurance. This means that capital-abundant countries interested in exporting capital-intensive goods and services have the greatest incentives not only to open themselves to trade but to lead liberalization of international trade.[29]

Resolving the Puzzles of Liberal Hegemony

A liberal leader is a country with the strongest interests in establishing a liberal subsystem and also with the capabilities to do so. From the arguments above, we can identify the states with the strongest desire to lead such subsystems; we should perhaps label these *prospective liberal leaders*, though, because only those capital-abundant republics with enough international power are able to carry out leadership functions successfully. The degree of success a prospective liberal leader has depends not only on its own capabilities but also on the dispositions of other states, for the other combinations of interests and capabilities of other states determine the strength of the opportunities and obstacles the prospective liberal leader faces. The manner in which this model can explain why states become prospective liberal leaders and then achieve

29. This argument fits nicely with some of Rogowski's conclusions on capital abundance and hegemony in *Commerce and Coalitions*, p. 169. Also, one might argue that leadership functions (such as countercyclical market interventions) require abundant capital. See also Jeffry Frieden, "Capital Politics: Creditors and the International Political Economy," *Journal of Public Policy* 8 (1988): 265–286.

some measure of success can best be seen by addressing the very puzzles other theories have failed to resolve.[30]

First, why is the liberal leader interested in free trade? A country with republican institutions has a relatively open domestic economy; a capital-abundant republic has economic incentives to export capital. Being abundant in capital makes this country interested in expanding and organizing trade, since these are capital-intensive activities. A capital-rich republic gains economically from the impact of trade as well as from the act of trade expansion. In this way, the prospective liberal leader's relatively greater interest in liberalizing trade is a by-product of its interest in exporting capital-intensive goods and services. By expanding trade levels through liberalization, a prospective liberal leader increases the demand for its abundant factor of production.

This argument is intimately intertwined with a domestic process argument, thereby resolving the second puzzle. In a republic, the state provides order and protection in exchange for revenues under certain political constraints. Being sensitive to domestic political competition and trying to maintain a high level of internal political support, the state is unlikely to accede often to domestic pressures for rents, and when it does it cannot allow the rents to be too distorting. If they fail to get rents sanctioned, the capital-intensive sectors push for their next preferred policy, free trade in capital-goods and services. If the state has international power, it can use this capability to provide order and protection on an international scale in return for revenues, just as it does domestically. In capital-abundant republics, capital-intensive sectors lobby the state for help in finding new employment for capital at higher rates of return; if the state has international power, the state can perform its traditional functions beyond its borders to ensure the success of capital-intensive economic ventures.

By examining these state activities in the service of the capital-intensive sectors, we can reach a deeper understanding of the creation process of international regimes and thereby address a third puzzle. The capital-intensive sectors lobby the state to assist them not only in raising exports of capital-intensive goods but, more important, in increasing exports of capital-intensive services such as the organizing and financing of trade. The state assists these activities by attempting to provide order to international economic rela-

---

30. This point assumes that there are no liberal leaders already in existence. If a liberal leader has already established a liberal subsystem, it is far cheaper to join this subsystem and free ride on the existing leader's efforts rather than to try to be another liberal leader; moreover, in practice two such systems would simply merge.

tions—ensuring legal obligations are honored, trading relations are stable, investments are safeguarded, and so on.

One of the most efficient ways to achieve these goals is to establish rules and norms of international behavior (regimes) which the state then enforces when necessary. These regimes are based on cooperation as well as coercion, since the aims of the prospective liberal leader in exporting capital-intensive goods and services and in expanding trade complement the interests of many other states. The actions of the prospective liberal leader's capital-intensive sectors facilitate the entry of other countries into the liberal subsystem, thereby altering the domestic interests of other states vis-à-vis the subsystem. The prospective liberal leader also wants to protect this subsystem from external forces disrupting it or undermining its principles, since the operation of the subsystem is a major source of the prospective liberal leader's state revenues. Finally, the prospective liberal leader can use its power to coerce or cajole other states to agree to participate in the economically open subsystem.

Since liberal leadership is the expression of the combination of domestic economic interests and the state's international capabilities, we can focus on these to discover the sources of a successful liberal leader's relative decline. Either the economic returns (and therefore interests) or the capabilities to pursue those returns change. The motivation for creating a liberal subsystem results from capital abundance in a republic, so if for any reason either republican institutions or relative capital abundance are lost, the incentives for policies of liberal leadership are also lost. Unfortunately, changes in domestic political institutions are not very well anticipated in this model, but declining capital abundance can occur as a direct result of the *successful* pursuit of leadership in a liberal subsystem.

By extending the open international market, the liberal leader alters its own position over time. The very success in employing capital in new ways and forms outside national boundaries changes the relative returns to capital and labor within the liberal leader's economy. At first, extension of the international market increases returns to capital used outside the country, but specialization and imports combine to boost wages inside the liberal leader's economy. To prevent higher wages from causing unemployment, labor must be shifted out of labor-intensive sectors and into the expanding capital-intensive sectors. This policy can be maintained as long as trade continues to grow, although the costs of sectoral adjustment associated with international economic success can still be high. This argument predicts that the first domestic opposition to policies of liberal leadership should arise from the most labor-intensive sectors of the economy, since these are the first to have their returns eroded by foreign competition and are therefore the first to appeal for protection. There is an erosion of liberal trade principles because the state does not allow domestic rents but is willing to give some protection to sectors as long as this does not lead to retaliations harming other more competitive sectors.

This scenario seems to preclude examples of liberal leaders pursuing relatively free trade across all sectors for more than a short period (when rising trade induces specialization).[31] Since a republic should be pursuing policies of free trade in the goods and services produced intensively with the abundant factor and protecting the domestic market for goods and services made intensively with the scarce factor, an interesting situation occurs when the country's endowments of capital and labor shift from relative abundance in one factor to relative abundance in the other. Pressures should develop to shift from policies protecting the market for goods and services produced by the initially scarce factor to policies protecting the market for goods and services produced intensively with the newly scarce factor. Conversely, pressures should build to shift from free trade in goods and services produced by the sectors intensively using the once abundant factor to free trade in the goods and services made by the sectors intensively using the now abundant factor. When a republic shifts from labor abundance to capital abundance (i.e., into a position from which it should become a liberal leader), instead of quickly passing through free trade in both sets of sectors as part of the transition from protection of once scarce capital-intensive sectors to protection of the now scarce labor-intensive sectors, foreign economic policies may become "stuck." Policies close to true free trade may persist because of the benefits accruing to the capital-intensive sectors from the expansion of the liberal subsystem, which requires the promotion of liberal economic principles.[32]

Relative economic decline begins when other countries accumulate capital (through either domestic processes or importation from the liberal leader itself). As other countries become relatively abundant in capital, their products begin to compete with the liberal leader's. The high returns the liberal leader's capital-intensive sectors once received internationally start to fall, even though the liberal leader's economy may not be losing capital absolutely. As the returns to capital decline, the state leading the liberal subsystem is caught in the dilemma of providing order and protection to an international arrangement with declining returns.[33] The capital-intensive sectors of the liberal leader's

31. It should be noted, though, that even the countries traditionally portrayed as having pursued free trade always kept some sectors protected; in both the U.S. and British cases, agriculture received protection.
32. This point is elaborated well by Frieden in "Capital Politics."
33. Here I parallel the argument made by Arthur A. Stein, "The Hegemon's Dilemma: Great

economy must either continue investing in international activities to chase high returns or focus on the domestic market with its lower returns; the state could shift to imperium or block the outflow of capital, but these tactics would merely hasten the problem of economic uncompetitiveness and also undermine domestic political support for the state.

Meanwhile, other states in the system which represent capital-abundant countries are maximizing their revenues by allowing their constituents to participate in the liberal subsystem without committing themselves to the overhead costs of providing order and protection (the free rider problem). The state acting as the liberal leader is trapped, because dropping its leadership obligations would only further harm the interests of the most viable, competitive parts of its own economy.

It is clear that we need a dynamic argument, because over time the underlying economic interests shift, altering the state's revenues and domestic support. In the initial period of leadership, both capital and labor can be satisfied: capital earns higher returns, and labor can benefit by shifting into the sectors gaining from trade specialization. Over time, increased foreign competition in labor-intensive sectors causes labor to become dissatisfied with liberal leadership, since labor's returns are falling and labor is no longer being absorbed into capital-intensive sectors. Then capital tied to the domestic market becomes dissatisfied, as it too comes under pressure from international competition, until only capital going abroad or servicing the international economy is supporting the state's foreign economic policies. The state comes under political pressure as the costs of providing leadership (which presumably remain constant, if not grow) catch up to the falling level of returns. Even through these processes, though, one would expect domestic returns to capital and labor to equalize across countries in the international system; with perfect factor mobility, the distribution of capital and labor might even equalize (capital-labor ratios would be the same everywhere). The liberal leader only becomes capital-poor in comparison to other countries if those other countries accumulate capital at rates beyond what one might expect from equalization through trade (something difficult to explain through purely international processes, though quite possible if driven by domestic economic processes outside the scope of this model). Even with the economic processes leading toward decline of the liberal hegemon's incentives to lead, this model does not

Britain, the United States, and the International Economic Order," *International Organization* 38 (Spring 1984): 355–386. This point is also an avenue for addressing the need for hegemonic stability theory to specify when the hegemon's marginal losses from regime provision meet its marginal returns from nontrade tax collection; see Conybeare, "Public Goods," p. 12.

predict the complete end of these interests solely because of the outflow of capital or capital-intensive goods and services.

The state's capability to be a liberal leader can decline if other nation-states increase their military power. Any explanation of decline based on changing relative capabilities must explain why other countries convert more material and energy into military power directed against the liberal leader. Using the same two political and economic variables (domestic political institutions and the endowment of the factors of production), I explain states' interests in politically challenging the liberal leaders when they are able to attain the requisite international power. This sort of challenge involves military rivalry, which drives up the liberal leader's costs of providing protection to the liberal subsystem. Political challenge leads to war, which may raise the costs of liberal leadership beyond acceptable limits or even destroy the capital richness of the liberal leader's economy. Either outcome spells the end of liberal leadership. What economic decline alone cannot be expected to do, challenge (whether successful or not) can force on the liberal leader.

Supporters and Challengers of Liberal Leadership

Most other countries have interests in following a liberal leader rather than challenging it.[34] This is especially true of other countries with republican states, which have relatively open domestic markets. By joining the open subsystem, republican states representing capital-scarce countries can obtain greater political support and increase revenues without raising their own costs. Joining the liberal subsystem means lowering the costs of capital and raising the domestic returns to abundant labor. Such a state truly maximizes support if it is able to join the liberal subsystem and still partially protect domestic capital-intensive sectors, for this minimizes any negative effect from higher levels of trade. The labor-abundant republics are most willing not only to follow but to be active *supporters* of the liberal leader, since their economic interests complement the liberal leader's.

Other capital-abundant republics willingly follow the liberal leader's inter-

34. Several writers have noted the inability of existing arguments to identify supporters of hegemony as well as challengers; see McKeown, "Hegemonic Stability Theory," p. 76, and Raimo Väyrynen, "Economic Cycles, Power Transitions, Political Management, and Wars between Major Powers," *International Studies Quarterly* 27 (1983): 389–418. Also, the hegemon's need for supporters has been noted several times, as for instance in Beth V. Yarbrough and Robert M. Yarbrough, "Free Trade, Hegemony, and the Theory of Agency," *Kyklos* 38 (1985): 350, and Stein, "The Hegemon's Dilemma," p. 358.

national rules but are *economic competitors* with the liberal leader within those rules, since they produce similar goods and services. These countries have the same economic and political characteristics as the liberal leader; in the absence of an established leader such a state would step forward to attempt to fill that role. But in the presence of a liberal leader and an existing liberal subsystem it makes no sense for these states to create other subsystems or convert potential into actual power, for they can gain benefits by simply competing economically within the subsystem and avoid the costs of leadership. Such a country challenges the liberal leader in the economic realm only. Politically, it follows the liberal leader.

Countries with autocratic states are more likely to have policies granting rents to capital-intensive sectors, which alters their interests in joining a liberal subsystem. Autocratic states in capital-poor countries are *ambivalent* toward the liberal leader and the open subsystem.[35] These states could raise revenues and domestic support by exporting labor-intensive goods, so the benefits of joining the liberal subsystem match those of the supporters described above, although the costs to the autocratic state are potentially higher. If domestic capital-intensive sectors' rents are threatened, that undermines the state's revenues as well as its strongest base of political support (i.e., from the groups to which it has bestowed privileges). One way around this dilemma is to allow foreign capital to capture domestic rents too.[36] In either case, autocratic capital-poor countries' actions reflect ambivalence to the liberal leader and the liberal subsystem, since the best export markets are in capital-rich countries (especially the open market of the liberal leader itself), but opening up to capital-intensive imports is not acceptable, and the autocratic state is also tempted to pursue illiberal policies to expand its capability to sanction rents.

Finally, we turn to capital-rich countries with autocratic states, which were previously identified as the political challengers to liberal leaders. These states would rather not accept participation in the liberal subsystem, since participation offers only second-best alternatives for both the capital-intensive and labor-intensive sectors. Capital-intensive sectors are receiving preferential treatment and higher returns via domestic rents; even though capital is abundant, its returns are artificially high. Exports of capital-intensive goods and services

35. Snidal, "Limits of Hegemonic Stability Theory," pp. 612–613, discusses how many Third and Fourth World countries might fit into such a category of ambivalence toward the hegemon.

36. This scenario fits the description of relations found in some modified dependista arguments, in which international capital dominates local economic activities through an alliance with local political authorities, and it also parallels the works building from the ideas of Richard L. Sklar, "Postimperialism: A Class Analysis of Multinational Corporate Expansion," *Comparative Politics* 9 (October 1976): 75–92.

(which by extension of the logic of the argument is dumping) are welcomed, but any imports of the same sorts of goods and services would upset domestic arrangements. Continued pursuit of domestic rents is preferred over participation in a liberal trading system. Meanwhile, the labor-intensive sectors are not competitive internationally and prefer protection over participation in liberal trade. At a minimum, these states reject participation in the liberal subsystem.

This description of the interests of autocratic capital-rich states carries the basis for addressing another puzzle posed earlier: why some but not all countries challenge the liberal leader. I have already shown why other types of countries prefer to accept the leadership of a capital-abundant, powerful republic in a subsystem based on liberal principles. A capital-rich autocratic state might choose not to join such a subsystem, but why would it wish to fight a major war against a liberal leader? The answer lies in the domestic rents granted to the sectors using the *abundant* factor of production intensively, which creates pressures in keeping those sectors fully employed. Participating in freer trade relieves the employment problem, but only by offering significantly lower returns. If the state has international power, other options are open. The most satisfactory option is one that resolves the employment problem without reducing rates of return; this can be done only by expanding the amount of rents sanctioned. Capital-rich autocracies with international power accordingly become insatiable *expansionary powers*, because successful expansion only temporarily relieves these domestic pressures, as further capital accumulation causes the same problems to reemerge.[37] This expansion drives the autocracy into conflict with the liberal leader, since the liberal leader is protecting the open subsystem from just the sort of encroachment these insatiable expansionary powers exercise. The two lock into major wars because there is no ground for accommodation; the liberal hegemon has nothing to offer the expansionary power that would not undermine its own position.

Why do expansionary powers always seem to lose major wars? We merely have to construct depictions of the likely alliances the liberal leader and the expansionary power are each able to create. The liberal leader can draw on supporters, since these have not only strong direct links to the liberal leader but also interests in defending the liberal subsystem. Economic competitors

37. This explanation parallels the argument propounded by Lenin in "Imperialism: the Highest Stage of Capitalism," except that the argument here applies only to those countries in which the impact of rents is pervasive, whereas Lenin thought all capitalist countries would act in the same manner. Note too that the expansionary powers would create international subsystems based on expropriation through political force, or at least through markets that were severely distorted via political intervention.

do not rush to the aid of the liberal leader in major war, since they accept erosion of the liberal leader's economic competitiveness, but they do come to the defense of the subsystem if they believe its existence is threatened. In any case, other powerful republics always join the liberal leader's alliance and are never part of the expansionary power's alliance.[38]

Ambivalent powers follow a bandwagoning strategy during major wars. These states' interests can be served by expanding their ability to grant rents, although they can also gain by participating in the liberal subsystem. Expanding the state's political authority to extend rent-sanctioning can best be achieved by being on the winning side at the war's end. Unlike supporters or economic challengers, these states can be expected to switch sides during major conflicts as the fortunes of war shift.

Expansionary powers have difficulty creating any stable alliances, even with each other (if two or more coexist). Such powers are potential threats to all their neighbors, and unlike liberal leaders they do not share interests with any other country (since they are rival monopolists). Whereas ambivalent powers may side with expansionary powers, such alliances are not stable, because of the war aims of the expansionary power. This political challenger is trying to redistribute wealth; it builds an alliance just large enough to win, since building a larger one dilutes the gains from winning.[39] The liberal leader, in contrast, is defending the status quo and builds as large an alliance as possible (a maximum-winning coalition). The liberal leader is always ready to accept ambivalent powers as allies. For these reasons, expansionary powers most likely face a stronger coalition in major wars.

These arguments can be taken a step farther, since the combination of war aims and relative alliance size determines the military strategies each side finds attractive. The expansionary power must use an offensive strategy to achieve its goals; since it most likely faces a stronger coalition, it adopts a strategy emphasizing offense to compensate for weaker numbers (utilizing speed, surprise, and other techniques to achieve local superiority). The liberal leader's alliance has mainly defensive goals and can bring in a wider array of partners against the expansionary power; this alliance finds an attrition strategy most attractive, since this enables it to use its size to advantage. Facing these strategies off against each other illustrates why challengers always seem to lose the

---

38. The fact that liberal democratic states stand together in major wars has been pointed out by several authors, including Michael W. Doyle, "Liberalism and World Politics," *American Political Science Review* 80 (December 1986): 1156.

39. Thus, when the expansionary power is winning, at the very times when ambivalent powers seek to join its alliance, the expansionary power has reasons not only to refuse these possible partners but to break off any existing alliances it no longer needs.

major wars they start. The offensive strategy of the expansionary power is a gamble: failure in the short run dooms the expansionary power to be slowly squeezed or even overwhelmed as the war is prolonged.[40]

The final puzzles I consider here concern major war as a source for liberal leadership and the apparent cyclical form liberal leadership has taken with major war as a functional part of the transition from one liberal leadership to another. Major war *may* be significant in creating new liberal leaders, since such conflicts can obviously affect the distribution of power in the international system, alter the relative capital abundance of countries, and even cause changes in domestic political institutions (particularly for the losing states). Any one of these changes could cause an existing liberal leader to discontinue its international role, in which case another leader might appear—but there is no assurance of such a transition occurring. Depending on the war's outcome, anything is possible. If an expansionary power emerges victorious, it does not take over or otherwise recreate a liberal subsystem—it constructs an empire instead. Although major war may influence transitions of leadership in liberal subsystems, it is not a necessary factor. Any route to the conjunction of capital abundance in a powerful republic, including peaceful means, can instigate new leadership.

Terms and Cases

Before I address historic cases, I must specify the key variables and definitions raised in the argument above. Given that the phenomena I analyze and explain are found only in long historical patterns, the model must deal with variables relevant to each historical period. In applying the model to such a long temporal sweep, my emphasis is on explaining as much of the international activities of states as possible with these few variables. Thus I deemphasize other variables specific to only certain time periods; this does not mean that I am arguing, for instance, that religious factors were insignificant in international affairs during the seventeenth century, or that ideological rivalries were insignificant in recent decades, but rather that the explanatory power of these factors has ebbed and waned over the past three and a half

---

40. Size of alliances and attrition alone do not determine which side will win in a war: "To be sure, generals [in World War I] still had to direct (or misdirect) their campaigns, troops still had to summon individual courage to assault an enemy position and sailors still had to endure the rigors of sea warfare; but the record indicates that such qualities and talents existed on both sides, and were not enjoyed in disproportionate measure by one of the coalitions" (Kennedy, *Rise and Fall of Great Powers*, p. 274).

centuries whereas the rise and decline of liberal leaders and economically open subsystems has been relatively continuous. Thus the explanatory variables I feature are those that are applicable across the last three and a half centuries.

The two most important types of international behavior I am interested in explaining are major wars and leadership of liberal subsystems. Since I look at domestic political institutions, relative endowments of the factors of production, and international power to explain when liberal leadership or major war occurs, these too must be defined.

I define major wars as being almost unlimited in scope, in terms of both the war aims of the participants and the means employed. I quantify and operationalize these ideas in two ways: the wars must involve almost all the major powers in the international system, and they must have an intensity of at least 10,000 battle deaths per million of European population.[41] This definition captures the widespread nature and destructiveness of major wars.

The timespan under consideration is limited to the centuries after the Peace of Westphalia (1648). The Thirty Years' War also fits my definition of major war, but that war transformed international relations. It created the modern (nonhierarchical) interstate system that made hegemony possible.[42] The wars that fit the definition of major wars since 1648 are the War of the Spanish Succession (1701–1713), the Napoleonic Wars (1803–1815), World War I (1914–1918), and World War II (1939–1945). This selection conforms to most other lists of major wars; arguably, these wars shaped the modern world.[43]

I have already defined liberal leadership as leadership of an economically open international subsystem. A liberal subsystem is one in which interna-

41. These criteria are based on Jack Levy's definition in *War in the Modern Great Power System, 1495–1975* (Lexington: University Press of Kentucky, 1983), p. 75, but with the intensity level increased by a factor of ten.

42. Hegemony is normally defined in terms of one state being dominant or exercising leadership over other states—with all states in the system performing basically the same sorts of tasks vis-à-vis their subjects. Before the Peace of Westphalia, the international system was composed of members linked hierarchically, with differing definitions of sovereignty. I suspect that hegemony or liberal leadership in such a situation would look quite different from that as commonly discussed in the literature.

43. For other lists, see Goldstein, *Long Cycles*, and Jack Levy, "Theories of General War," *World Politics* 37 (April 1985): 344–374. Two major points distinguish my list from others. First, my time frame precludes the Thirty Years' War or any earlier wars. Second, I look at specific wars rather than periods of war. I stress intensity, not duration. Periods of war may signal the approach of major war, but not in all cases. Also, although I believe that World Wars I and II are definitely related, they should be treated as distinct events, if only because major power alliance memberships shifted. One final point: the Seven Years' War does not make my list because, although it had widespread participation, it failed to have the intensity or destructiveness of a major war.

tional trade in goods and services and flows of capital are relatively free from governmental restraint; if capital is to flow freely, currencies must also be convertible.[44] This situation certainly existed in the periods of the past two centuries broadly entitled *pax Britannica* and *pax Americana*, but brief attempts at leadership have occurred at other times as well. It is not necessary to identify explicitly periods when liberal subsystems existed, since I am interested in attempted liberal leadership—especially when that leadership has faced difficulties in producing a sizable liberal subsystem. Indeed, one aspect of my approach is to distinguish interests from capabilities. Prospective liberal leaders with the combination of factors supporting interest in establishing open economic subsystems may be identified; but the necessary power they need to achieve their goals depends not only on their own capabilities but also on the distribution of other states. Where there are few supporters among the other major powers, a liberal leader may have to be quite strong in order to establish some sort of effective liberal regime. In a situation with many supporters, even a weak liberal leader may be successful. Unlike previous scholars, I wish to examine conditions under which prospective liberal leaders have succeeded *and* failed. Since successful liberal leadership depends on such a variety of international interactions and cannot be easily quantified, I do not list such periods here; that task remains until it can be dealt with much more effectively in specific cases.

I categorize countries by their domestic political institutions, their endowments of the factors of production, and international power. I place attention almost solely on the major powers, since these are the only possible liberal leaders or significant participants in the major wars. My arguments above could also be applied to less powerful states with significant results, but this lies outside this book's focus.

Power has been defined as the ability of one actor to get a second actor to do what this second actor would not do otherwise. Since in this book I am interested in explaining major war, realized military power is most relevant. This is relatively easy to quantify, although perhaps leading to bias against military establishments that are qualitatively superior to their rivals. The quantitative indicators I use are size of military budgets, number of men in uniform, and numbers of major weapon systems. The goal is to identify not a single dominant power but the upper echelon of stronger powers.

Capital abundance or scarcity refers to the capital-labor ratio within the country, compared to elsewhere. Capital abundance means capital is abundant

44. Here I follow Krasner's definition in "State Power."

relative to labor (and the ratio is above the world level). As an indicator of this ratio, hard measures are preferred, in order to compare across countries. Labor productivity is a good proxy measure for capital abundance, since it measures capital per worker, including human capital and land per worker. Measures such as fixed capital per employee also give a comparable indication of capital-labor ratios, although these measures are not as inclusive as the first.

In earlier periods, where such statistics are not available for cross-country comparison, two alternative courses can be followed. Edward Leamer suggests considering the capital and labor components of a country's exports in order to deduce something about its endowments.[45] A second course is to compare the returns to capital and labor within each country. This can be done for earlier periods, so it proves useful here. But, wages and interest rates are influenced by nonmarket forces, which reduces their reliability. As key points in the argument suggest, governmental interference is a significant factor upsetting this sort of information. Since pivotal points in the argument rest on surges in capital abundance (at the heart of the dynamic arguments on liberal leadership and expansionary challengers), I pay particular attention to times when countries' capital accumulation rates rise.

Defining countries as representative or autocratic requires an investigation into the institutional setup of the state. In particular, I examine whether representative institutions control the budget, have the ability to set foreign policy, and otherwise exercise some control over the executive bodies of government. Since these terms are qualitative rather than quantitative, their application awaits the actual cases. No list of the relevant republican states is given here, but possible similar lists can be found in the works of Michael Doyle, among others.[46]

---

45. Edward Leamer, "The Leontief Paradox, Reconsidered," *Journal of Political Economy* 88 (June 1980): 495–503.

46. See Doyle, "Liberalism and World Politics," and William K. Domke, *War and the Changing Global System* (New Haven: Yale University Press, 1988). The significant differences between Doyle's list and the material brought to bear in the cases here are my treatment of the Netherlands before the 1790s and Britain from 1688 until 1830 as republics.

TWO

Liberalism in an Age of Mercantilism:
Dutch Attempts at Leadership and the French Challenge, 1648–1713

The first historical period I consider encompasses much of the seventeenth century, beginning with the establishment of the modern international state system at the settlement of the Thirty Years' War (1648) and concluding with the next major war (1701–1713). During this period the United Provinces of the Netherlands, or Dutch Republic, tried to establish a liberal subsystem. Both England and France lagged behind the Dutch in capital abundance but were catching up by the end of the century. With capital accumulation, England's policy vacillated between purely economic competition and expansionary challenge, depending on the shifts between Parliament and the monarchy for control of the domestic political system; in France, capital accumulation combined with absolutist political institutions to culminate in the first major war challenging an established liberal leader.

The United Provinces and the First Attempt at Liberal International Leadership

The seventeenth-century Dutch Republic was rich in capital, ruled by republican institutions, and a major international power. It was the first nation-state to combine these characteristics in the modern era and, therefore, the first major power with interests in the construction of a liberal international economic subsystem.

The Republican Nature of the Dutch State

The domestic political attributes of the Dutch Republic fit the definition of a representative government detailed in Chapter 1. It was a loose confederation of the seven provinces that had successfully rebelled against Spain. Each province had its own particular representative body, with layers of representative government down to the town, or corporate, level. Towns and provinces had a variety of rules about voter eligibility and the distribution of representatives, so it is practically impossible to give a brief, clear, and accurate picture of the overall structure of Dutch government. For instance, of the nineteen delegates representing the province of Holland, eighteen represented towns and only one represented the nobility; Zeeland also had only one delegate for the nobility, but Gelderland and Overijssel gave the nobility greater representation. In the provinces of Friesland and Groningen, which had never experienced feudalism, even property-owning peasants had a voice in the lower levels of government.[1]

The main federal body of government was the States-General, a representative body of delegates from the seven provinces. Among the provinces, Holland held the most power, since it was the largest and wealthiest. Holland was well represented in terms of the number of delegates in the States-General, but the real strength of its politicians was their ability to influence the budget. Holland contributed almost half the federal monies, which enabled its grand pensionary, or state secretary, to be the key political figure both for the province and for the States-General during most of the seventeenth century.[2]

The other important political actor was the stadhouder, a military-political leader chosen by each province during wartime and usually combined with the posts of admiral-general and captain-general. This position was inheritable and in the hands of the princes of Orange, who had led the revolt against Spain. But as republicans, the Dutch gave powers to and took powers away from the stadhouder as the situation dictated. At times antirepublican sentiments ran high, and coup d'état were even attempted. But during most of the time considered in this chapter, the stadhouder worked within the Republic's laws.

The city of Amsterdam dominated politics within the province of Holland. In a very indirect manner, Amsterdam could control much of what the federal government did. Again, this was because of the budget: Holland's contributions accounted for up to half the federal budget, but Amsterdam's contributions were half of Holland's total. Merchants dominated Amsterdam's munici-

1. For a discussion of some of these relationships, see E. N. Williams, *The Ancien Regime in Europe: Government and Society in the Major States, 1648–1789* (New York: Harper & Row, 1970), pp. 36–37.

2. Stephen B. Baxter, *William III and the Defense of European Liberty, 1650–1702* (New York: Harcourt, Brace & World, 1966), pp. 4–5; Williams, *Ancien Regime*, p. 38.

pal government; because of democratic institutions, provincial and federal policies never strayed far from their interests. Since defending trade required a navy, Amsterdam was always ready to pay for ships, but it often resisted the expense of building an army, to the chagrin of the landlocked provinces.[3]

Not all men (and certainly no women) could vote in the Dutch Republic. But the degree of representation was astonishingly high, sometimes bothersomely so. When major policies were being considered in the States-General, delegates were often required to return to their lower-level constituencies for guidance; these lower-level bodies might have to do the same in turn, and so on, until the question worked its way down to the lowest levels. On major questions of war and taxation, one province could block a decision by the States-General, and often one town could block a decision of a single province.[4] This sometimes prevented decisive action, but it is a strong indication of how representative the government of the Dutch Republic was.

The Capital Abundance of the Netherlands

The Dutch economy was rich in capital; it was probably the most capital-abundant national economy from 1600 until the middle of the eighteenth century. In the single clearest statistic, the Netherlands had the highest estimated levels of labor productivity, measured in terms of gross domestic product per man-hour, until the 1780s.[5]

The eighty-year war of independence from Spain (which ended with a truce in 1609 but was not settled until 1648) and the Thirty Years' War that ravaged Germany between 1618 and 1648 helped concentrate capital and economic activity in the Netherlands. The Netherlands' successful blockade of the Scheldt during the war with Spain eliminated Amsterdam's great financial and trading rival, Antwerp. Refugees from the Southern Netherlands, where much of the fighting had taken place and where the revolt against Spain had failed,

3. Shepherd B. Clough and C. W. Cole, *Economic History of Europe* (Boston: Heath, 1946), pp. 166–167; Charles H. Wilson, *The Dutch Republic and the Civilisation of the Seventeenth Century* (London: World University Library, 1968), p. 33; Leon van Buyten and J. A. van Houtte, "The Low Countries," in *An Introduction to the Sources of European Economic History, 1500–1800*, ed. C. H. Wilson and Geoffrey Parker (Ithaca: Cornell University Press, 1977), p. 112; Ivo Schöffer, "Did Holland's Golden Age Coincide with a Period of Crisis?" in *The General Crisis of the Seventeenth Century*, ed. Geoffrey Parker and L. M. Smith (Boston: Routledge Kegan Paul, 1978), p. 104; Williams, *Ancien Regime*, p. 39.

4. Alice Carter, *Neutrality or Commitment* (London: Edward Arnold, 1975), p. 4; Baxter, *William III*, p. 181.

5. Angus Maddison, *Phases of Capitalist Development* (New York: Oxford University Press, 1982).

resettled in the United Provinces. In 1622, one third of Amsterdam's population of 100,000 were immigrants. At a minimum, this flow of people would have added to the labor force, so one might think these refugees lowered the capital-labor ratio; in fact, most were highly skilled workers or merchants who brought with them knowledge, personal contacts, and capital. Up to one half the capital put up to support the Bank of Amsterdam in 1609 came from immigrants from the Southern Netherlands. One contemporary went so far as to say, "Here is Antwerp become Amsterdam."[6]

Dutch capital abundance appears in several distinguishable ways. Dutch interest rates were among the lowest of the time, and they consistently declined in the seventeenth century. For example, on government bonds in 1600, the rate was 8.33 percent; in 1611, it fell to 6.25 percent; in 1640 to 5 percent; by 1672 it fluctuated between 3 and 3.75 percent—and government bonds at that time were continually oversubscribed. At one point, the government of the province of Holland was able to expand its debt 225 percent, without having to alter the percentage of revenues allocated for debt service.[7] Dutch long-term commercial rates remained below those in England and France until well into the eighteenth century.[8] Josiah Child, an Englishman writing in 1668, considered the low rate of interest in the Netherlands to be the keystone of Dutch economic success. Gregory King, another Englishman writing in the late seventeenth century, estimated the Dutch savings rate to have been over 11 percent of national income in 1688, compared to only 4 percent in England and France.[9] As trade developed and prospered, capital accumulation increased, and eventually there was a shortage of safe investment opportunities—as witnessed by the vast sums expended on land reclamation, investment in the

6. Wilson, *Dutch Republic*, p. 26, and also Wilson, *The Transformation of Europe, 1558–1648* (Berkeley: University of California Press, 1976), p. 43; Fernand Braudel, *The Perspective of the World* (New York: Harper & Row, 1984), p. 187; David Maland, *Europe in the Seventeenth Century* (London: Macmillan Education, 1983), p. 245; J. A. van Houtte, *An Economic History of the Low Countries, 800–1800* (London: Weidenfeld & Nicolson, 1977), p. 135; B. H. Slicher van Bath, "The Economic Situation in the Dutch Republic during the Seventeenth Century," in *Dutch Capitalism and World Capitalism / Capitalisme hollandais et capitalism mondial*, ed. Maurice Aymard (New York: Cambridge University Press, 1982), pp. 27, 29.

7. Jan de Vries, *The Economy of Europe in an Age of Crisis, 1600–1750* (New York: Cambridge University Press, 1976), pp. 211–212; James C. Riley, *International Government Finance and the Amsterdam Capital Market, 1740–1815* (New York: Cambridge University Press, 1980), pp. 3, 72.

8. Sidney Homer, *A History of Interest Rates* (New Brunswick: Rutgers University Press, 1963), p. 178.

9. For Child's comments, see Charles H. Wilson, *England's Apprenticeship, 1603–1763* (New York: St. Martin's, 1965), p. 210; for King's comments, see Maddison, *Phases of Capitalist Development*, p. 31.

Dutch East India Company, stock market and tulipmania speculation, and other high-risk capital-intensive ventures.

As another indication of capital abundance, the Netherlands had the highest wage rates of any country in the seventeenth century. In 1667 a publicist for the Leiden textile industry complained that "day wages in combing, carding, spinning and weaving are about half as much in England as must be paid here."[10] There were large wage gaps between common laborers in Amsterdam and other places, and these gaps are observable among salaried positions as well.

The Netherlands as a Major International Power

The discussion above suggests that the Dutch would have an interest in liberalizing trade, but what international capabilities did the Dutch state have? Despite the Republic's small physical size, it was relatively powerful in the seventeenth century.[11] According to Jack Levy, the Dutch were a major power from 1610 until 1713. George Modelski and William Thompson's figures show that the Dutch fleet was one of the three strongest during the seventeenth century—and these figures do not take into account the higher quality of the men and ships in the Dutch fleet. The Dutch army was also sizable, for the Dutch could afford to arm many citizens and hire mercenaries. In the 1670s only Russia and France could field larger land armies than the Republic. Also, the Dutch Republic was the shipbuilding and arms center of Europe during much of the seventeenth century.

As a republican state with a capital-abundant national economy, the Dutch emerged as a prospective liberal leader. They would use what international power they had to try to establish an open international subsystem. The domestic process argument for liberal leadership presented in Chapter 1 suggests that (1) domestic rent-seeking would be limited by the state, (2) capital-intensive sectors would look for foreign outlets to employ capital, in order to drive up capital's relative returns, and (3) capital-intensive sectors would therefore

10. Jan de Vries, "An Inquiry into the Behaviour of Wages in the Dutch Republic and the Southern Netherlands from 1580 to 1800," in *Dutch Capitalism and World Capitalism*, ed. Aymard, pp. 43–45.

11. This paragraph draws on the following sources: Jack Levy, *War in the Modern Great Power System, 1495–1975* (Lexington: University Press of Kentucky, 1983), pp. 37–38; George Modelski and William R. Thompson, *Seapower in Global Politics, 1494–1993* (London: Macmillan, 1988), pp. 187–193. The figures given in Geoffrey Parker and L. M. Smith, "Introduction," in *General Crisis*, ed. Parker and Smith, p. 14, are 110,000 men for the Dutch, 120,000 for France, and 130,000 for Russia.

appeal to the state to provide services facilitating the international expansion of capital-intensive economic activities.

Monopolies in the Dutch Economy

Although the Dutch state's institutions were republican, and overall rent-seeking was low (there were relatively fewer guilds, for instance[12]), there was one major exception to this pattern. The Dutch East India Company was given certain grants to monopolize the trade with the East Indies. This exception fits within the expectations of the model, though. First, this was a capital-intensive venture, particularly in comparison with the other East India companies in other countries (the Dutch were the first to sink capital into permanent positions in the East Indies, such as forts), so it reflects the factor endowments of the Dutch economy.[13]

Second, the grants were given in order to form the United East India Company (the Verenigde Oostindische Compagnie, or VOC). The uniting of existing companies was a response to ruinous competition. Competition was not destroyed but regulated: the different chambers of the VOC operated as semi-independent profit centers, each with its own monies and in competition with the other chambers. As Robert Ekelund and Robert Tollison point out, the Dutch companies' efficiency followed from the inability to suppress competition among separate Dutch towns.[14] The VOC was not a complete marketing syndicate: monopoly rights did not prevent competition between its chambers operating in different locales within the United Provinces.

Third, the state was willing to grant these special rights for several reasons. Not least of these was the special loans and access to capital and equipment the state received in exchange for these rights. More important, the VOC was allowed to form because the state could not provide the services of protection and order in the far-off waters of Africa or Asia; the special rights granted to the united company empowered it to provide these services for itself. This also explains the timing of the original grants to the VOC: the company was uni-

---

12. Jan de Vries, "Holland: Commentary," in *Failed Transitions to Modern Industrial Society: Renaissance Italy and Seventeenth Century Holland,* ed. Frederick Krantz and Paul M. Hohenberg (Montreal: Interuniversity Centre for European Studies, 1975), p. 56.

13. The Dutch company was able to sink money permanently into its projects because of the form of its capitalization, see Larry Neal, *The Rise of Financial Capitalism: International Capital Markets in the Age of Reason* (New York: Cambridge University Press, 1990), pp. 8–9.

14. Robert B. Ekelund and Robert D. Tollison, *Mercantilism as a Rent-Seeking Society* (College Station: Texas A&M University Press, 1981), p. 112.

fied when the Dutch were still at war with Spain, when the state's ability to protect these far-flung interests was especially low.

These special rights did not curb competition with foreign companies. Unlike other countries, the Netherlands did not prevent its citizens from investing in other countries' trading companies. Dutch investors, for instance, were consistently strong backers of the rival English East India Company. The Swedish African Company organized in 1649 received five-sixths of its original capital from Dutch sources. The Danish West India Company was established by a Dutchman (Jan de Willem) and was prepared to send out its first expedition without any Danish capital backing.[15]

The VOC's monopoly also came under attack several times. Some of the most articulate criticisms were made by Pieter de la Court in *The True Interest and Political Maxims of the Republic of Holland*. By the 1660s, the state was accustomed to special treatment by the VOC and vice versa, and stock ownership in the VOC had become quite widespread, so the VOC's political position was difficult to challenge. Although the VOC did have some exceptional rights, its role in the Dutch economy is often overemphasized. Huge profits were made, but the VOC's pre-1730 profits were moderate when compared to those made by shipping and commerce within Europe itself.[16] When put in such terms, it is clear that some scholars have lost sight of the greater relative importance of the intra-European trade.

Other instances of monopoly rights granted during the war years and the early period of attempted liberal international leadership show that monopoly rights could be withdrawn. For instance, monopoly rights were given to the Bank of Amsterdam in some areas of foreign exchange within the city of Amsterdam, in order to ensure that institution's survival. These monopoly rights were rescinded after a relatively short period. As de la Court argued, monopolies should not be indulged because they made the rest of the economy less competitive in international trade: "For how much soever those members [of guilds or monopolies] sell their pains or commodities dearer than if that trade or occupation was open or free, all the other better inhabitants that gain their subsistence immediately, or by consequence by a foreign consumption, must bear that loss."[17]

Except for the long-distance trading companies, other economic activities in

15. Violet Barbour, *Capitalism in Amsterdam in the Seventeenth Century* (Ann Arbor: University of Michigan Press, 1963), p. 134; Braudel, *Perspective of the World*, p. 205.

16. De Vries, *Economy of Europe in an Age of Crisis*, p. 143.

17. Pieter de la Court, *The True Interest and Political Maxims of the Republic of Holland* (New York: Arno Press, 1972; reprint of the 1669 English version of the 1662 original), pp. 63–64.

the Netherlands were highly competitive. In the preindustrial economy of the time, this economic competition centered around trade. Abundant capital in the Netherlands allowed Dutch traders to raise money cheaply—at about half the interest rates Frenchmen or Englishmen faced. Access to cheap capital made Dutch merchants competitive in several ways. They had an easier time buying ships and financing trade. They could handle more commerce by being the only ones prepared to pay cash for goods, and particularly by being prepared to pay cash in advance. They could afford to stockpile goods when prices were low, to invest in fixed capital necessary to store goods for long periods of time, to wait for market prices to rise; and they could use capital to balance the trade in goods.[18] As de la Court wrote,

> it is a great advantage for the traffick of *Holland*, that money may be taken up by merchants at *3 1/2 per cent* for a year, without pawn or pledge; whereas in other countries there is much more given, and yet real estates bound for the same: so that it appears, that the *Hollanders* may buy and lay out their ready money a whole season, before the goods they purchase are in being, and manufactured, and sell them again on trust (which cannot be done by any other trading nation, considering their high interest of money) and therefore is one of the greatest means whereby the *Hollanders* have gotten most of the trade from other nations.[19]

Cheaper capital meant greater efficiency in day-to-day operations, which increased the accumulation of profits, which allowed for even greater inroads in markets, which again raised efficiency.[20]

The Economics of Dutch Trade Policy

Dutch foreign policy came to reflect the developing international interests of the capital-intensive sectors. The States-General was heavily influenced by the province of Holland, which in turn was dominated by the city of Amsterdam. Amsterdam was run by burghers who were dependent, directly or indirectly, on international trade. The burghers continually pushed the federal

---

18. Clough and Cole, *Economic History of Europe*, p. 166; Artur Attman, *The Bullion Flow between Europe and the East, 1000–1750* (Göteborg: Kungl. Vetenschaps—och Vitterhets Samhället, 1981), p. 84. In *Capitalism in Amsterdam*, chap. 5, Barbour discusses these in detail.
19. De la Court, *True Interest of Holland*, p. 28.
20. Immanuel Wallerstein, *The Modern World-System II: Mercantilism and the Consolidation of the European World-Economy, 1600–1750* (New York: Academic Press, 1980), p. 53.

government to support and protect trade. Charles H. Wilson notes that, since trading interests dominated, the state's foreign economic policy was to create free trade that reflected the requirements of an entrepôt system.[21] In this early period of attempted liberal leadership, the state supported and protected the expansion of trade: wages were high compared to other countries, and with expanded trade prices of consumer goods (especially foodstuffs) fell; capital's gains relative to labor increased; and the state's tax base grew with increased economic activity. In the short run, the liberal trade policies could be construed to be in everyone's interest.

The extension of trade continually worked to the United Provinces' advantage. Since the country had a large urban population and few if any raw materials, certain imports were necessities. Grain was brought from the Baltic, which lowered the costs of basic foods; the Dutch agricultural provinces were not upset by this, because it allowed them to specialize in more capital-intensive types of agriculture, using their comparative advantage.[22] Dutch agriculture became technically advanced, learning to rotate crops, developing new strains, increasingly employing seed selection, using higher manurial treatment of the soil, producing a greater mix of agricultural products, and also investing vast sums of money to extend the acreage under cultivation through poldering. Before the 1660s the draining of 36,000 hectares in the northern peninsula of Holland increased the cultivable land area by more than 25 percent—and took more capital than the combined capitalization of the Dutch East and West India companies.[23]

To import grain and the naval stores necessary to build ships (the Netherlands lacked these, too, including wood), other goods or capital had to be exported to the Baltic. Since the Baltic trade was hard to balance with domestically produced goods, and expensive to balance with capital, the Dutch sought out third parties with goods they could carry to the Baltic. Dutch merchants handled some 75 percent of the total Baltic grain trade, 50–75 percent of the Baltic lumber trade, and 33–50 percent of the exports of metal from Sweden; in exchange, the Dutch carried around 75 percent of the salt from France and Portugal that went to the Baltic, and more than half the textiles brought to the Baltic were manufactured or finished in the Nether-

21. Charles H. Wilson, *Anglo-Dutch Commerce and Finance in the Eighteenth Century* (Cambridge: Cambridge University Press, 1941; reprinted in 1966), p. 4.
22. The best discussion is in Jan de Vries, *The Dutch Rural Economy in the Golden Age, 1500–1700* (New Haven: Yale University Press, 1974).
23. Wilson, *Transformation of Europe,* pp. 17–18; Braudel, *Perspective of the World,* p. 178; De Vries, *Economy of Europe in an Age of Crisis,* p. 37.

lands.[24] Danzig was the main trading center on the Baltic, and its trade was dominated by Dutch shipping. Between 1565 and 1646, 66–80 percent of Danzig's exports to other parts of Europe consisted of grain, most of which went to the Netherlands. The large volume of exports from the Baltic was controlled by the Dutch because only they could counterbalance exports with other goods *and capital.*[25]

The need for imports helped to direct trade into the Netherlands as an entrepôt, which when combined with cheap capital stimulated advances in shipbuilding and operations. Capital was cheap, but men and material for ships and crews were relatively expensive. So the Dutch developed the *fluit*, an easily constructed, cheap-to-operate bulk carrier. The *fluit* drove down the costs of importing timber and other naval stores, which lowered the costs of ship construction even further. Cheap shipping operations plus access to cheap capital for financing trade made Dutch shipping rates one-third to one-half lower than English rates. The Dutch merchant fleet grew to be the largest in the world, comprising one-half or more of the European total, and was more than twice as large as England's and eight to nine times the size of France's.[26]

Cheap freight rates, the ability to carry bulky cargoes, and the use of cheap finances also allowed an ever greater range of goods to be brought into international trade. This made trade easier to balance. Since markets work with economies of scale, adding to the range of goods increased the market's efficiency, and the entrepôt function worked more smoothly. Domination of the carrying trade stimulated industrial advances within the Dutch economy. Cheap capital made investment in new technologies easier to undertake; technological advances became industrial power. Circulating capital created the demand for fixed capital: organizing international trade required not only the building of ships but also the construction of warehouses for stapling goods. Goods shipped through the Netherlands were often processed or refined while they were there, so the entrepôt function naturally aided industrialization: Dutch ports developed mills, sugar refineries, breweries, and distilleries.[27]

---

24. Wilson, *Profit and Power*, p. 41.
25. Attman, *Bullion Flow*, pp. 71–72, 90.
26. De Vries, *Economy of Europe in an Age of Crisis*, pp. 117–118; Wilson, *Profit and Power*, p. 42; Violet Barbour, "Dutch and English Merchant Shipping in the Seventeenth Century," in *Essays in Economic History*, ed. E. M. Carus-Wilson (London: Edward Arnold, 1954), p. 249; Charles H. Wilson, *Economic History and the Historian: Collected Essays* (New York: Praeger, 1969), p. 24.
27. De Vries, *Economy of Europe in an Age of Crisis*, pp. 92–93, 118, 192; Wilson, *Economic History and the Historian*, p. 25.

The carrying trade especially facilitated development of the textile sector, the single largest industry of the seventeenth century. The Dutch did not raise sheep, so they did not produce wool; nor did they spin or weave wool. Instead, they dominated the higher, most capital-intensive stages of production (the dyeing and dressing of cloth), which accounted for nearly half the final price of woolens.[28] In this the most important manufacturing industry of the period, the Dutch developed a strong international position.

Just as industrial rise was fueled by the carrying trade and cheap capital, so was financial ascendance. In an effort to create a more sound currency for merchants' use, the Bank of Amsterdam was established in 1609. The Bank was intended to be a giro bank, keeping bullion to the exact extent of the money owed depositors. Transfers between depositors were to be made on the books only. Early on, however, the Bank loaned money to the VOC, Amsterdam's Lombard Bank (which had been established in 1614 to handle loans but now needed help), and the Amsterdam municipal government.[29] None of these activities threatened the Bank's solvency.

The Bank became a source of stable media of exchange, a secure depository with book transfers, and a central clearing house for international payments. This success helped make Amsterdam the financial center of Europe. Because the Bank of Amsterdam was secure and stable and the Amsterdam market had a greater variety of goods to offer than any other market, bills of exchange from Amsterdam were much more attractive than bills originating elsewhere. The use of bills of exchange was strengthened and encouraged when the Bank extended its services to bullion traders in the 1680s; this had the effect of increasing the stock of precious metals, which dampened the fluctuations in the price of circulating money. Inasmuch as the Amsterdam market *was* the international market, the Bank of Amsterdam provided some of the market stabilizing functions Charles Kindleberger has argued a hegemon must perform.[30]

The importance of the Bank and the market in Amsterdam made that city the undisputed center of European trade and the heart of the first modern

28. De Vries, *Economy of Europe in an Age of Crisis*, p. 88; Wilson, *Dutch Republic*, p. 31.

29. Clough and Cole, *Economic History of Europe*, pp. 168–169; Wilson, *Dutch Republic*, p. 25; Jonathon I. Israel, *Dutch Primacy in World Trade, 1585–1740* (Oxford: Clarendon, 1989), pp. 77–78.

30. Riley, *International Government Finance*, p. 28; Clough and Cole, *Economic History of Europe*, p. 316; De Vries, *Economy of Europe in an Age of Crisis*, pp. 121, 230; Geoffrey Parker, "The Emergence of Modern Finance in Europe, 1500–1730," in *The Fontana Economic History of Europe: The Sixteenth and Seventeenth Centuries*, ed. C. M. Cipolla (Glasgow: Collins/Fontana, 1974), p. 551.

multilateral payments system.[31] As the center of an open international economic subsystem, the Netherlands became a center for the flow of information. Early in the seventeenth century, current prices of goods were being printed in Amsterdam for merchants' use; this information influenced wholesale prices elsewhere as merchants left the Netherlands and traveled abroad. Improvements in making and receiving payments, in finding and matching buyers and sellers, and in centralizing information all contributed to give Amsterdam a commanding position in trade. By the end of the century, the service sector would develop large-scale transactions in banking, insurance, shipping, and warehousing.[32]

The Dutch Republic as a Prospective Liberal Leader

To enhance the effectiveness of expanding economic activities, the state was to provide order to the open international economic subsystem and protect it from outside interference. Although the Dutch Republic was not the dominant military power in the international system, the Dutch did in fact use what power they had in an attempt to establish an international political order to further and then maintain an economically open subsystem. Their inability to dominate meant that their leadership was not totally successful, yet it is significant that they were so active in trying to establish a subsystem with distinctly liberal economic principles despite the international political opposition they faced.

Dutch foreign policy differed from that of the other continental powers because the Netherlands was rich and ruled by republican institutions. The state could use its power only in ways the citizens wished—in other words, to support expansion of capital-intensive economic activity. One historian describes how seventeenth-century Dutch statesmen understood the domestic constraints on policy: "The fleets and armies of the Republic could be used only for purposes which commended themselves to those who paid for them—and whose cooperation had to be laboriously gained—in other words, to preserve the freedom of the seas (at least in European waters) and to ensure

31. Parker, "Emergence of Modern Finance," p. 551, discussing the period 1660–1710; C. H. Lee, *The British Economy since 1700: A Macroeconomic Perspective* (New York: Cambridge University Press, 1986), p. 121.

32. Van Houtte, *Economic History of the Low Countries*, p. 207; De Vries, *Economy of Europe in an Age of Crisis*, p. 121; Maddison, *Phases of Capitalist Development*, pp. 29–30; Neal, *Rise of Financial Capitalism*.

security from invasion."[33] Unlike the neighboring monarchies, the Dutch state always had to bear in mind the concerns of its citizens. Those concerns were for the development of an open economic subsystem that would use the abundant Dutch capital.

Providing order meant preventing the disruption of trade. The Dutch took the lead in trying to eliminate piracy. As de la Court explained, the Netherlands' greatest interests were bound up with "the guarding and clearing of the seas." The United Provinces was the first northern European power to send a fleet to the Mediterranean to punish Barbary pirates, in 1617.[34]

Wars between nation-states, as well as piracy, could disrupt trade. Thus the Dutch state sought to stabilize relations in areas where Dutch trading interests were particularly high. Again, in de la Court's words: "But if the scouring of the seas against sea robbers or enemies is so necessary for Holland during peace, then much more peace itself. For besides that all sea robbing is more frequent in war, it deprives all our inhabitants at once of all their trade to the enemy's country, and carries it to the inhabitants of neutral nations."[35] A Dutch fleet imposed a peace on Sweden and Denmark in 1645, when conflict in Scandinavia was upsetting the vital Dutch trade with the Baltic. The Dutch state continually did its best to maintain peace internationally, to promote the stability of trade. The Dutch state also promoted the idea of the right of neutrals to trade with either side in a war. This is clearly an indication of the Dutch willingness to profit from the troubles of others, but it can also be seen as an attempt to promote the right to trade at all times, including wartime.

The state's concern for international order and protection of the open trading subsystem encouraged it to create international regimes. The Dutch helped establish the international law of the sea to attain these goals. This development parallels, and indeed was a necessary precursor to, the free trade rules of our own time.[36] Hugo Grotius, a lawyer for the VOC, successfully argued for "open seas" against the position of *mare clausum*—closure of the seas—developed by the English and Scots, who felt unable to compete with the Dutch. Grotius's interpretation of the limits of sovereignty certainly rested firmly with Dutch interests, since the Netherlands was the primary sea-fishing

---

33. K. H. D. Haley, *The Dutch in the Seventeenth Century* (London: Thames & Hudson, 1972), p. 176.

34. De la Court, *True Interest of Holland*, p. 133; G. D. Ramsay, *English Overseas Trade during the Centuries of Emergence* (London: Macmillan, 1957), pp. 55–56. Since the Barbary pirates were a constant threat to international trade for several centuries, one could use punitive attacks on these pirates as an indicator of a country's degree of support for a free trade system.

35. De la Court, *True Interest of Holland*, p. 195.

36. Wilson, *Dutch Republic*, pp. 62–68.

and sea-trading nation, whereas the Britons hoped to exercise sovereignty over the seas in order to bar Dutch fisheries and merchants.[37] The new international rules were accepted by other nation-states because Dutch naval strength and economic policy could support this legal position. This is important as an example of regime creation: rather than claim the oceans as their own, the Dutch declared them open to all; rather than formal control, the Dutch established international rules—but they were prepared to back up those rules with national power and the enticement of economic connections with their own country.

Although the Dutch were not able to establish a free trade network for all nation-states, they did their best to barter or force down barriers to trade; again, as the nation-state most involved in trade, the Netherlands benefited particularly from lower tariff barriers.[38] The Dutch used force and persuasion to defend local liberties in the north German towns of Hamburg, Bremen, Cologne, and Coblenz from Swedish and Danish efforts to raise tariffs and tolls.[39] When, in the eighteenth century, Adam Smith wanted a real example that best approximated the character of a free-trade country, he chose the Netherlands.

Dutch policies were based on interests, not altruism. If rules could be established to ensure that Dutch trade had access to a market while other nations did not, the Dutch would not act altruistically. Dutch trading companies outside Europe often violated the principles of free trade and free navigation when it was to their advantage. But in the more important intra-European trade, Dutch foreign policy fits the general expectations of the model. Since the Dutch did not have the relative strength of later liberal leaders, their success was limited. The Dutch state used its power to open as much of the international system to greater levels of trade as possible, provided order to this open subsystem, and eventually was forced to protect it from the en-

37. Andre Gunder Frank, *World Accumulation, 1492–1789* (New York: Monthly Review Press, 1978), p. 82; George Modelski, "Dependency Reversal in the Modern State System: A Long Cycle Perspective," in *North/South Relations: Studies in Dependency Reversal,* ed. Charles F. Doran, Modelski, and Cal Clark (New York: Praeger, 1983), p. 67.

38. Clough and Cole, *Economic History of Europe,* p. 223; for the Dutch realization of this, see de la Court, *True Interest of Holland,* chap. 21 in pt. 1. It must be remembered that later, more familiar examples of hegemony were laid on the foundations the Dutch created; just as American hegemony may be faulted for its failure to lower not only tariffs but also nontariff barriers to international trade, the difficulties the Dutch faced in reducing tariffs must be considered in light of their success in establishing open trade on the high seas—without which large trade flows would have been difficult to achieve in the first place.

39. Wilson, *Anglo-Dutch Commerce,* p. 8; Ramsay, *English Overseas Trade,* p. 124.

croachment of closed subsystems led by stronger states such as England and France.

England's Rise in Power and Wealth

At the beginning of the seventeenth century, England was a capital-poor monarchy, with considerable international power before 1650. Although England is sometimes thought of as one of the stronger European countries during this period, its ability to project power was not yet well developed. Before the 1660s, England could not raise armies or fleets equal to the Netherlands'. Depending on relations with Scotland, many English troops had to be kept inside England, and more were garrisoned in Ireland. England could not yet rely solely on a strong navy for defense, and it could not afford to send many troops on foreign adventures. The English navy, which had helped break Spanish naval power in 1588, was still in its infancy.

In converting the nation's potential into military might, the greatest obstacle was the continual institutional struggle for control of the state itself. Neither Parliament nor the crown would allow the other to create a large army it might not be able to control. This struggle also shifted the state's policies, as first one then the other institution had control. Shifts in the type of government directly affected the ability of different economic interests to be heard.

In terms of the model presented here, when the crown dominates England should be (as a capital-poor, powerful country with a more autocratic state) ambivalent toward Dutch liberal leadership. When Parliament has the upper hand England should be (as a capital-poor, powerful country with a representative state) a supporter of Dutch liberal hegemony. Specific shifts in domestic politics should result not only in changes in the amount of domestic rents sanctioned but also in specific changes in foreign economic policies.

Changes in foreign policy due to political shifts differed as the economic endowments of England changed over the course of the century. As agricultural productivity increased, the ability to accumulate capital changed; England moved into the category of relatively capital-abundant countries. Unfortunately, internationally comparable data for this period is hard to come by. Although England appears to have been narrowing the gap in terms of the capital-labor ratio in comparison with the Netherlands, it never passed the Dutch in the seventeenth century.[40] Trends do indicate that English capital

---

40. Wilson, *Economic History and the Historian*, p. 118, shows that as late as 1690 Dutch wages

accumulation increased up to the last few decades of the seventeenth century. There was, for example, no shortage of funds to rebuild London after the Great Fire or to invest in the trading companies, in the 1660s and 1670s.[41] Therefore, toward the end of the century, when the dominant political institutions changed, we would expect foreign economic policies to change drastically, as England alternated between the roles of expansionary enemy of the Dutch and peaceful economic competitor. Two domestic changes altered England's international position late in the seventeenth century: vacillation in control of the state between institutions more autocratic and more republican, matched with steady capital accumulation. Capital accumulation brought about economic competition with the Dutch, but the concomitant political character this competition took depended on the nature of the domestic political system.

England as an Ambivalent Power

England started the seventeenth century ambivalent toward Dutch international leadership. Clearly, the English felt economically dominated by the Dutch, as expressed in their own words and actions. The writings of early English "economists" stress sovereignty and economic nationalism and continually emphasize the balance of trade argument; all are directed at the Dutch control of international trade and finance. As in other countries, mercantilism in England was largely a reaction against Dutch attempts to liberalize the international economy. Mercantilist regulations were a viable option earlier in England than elsewhere because of the earlier centralization of government there.[42]

Contemporary English assessments of the Baltic trade focus on the advantages Dutch traders exercised. The difficulties of competing in international services when capital is scarce come through clearly. In the first half of the seventeenth century, the Dutch had an estimated five to six times as much total shipping tonnage as England and up to thirteen times more tonnage

---

were 16 percent higher than English. In *Phases of Capitalist Development* (p. 29), Maddison claims that Britain did not surpass the Netherlands in labor productivity until the 1780s.

41. Phyllis Deane, "Capital Formation in Britain before the Railway Age," in *Capital Formation in the Industrial Revolution*, ed. F. Crouzet (London: Methuen, 1972), p. 115.

42. Clough and Cole, *Economic History of Europe*, p. 223. The point is that having a centralized government makes rents easier to sanction (consistent with Ekelund and Tollison's arguments), and that England reached this point of centralized government at a much earlier date than other countries. Mercantilist policies had been in position for a longer time in England than elsewhere by the period in question, though the bureaucracy was still inefficient.

engaged in the Baltic; half the goods transported from the Baltic to England were carried in Dutch ships.[43] The Dutch had several advantages associated with their capital richness: cheaper ships, and other goods to trade, which they amassed through their entrepôt role. Thus the Dutch controlled the inward traffic, so that English ships often went to the Baltic with ballast; with higher operating costs in the first place (being harder to maneuver and needing a larger crew), English ships were bound to be uncompetitive. Some contemporary English writers wanted to copy Dutch shipping and shipbuilding techniques to reverse this situation.[44] But to replace older ships with new ones and to adopt new technology and styles of production would have required more investment than the English could then afford.

Control of international trade gave the Dutch merchants advantages in influencing what was produced in capital-poor markets for international trade. England's key export was wool, and in this trade the Dutch economic dominance of England in the first half of the seventeenth century is obvious; nowhere else did England try to break the Dutch economic grip yet fail so strikingly.

Cloth has been estimated to have been up to 90 percent of English exports by value between the years 1600 and 1660. The largest single market for English cloth was the Netherlands. Rather than finished products for final markets, English exports consisted primarily of unfinished cloth that passed through the Dutch entrepôt. At the end of the sixteenth century, London had exported some 105,000 cloths, sending 75,000 to the Netherlands and Germany but only some 12,000 directly to the Baltic, 6,500 directly to the Levant, roughly the same number directly to France, and around 2,000 each directly to Italy, Russia, and Barbary. Attempts to win back the direct trade with the Mediterranean (and the Baltic, too) which England had held in the sixteenth century were implemented in 1615 and 1622, via legislation that was a precursor to the Navigation Act of 1651.[45] These attempts to legislate a direct carrying of cloths to final markets failed in the face of Dutch competition. English cloth merchants were not to make strong direct links to markets until the 1730s, after Dutch attempts at liberal leadership had ended.[46]

43. Frank, World Accumulation, p. 79.

44. Wilson, England's Apprenticeship, p. 168; Wilson, Profit and Power, pp. 94–96.

45. Wilson, Economic History and the Historian, p. 144; Wilson, Profit and Power, p. 8; Wilson, England's Apprenticeship, pp. 38, 69–70; Ralph Davis, English Overseas Trade, 1500–1700 (New York: Macmillan, 1973), pp. 22–24, 29.

46. J. G. van Dillen, "Economic Fluctuations and Trade in the Netherlands, 1650–1750," in Essays in European Economic History, 1500–1800, ed. Peter Earle (Oxford: Clarendon Press, 1974), p. 204.

The most famous English cloth merchants were in an organized marketing association known as the Merchant Adventurers. The Merchant Adventurers had monopolistic rights (purchased from the crown) to sell unfinished cloth internationally. Their primary customers were Dutch middlemen. The domination of Dutch merchants, in alliance with local political and economic interests as seen in other countries such as Sweden, could be seen in England too. This type of alliance creates trade with the liberal leader even when the state is ambivalent toward the liberal international trading system.

Rent-Sanctioning and the Cockayne Project

To increase revenues, King James I decided to end the Merchant Adventurer's rent sanction, to replace it with another. A government report prepared in 1614 estimated that the potential gains from carrying out the higher stages of cloth production in England before export could be anywhere from 50 to 100 percent in the total value of the good.[47] In that year, the king forbade the export of "cloth in the white" (unfinished cloth) in order to stimulate English efforts to attain the higher steps of production (dyeing and bleaching), where so much of the final value accrued. The Dutch responded by prohibiting the import of finished goods from England, to which James responded by banning the export of wool.[48] The Dutch state had clearly responded to the English state's attack on Dutch trade.

What the English state (or, more specifically, what James I) was trying to do was take away the rights of the Merchant Adventurers, who had cozy relations with the Dutch, and give those rights to a group of investors led by a man named Cockayne. The official aim of this group was to develop the higher stages of cloth production, to enable England to export finished cloth.[49] Rivals of the Merchant Adventurers were quick to support Cockayne; the domestic clothworkers and dyers, who would also receive rents, shared this support. Finally, James saw an opportunity to increase state revenues—by as much as £20,000 from the customs on dyestuffs and another £20,000 on the higher value expected from exports, according to his advisers. Bribery by Cockayne, or at least timely cheap loans, undoubtedly influenced the king's decision.[50] Of course, the replacement of one monopoly with another did not actually ap-

47. Wilson, *England's Apprenticeship*, p. 38.

48. Immanuel Wallerstein, "Dutch Hegemony in the Seventeenth Century World-Economy," in *Dutch Capitalism and World Capitalism*, ed. Aymard, p. 99.

49. B. E. Supple, *Commercial Crisis and Change in England, 1600–1642: A Study in the Instability of a Mercantile Economy* (Cambridge: Cambridge University Press, 1964), p. 35.

50. Wilson, *England's Apprenticeship*, pp. 72–73.

pease all the rivals of the Adventurers, and the creation of economic problems with the Dutch made the new monopoly's tasks that much harder.

The Cockayne project ended in failure for several reasons. Cockayne's group lacked sufficient capital to finance the investments in technology to develop and expand the dyeing and bleaching operations; the necessary technology and skilled workers were not available in sufficient numbers to process the quantity of cloth that had previously been exported to the Dutch. Unable to change the actual mix of English exports in the short run, Cockayne's group used their monopoly rights to do exactly what the Merchant Adventurers had done—export unfinished cloth.[51] All the project achieved was a change in who handled these exports and a bigger state share in the rents.

Meanwhile, the Dutch merchants and state were putting pressure on England to change its policies. Cockayne's group could not buy up all the unfinished cloth, so unemployment in the English cloth industry started to rise. The finished cloth Cockayne did produce was not priced competitively for international trade anyway—reflecting how domestic rents can distort markets and push domestic prices from below international levels to well above them. Trade disruption and unemployment made the king's position vis-à-vis Cockayne less tenable. Since cloth production was one of the largest sectors of the national economy, disruptions in employment created social disorder the crown could not accept. By 1624, Parliament had gotten freedom for anyone to export cloth; the Merchant Adventurers were only able to repurchase their charter from the king (in 1634, after borrowing the necessary funds from the Dutch) when Parliament was not in session.[52] The relative scarcity of capital in England compared to the Netherlands made it difficult to compete against the Dutch in capital-intensive industries, despite the state's efforts to create national monopolies in exactly those sectors.

England's Navigation Acts

Another famous attempt by the English to end the domination of their economy by Dutch middlemen was eventually much more successful, although this policy would not achieve its goals until the Dutch had abandoned attempts to create a liberal subsystem. The Navigation Acts of the seventeenth century were designed to eliminate the Dutch from distribution functions within England's realm, which the English hoped would then correct their

51. Wilson, *Profit and Power*, p. 29; Supple, *Commercial Crisis*, p. 36.
52. Wilson, *Transformation of Europe*, pp. 37–38; Wilson, *England's Apprenticeship*, pp. 54, 149. Barbour, *Capitalism in Amsterdam*, p. 123, gives a different date.

problematic balance of payments by lowering Dutch gains on invisibles (services). The Navigation Acts were to give a monopoly to English shipping by decreeing that imports had to come straight from the source country and be carried in ships from the source country or England. The prohibitions on the use of foreign ships and the importation of fish in foreign boats were aimed specifically at the Dutch.[53]

The initial Navigation Act (of 1651) had gained domestic support because of economic depression in England and because the Dutch and English governments had just failed to reach settlement on ways to restrain Dutch trade with England.[54] Like the earlier Cockayne project, the series of navigation acts that were eventually passed during the seventeenth century tried to combine economic jealousy of the Dutch with the rhetoric of strategic interests. Through the sanctioning of these rents, some domestic economic interests would benefit, as would the state. By establishing domestic monopolies favoring the already scarce resource of capital, the crown hoped to increase its revenues (by excluding Dutch profits), make tax collection easier, and use claims of national interest to reduce criticism of the policies.[55]

The Dutch had several ways around the Navigation Acts. First, the commercial rivalry developed into a series of limited wars (discussed below).[56] By doing well in the second of these wars, the Dutch were able to introduce loopholes into the Navigation Act. The Treaty of Breda (1667), which ended the Second Anglo-Dutch War, made goods produced in the Dutch hinterland exempt from the Navigation Act. Since the Dutch hinterland included not only the Netherlands but the Rhine and other river valleys that reached the sea in the Netherlands, most of Germany fell into this category—so goods produced not only in the Netherlands but also in much of Germany could legally be transported to England in Dutch ships.

The Navigation Acts were often relaxed during wartime, when England required greater amounts of foreign material to prosecute wars. In such times, foreign ships were allowed to carry goods from a third country to England. One can easily understand how this worked. If England's war effort required iron from Sweden, the Navigation Acts would have permitted only English or Swedish ships to carry that iron to England. Since the Swedish merchant fleet was small, if England wanted larger amounts of iron quickly it would most

---

53. Wilson, *Profit and Power*, pp. 53, 99, 102; Wilson, *England's Apprenticeship*, p. 62.
54. Wilson, *England's Apprenticeship*, pp. 61–62.
55. Supple, *Commercial Crisis*, pp. 242–243, makes the argument on the cost-effectiveness of regulated companies for the state.
56. Each of these can be found in Wilson, *Anglo-Dutch Commerce*, pp. 6–7.

certainly have been forced to rely on Dutch ships. Since the seventeenth century was a time of almost continual warfare, exceptions to the Navigation Acts abounded.

The other way the Navigation Acts could be avoided was for Dutch ships to become English. This could be done by establishing a branch office of a Dutch firm in England, then simply transferring ships from one branch of the firm to the other. Since most business firms of the time were family operations, the risks of doing multinational business were kept low; a son or brother would be placed in control of the foreign branch. After a generation or two, this branch of the family was probably as English as it was Dutch. Yet this was an actual way of evading the maritime prohibitions.

The Navigation Acts did not provide positive results until the eighteenth century, after the Dutch gave up attempts at liberal leadership. In fact, one may view the continual reissuance of navigation controls as a sign that the previous ones had failed.[57] As late as 1721 there were still more Dutch than British ships carrying trade between Britain and France.[58] The Dutch control of the Baltic trade lasted even longer, although the prominence of Dutch ships slowly declined. Although English ships began carrying more of the goods, the Dutch still provided the financing and insurance for trade. Until the late 1700s, Russian customs had to be paid in Dutch currency, although English merchants were the first to be allowed exceptions to this rule. No exchange rate was quoted between London and St. Petersburg until 1763; up to that time, Anglo-Russian trade payments went through Dutch banks. English shipping would not rapidly increase in numbers until the production of colonial goods rose dramatically and the Dutch fleet (and Dutch power) had been damaged by the political challenge of France.[59]

In history texts, the Navigation Acts are connected with discussions of the three wars fought between England and the United Provinces in the seventeenth century. In a sense, these wars were challenges to the liberal leadership exercised by the Dutch, but they were limited in aims. As England accumulated more capital and came to compete more directly with the Netherlands, there was a strong possibility that England would become an expansionary challenger. This was especially true when the crown had the upper hand domestically (as in the Third Anglo-Dutch War). Capital abundance in the later

57. Eli F. Heckscher, *The Continental System: An Economic Interpretation* (Oxford: Clarendon, 1922), p. 15.

58. Wilson, *Anglo-Dutch Commerce*, p. 6; Van Houtte, *Economic History of the Low Countries*, p. 275.

59. Wilson, *Economic History and the Historian*, pp. 28, 59; Christopher Hill, *The Century of Revolution, 1603–1714* (New York: Norton, 1966), p. 211; Davis, *English Overseas Trade*, p. 10.

seventeenth century meant that, when the monarch had control, England would follow policies of expansionary challenge.

England's Domestic Changes and the Anglo-Dutch Wars

England vacillated between control by a strong monarchy and by a strong Parliament until the issue was finally settled in 1688. The monarchy's power was challenged by Parliament early in the seventeenth century, as both parties tried to raise revenues independently of the other. The English king was more desperate for revenue than his continental peers because he had relatively limited personal resources. The seizure of monastic and ecclesiastic lands by the Tudors had given the crown an economic base, but much of this had been sold off by the 1600s. Moreover, the changes in agricultural productivity had eroded the privileged position of the nobility in Parliament; the hereditary distinctions were disappearing.[60] Parliament became an institution representing a broader range of interests, which served to heighten the tension between it and the crown.

The crown's efforts to raise revenues through the sanctioning of rents were undercut by Parliament's efforts to do the same. Each tried to establish monopoly rights and grant special charters—but they wound up creating two "monopolies" in many cases, which made neither of the rival companies as successful as it otherwise would have been. The crown supported company regulation and monopolies in order to increase its own rents (not just in terms of government revenues but also in bribes, loans to government, loans to government agents, and greater control and monitoring of other forms of tax collection, such as with customs). Based on the expectations for autocratic states formulated in Chapter 1, the king should favor increased sanctioning of rents, for this raises his revenues and lowers collection costs without changing the costs of providing protection and order. The only damage wrought is to his popularity and support, which he can counter with rhetoric about national interests. The Cockayne project is an example of this type of policy.

In 1625, Charles I came to the throne and began reasserting the rights of the crown; in doing so he started a battle between the crown and Parliament that would run its course with English Civil War and eventually his own beheading. In the economic sphere, his attempts to reassert the royal power to grant monopolies failed for several reasons; the most important was the in-

---

60. Perry Anderson, *Lineages of the Absolutist State* (London: Verso, 1979), pp. 124–126; Hill, *Century of Revolution*, p. 51.

ability to suppress competition, both within and outside cartel arrangements.[61] This inability directly reflects the broader competition between the two political institutions.

Parliament also had a desire to sanction rents in order to raise its revenues, but it was less able to arrange monopolies, since it was listening to a broader range of interests, and less able to overcome the higher costs of democratic rather than monarchic decision making in this area. The king increasingly resorted to the use of prerogative powers to enforce royally sanctioned rents. In 1628/29, Parliament responded with the Petition of Right, which declared arbitrary imprisonment and the collection of taxes without Parliament's consent illegal, in order to get some control over the king and his rent-enhancing actions.

Charles I, through some ingenious maneuvers, managed to raise enough revenues to survive without Parliament—but his limited success only served to generate Parliament's resentment. Charles resurrected many feudal dues and even resorted to the sale of offices (which came to account for roughly a third of royal income).[62] But in the summer of 1640, Charles needed yet more money and could not secure any loans without promising to recall Parliament. Once in session, Parliament immediately initiated a constitutional struggle with the crown. Parliament began by passing the Triennial Act in 1640, which declared that Parliament would meet regularly (every three years) whether the king summoned it or not; another act passed at the same time declared that Parliament could not be dissolved without its own consent; nonparliamentary taxes were declared illegal, and the prerogative courts (such as the infamous Star Chamber or the Council of the North) that had been enforcing the king's laws were abolished. This was an all-out attack on the king's assumed privileges. The struggle for political supremacy urged Parliament to protect itself by establishing religious, civil, and political liberties.

The struggle between Parliament and the monarchy should not be construed as simply a struggle between free trade and monopolies, or for that matter as simply a struggle over the right to sanction rents. Instead, it should be seen as a conflict over which institution would control the state; the right to sanction and share in rents was simply one attribute the winner of this struggle could collect. Although some see Parliament victorious by the 1640s, flirtations with centralized monarchic power would continue until the Glorious Revolution of 1688.

---

61. Anderson, *Lineages of the Absolutist State*, p. 139; Ekelund and Tollison, *Mercantilism as a Rent-Seeking Society*, pp. 63–64.

62. Anderson, *Lineages of the Absolutist State*, p. 141.

Civil War, Cromwell, and the First Anglo-Dutch War

The civil war that erupted out of the institutional rivalry between crown and Parliament has been interpreted in many different fashions, all of which contain elements of truth. The simple fact is that the civil war was over control of the state. Religious and economic divisions mattered, but the central issue was political sovereignty (and therefore control) over several key areas, such as government finance, the armed forces, and the bureaucracy. Economic interpretations stress that Parliament's support came from the economically advanced south and east whereas Royalist support was mainly from the north and west; industrial and agricultural areas mirrored this split in general.[63] One recent interpretation of the geographic split notes that parliamentary support came from the areas most integrated into wider markets.[64]

Parliament's victory in the civil war did not create a stable representative government. Instead, Oliver Cromwell assumed dictatorial powers. Although Parliament represented a broader range of manufacturing, commercial, shipping, and naval interests than the crown had, it proved quite willing to support Cromwell's anti-Dutch policies in the 1651 Navigation Act. This act was only one point of contention between the two countries; rival trading companies had started low-level conflicts outside Europe. Also, Cromwell continued disputes over sovereignty of the seas begun by the king, which led to clashes over North Sea fishing rights and maritime etiquette.[65]

The change from royal rule to the rule of a dictator did not lead to a change in England's ambivalence toward Dutch liberal leadership. Instead, the actors in control of state-sanctioned rents changed. Cromwell led the now more powerful England into the First Anglo-Dutch War (1652–1654) to try to limit Dutch economic competition. English feeling was that the only way to eliminate Dutch advantages in trade was through the application of armed force.

As the established liberal leader, the Dutch controlled an international political-economic system that was vulnerable to attack. One Dutch statesman described the beginning of the First Anglo-Dutch War thus: "The English are about to attack a mountain of gold; we are about to attack a mountain of

---

63. Hill, *Century of Revolution*, pp. 106, 121–125. But no single explanation captures the wide variance in the sources of support going to either side; contrasting examples to any simple explanation can be found easily. See Wilson's discussions in *England's Apprenticeship*, p. 126, and *Economic History and the Historian*, p. 11.

64. Leonard Hochberg, "The English Civil War in Geographical Perspective," *Journal of Interdisciplinary History* 14 (Spring 1984): 729–750.

65. Wilson, *Profit and Power*, p. 61; Wilson, *England's Apprenticeship*, pp. 63–64; Frank, *World Accumulation*, p. 83.

iron." Since the Dutch had merchant ships throughout European waters and had built an international economic subsystem by balancing European trade, the English could apply economic pressure by harrassing that shipping and unbalancing that trade; the Dutch had no comparable, easy way to compel the English to stop, though they successfully pressured Denmark to close the Baltic from English shipping in 1653. Because English war aims were limited, the two sides came to terms after only two years of fighting.[66] The English were not trying to destroy the Dutch-led subsystem; they were trying to alter Anglo-Dutch relations within it.

Cromwell was accused by some of his fellow Englishmen of going too lightly on the Dutch. They felt that he could have extracted more from the Dutch but had chosen not to out of partiality to the other major Protestant non-monarchy, which England might need as an ally some day. Because the major Dutch concession was the elimination of the position of stadhouder (which would weaken Dutch military leadership, though some Dutch republicans would not mind this since they saw the stadhouder as a political rival domestically), it was hardly a major English victory. All other economic or colonial demands were dropped.[67] The fact that Cromwell did not ask for more is also a good indication of the inability of the English economy to persevere without access to Dutch trade and Dutch capital; as an ambivalent power, England was trying to change the rules governing trade, but it still desired economic links with the liberal leader. The only significant gain for England was that the Danes agreed to charge them the same low Sound tolls the Dutch received.[68]

Restoration and the Second Anglo-Dutch War

The Cromwellian government collapsed into military dictatorship, and eventually the domestic turmoil led to support for a return to monarchy. The early years of the Restoration saw a vigorous reconstruction of the legal instruments of economic regulation and control. Parliamentary interests and the crown tried to work together, as these interests had worked with Cromwell. Moreover, the partial success of the First Anglo-Dutch War fueled ambitions. As Samuel Pepys quoted one merchant, "The trade of the world is too little

66. Wilson, *England's Apprenticeship*, p. 64; Wilson, *Profit and Power*, p. 77; Ramsay, *English Overseas Trade*, p. 125. Paul M. Kennedy, *The Rise and Fall of British Naval Mastery* (London: Lane, 1976), pp. 54, 48–51, claims that, if territorial security was the main criterion for determining enemies, both England and the Netherlands would have seen France as their main enemy.
67. Israel, *Dutch Primacy in World Trade*, pp. 210–213.
68. Wilson, *Profit and Power*, p. 77.

for us two, therefore one must down." When London merchants began to clamor for war and looked to the royal court for support, the court in turn thought the city was finally ready to finance royal policy.[69] In the meantime, the English navy was increased by some two hundred ships by 1665, and prizes from the First Anglo-Dutch War were added to the English merchant marine.[70]

England had been accumulating capital, so it was better placed in 1665 to compete economically with the Dutch; Englishmen could more easily finance their own trade now. And England had a larger military establishment than before, to help further economic competition with the Dutch. The duke of Ablemarle succinctly stated English war aims in the Second Anglo-Dutch War when he proclaimed, "What we want is more of the trade the Dutch now have." The owners of capital in England (concentrated in London) were looking for ways to keep capital employed and had turned to the state to lessen Dutch competition; these merchants, the Catholic followers of the royal court, and ambitious young naval officers formed the very core of English support for the war. The regulated companies of the Restoration were symbols of the linkage between the new capital richness of England and the monarchy, for these companies were made of just such an alliance—and these companies led the way into the Second Anglo-Dutch War by starting unofficial hostilities with the Dutch in non-European waters.[71]

The change in English interests between 1654 and 1665 (when the Second Anglo-Dutch War began) showed that England was becoming more important in international trade. As the Dutch had been vulnerable (and still were) to pressure via attacks on the far-flung Dutch merchant fleet, the English too were now vulnerable. This time, war proved disastrous for English trade. Because the English merchant marine was larger and English trading interests more developed, the Dutch could now attack exposed English economic interests. Despite the early support for the war by the city of London, Charles soon had difficulty securing loans for naval operations; the Dutch government, in contrast, raised funds easily. The Dutch navy took the offensive and brought the war to their enemies by ravaging the nascent English merchant fleet and attacking England itself—once penetrating the Thames all the way to London, seizing one of the largest English warships, and towing it away. The natural

---

69. Ibid., p. 93; Wilson, *England's Apprenticeship*, pp. 161–163; Wilson, *Dutch Republic*, p. 198. The Pepys quotation is as cited in Wilson, *Profit and Power*, p. 122.

70. Wilson, *Profit and Power*, p. 78; Hill, *Century of Revolution*, p. 157.

71. Lee, *British Economy since 1700*, p. 121. Quotation from Wilson, *England's Apprenticeship*, p. 165. Wilson, *Profit and Power*, p. 111; Wilson, *Dutch Republic*, p. 195; Derek McKay and H. M. Scott, *The Rise of the Great Powers, 1648–1815* (New York: Longman, 1983), p. 19.

calamities of the plague and the Great Fire of London combined with the poor military showing of English forces to make support for the war falter.[72]

The Second Anglo-Dutch War ended in more of a draw than a Dutch victory, for English forces had made some gains in colonial areas and the Dutch sought a speedy return to peace. The peace treaty took away and gave to both sides, perhaps reflecting the new balance of naval strength. The Navigation Acts were amended favorably for the Dutch, whereas the minor exchanges of colonial territory generally benefited England (as when New Amsterdam became New York).

The war proved to be a turning point in Anglo-Dutch relations, for it reopened the split between economic interests and the crown. As capital became more abundant, competition for rents in capital-intensive sectors increased. Since the state had failed to expand a closed economic subsystem for this growing group of capitalists to exploit through sanctioned rents, more economic interests were drawn toward participation in the Dutch-led subsystem. In this sense, the Second Anglo-Dutch War *might* be seen as a war of challenge that failed. In the words of Pepys, "trade and war could not be supported together."[73] The economic interests voiced in Parliament now chose trade and shifted that institution's position closer to the Dutch, but the king still controlled foreign policy.

The Third Anglo-Dutch War

Charles knew that he could no longer turn to Parliament for funds without giving up some of his independence. Instead, he turned to the French king for support. In 1670, England and France became allies through the Treaty of Dover. Louis XIV was preparing France for war against the Dutch and wanted the English as allies. Parliament and the commercial community wanted no part in this war, but Charles was drawn to Louis by religious leanings and the hope of financial aid. The royal court began expounding the virtues of France, absolutism, and Catholicism—policies the general English populace did not care for. Parliament countered with a protestant, pro-Dutch policy. Louis was only too happy to give Charles subsidies so that Charles could keep a firm grip on English foreign policy and ignore Parliament.[74]

---

72. Wilson, *England's Apprenticeship*, pp. 165, 185; Israel, *Dutch Primacy in World Trade*, p. 278; McKay and Scott, *Rise of the Great Powers*, p. 19; Baxter, *William III*, p. 42.

73. Pepys quotation from Kennedy, *Rise & Fall of British Naval Mastery*, p. 61.

74. Hill, *Century of Revolution*, pp. 215–216; Carter, *Neutrality or Commitment*, pp. 12–13; Kennedy, *Rise and Fall of British Naval Mastery*, p. 61; Carl J. Ekberg, *The Failure of Louis XIV's*

What Charles apparently did not realize was that subsidies from France, though possibly freeing him from Parliament, thrust him into dependence on Louis. By supporting the French war against the Dutch in 1672 (the Third Anglo-Dutch War), Charles would need even more money. He would either have to become Louis's puppet or face an increasingly angry Parliament. Charles found neither of these paths attractive, so the English war effort was underfunded and feeble at best. England eventually had to drop out of the war and sign a separate peace treaty with the Dutch. For all practical purposes, the Treaty of Westminster in 1674 restored the status quo ante, which reinforced contemporary public opinion that together the three Anglo-Dutch wars had been largely futile.[75]

England's position vis-à-vis the Netherlands changed dramatically over the course of the decades before 1674. England began as a capital-scarce, medium-strength country ruled by an autocratic institution. As such, it had ambivalent policies toward the Dutch and the Dutch-led liberal international economic subsystem—upsetting some of the rules the Dutch established but always returning to trade with the Dutch. Over time, capital accumulation in England increased, as did English military power; after the 1650s, interest rates in England fell to as low as 6 percent, although they were still lower in the Netherlands, at 4 percent.[76] Economic competition with the Dutch was continually increasing. Cloth exports grew absolutely, but so did the variety of English exports; by 1700, English shipbuilders were producing boats of the same quality as the Dutch at cheap prices; and between 1669 and 1700, England was able to turn a trade deficit into a stable trade surplus, along with growing profits from international services. The English began to be more vigorous in the trade with Russia, Spain, and the Levant. Capital services such as marine insurance began to develop in London in the 1680s. Whereas only a small part of English trade had been reexports of colonial goods in 1640, this figure rose to a quarter of the total by 1700.[77] In the absence of other changes, this would have encouraged England to become an expansionary challenger. Indeed, the

---

Dutch War (Chapel Hill: University of North Carolina Press, 1979), pp. 152–153; Frank T. Melton, *Sir Robert Clayton and the Origins of English Deposit Banking, 1658–1685* (New York: Cambridge University Press, 1986), p. 17.

75. Kennedy, *Rise and Fall of British Naval Mastery*, p. 63.

76. Parker, "Emergence of Modern Finance," pp. 539–540. Homer, *History of Interest Rates*, p. 178, also states that English interest rates fell, but stayed higher than in the Netherlands.

77. Wilson, *England's Apprenticeship*, pp. 160–161, 171, 185. The figures on trade balances do not include the war debts England owed to the Netherlands, which became formidable after 1710. Also Wilson, *Economic History and the Historian*, p. 28, and Hill, *Century of Revolution*, pp. 211, 273.

Anglo-Dutch wars appear as the preliminary rounds of just such a political challenge.

Growing economic competition with the Dutch might have fueled a challenge if the monarchy had retained complete control of the English state and rents in the capital-intensive sectors had been widely sanctioned. But the attacks on the monarchy's powers made commercial and industrial economic regulation less a tool of rent-seeking interests and made England's foreign economic policy more receptive to foreign trade. Parliament's increasingly important role in state policymaking would provide the crucial difference between peaceful economic rivalry and political challenge: once Parliament became the dominant political institution in 1688, England became an ally and supporter of liberal leadership by the Dutch.

The French State and Economy in the Seventeenth Century

The Third Anglo-Dutch War illustrated that, though England was not prepared to challenge Dutch liberal leadership politically, France was. This conflict was one facet of a wider conflict known as Louis's Dutch war. France had begun the seventeenth century as a capital-poor, powerful country with an autocratic state, and it was originally ambivalent toward Dutch liberal leadership. As capital accumulated, increased economic competition with the Dutch was not tempered by political institutions representing broader domestic interests as it had been by Parliament's rise in England. Quite the opposite occurred in France, where the monarchy gained absolute control. As capital accumulated, domestic political power was being centralized—and France became an expansionary political challenger against the Dutch and the open subsystem.

The battle between the central monarchy and other social-political groups (and especially the nobility) took a different course in France than it had in England. Although the monarchy lost control during the Frondes (1640s), when the new King Louis XIV was but a child, the crown was soon able to reassert its dominance. This was because the king could draw on his own resources to raise more than enough money to run the state; the king had enough funds to attack internal opposition and finance external expansion.

Once Louis came of age and assumed the throne, he undertook to overcome the monarchy's weakness versus the nobility and other domestic interests. With able advisers and servants, exemplified by Jean-Baptiste Colbert, Louis set out to establish the absolute monarchy. When necessary, he used force to silence the parlements, to reduce the autonomy of provincial estates and municipalities, and to remove the nobility from direct rule over the land.[78] One by one, Louis reduced rival claimants to power and authority within France; although this took resources and effort, it also enabled him to sanction and enforce a wider range of rents. Centralization of authority meant that Louis's arrangement of rents held for all of France, whereas previously the strength of other domestic political actors had created numerous exceptions to royally established rents.

Nowhere is the combination of the buildup of Louis's own resources to solidify his position and the prosecution of more extensive rents more evident than in the actions of Colbert. Under Colbert's administration, the French state increased its annual revenues from grants of monopoly and cartel rights.[79] Colbert was placed in charge of royal finances in 1661. His actions soon doubled the monarchy's revenues, moving the state's budget into surplus for the first time since 1610, where he kept it from 1662 until 1671.

Colbert's financial moves were successful in altering and increasing the sources of the crown's revenues, thus allowing the state to tap into the French economy and become important in accumulating capital itself. The crown drew money in five main ways: (1) revenue from crown lands, (2) the *taille* (a direct property tax on non-nobles and non-clergy), (3) the *gabelle* (a tax on salt), (4) the *aides* (residual feudal dues on sales, transportation, and internal trade), and (5) the *traites* (import-export customs). Colbert simplified these taxes and increased the revenues generated by the royal lands.[80]

Colbert's success in changing the state's actions is as one would expect from the discussion of an autocratic state's domestic interests in Chapter 1. As an institution that provides protection and order in exchange for revenue, the state increases its revenue by preventing rivals from offering the same services, lowering the costs of collecting revenue and providing services. Colbert's sim-

---

78. Anderson, *Lineages of the Absolutist State*, p. 100, and also Hilton Root, "The Redistributive Role of Government: Economic Regulation in Old Regime France and England," *Comparative Studies in Society and History* 33 (April 1991): 367.

79. Though Ekelund and Tollison, *Mercantilism as a Rent-Seeking Society*, p. 6, claim that these increases were more than half the state's revenues, other scholars such as William Beik, *Absolutism and Society in Seventeenth-Century France* (New York: Cambridge University Press, 1985), pp. 288–292, suggest that most of Colbert's monopolies and cartels failed to generate profits in the long run.

80. Laurence B. Packard, *The Commercial Revolution 1400–1776: Mercantilism—Colbert—Adam Smith* (New York: Holt, 1927), pp. 53–55. For more specific information, see Alain Guéry, "Les finances de la monarchie française sous L'Ancien Régime," as well as others in *Annales E.S.C.* 33 (March–April 1978): 216–239, Julian Dent, *Crisis in France: Crown Financiers and Society in Seventeenth Century France* (Newton Abbot: David & Charles, 1973), and J. F. Bosher, *French Finances, 1770–1795: From Business to Bureaucracy* (New York: Cambridge University Press, 1970).

plification of the tax structure lowered the costs of collection; the use of *inten-dants* to execute royal orders and inspect activities and services provided for and to the state raised the quality of the state's activities. At the same time, the *intendants* (who were dependent on the monarchy) replaced more indepen-dent servants of the crown. The money raised and power created was used to lessen internal rivals' power and to monopolize the functions of providing protection and order, by establishing the monarchy's complete control over the military.

What developed in France was one of the better examples of an autocratic state—the absolutist monarchy.[81] More important, this particular monarchy ruled a large country with a large population (which was perhaps the single greatest military asset of the time). At some time between the 1630s and the 1670s, as Spain's ability to field large armies declined and France's rose, France became the greatest land power. If it had any military weakness, it was its small navy. But even here France grew stronger: the navy rose to be the third largest fleet in the 1670s, although the numbers belie its poor quality. The large army, however, was first rate. No other monarch could match Louis's ability to raise money and troops and then use them independently.[82]

Assessing seventeenth-century France's relative capital abundance is a diffi-cult task. Hard comparable figures are not available. And, in this case, exten-sive rents distort the historical indicators derived from market transactions. Interest rates or other market indicators of the relative scarcity of capital in France are likely to be influenced by several nonmarket factors. First, the state granted some exclusive economic privileges, which could serve to drive up some interest rates beyond normal market returns, meaning high interest rates may not be evidence of an actual capital scarcity. Second, the state was also able to impose forced loans at cheap rates, so at times certain interest rates may look deceptively low and not reflect actual capital abundance. For in-stance, the French are quite well known for the tradition of hoarding capital, particularly bullion, and keeping it off the market; this was a prudent move in the seventeenth century, for when the market was not necessarily open the

81. It should be remembered that even the absolutist state was constrained by other social actors; for an elaboration of this point in this particular case (but focusing on slightly earlier periods), see James B. Collins, *Fiscal Limits of Absolutism* (Berkeley: University of California Press, 1988), and Beik, *Absolutism and Society*.

82. For the figures on land forces, see Parker and Smith, "Introduction," in *General Crisis*, ed. Parker and Smith, p. 14. For naval forces, see William R. Thompson, "Succession Crises in the Global Political System: A Test of the Transition Model," in *Crises in the World-System*, ed. Albert Bergesen (Beverly Hills, Calif.: Sage, 1983), p. 107. Also see McKay and Scott, *Rise of the Great Powers*, p. 15.

state might requisition one's capital. It was often in the owner's best interest to keep capital out of sight.[83]

To determine France's capital-labor ratio at this time, it is necessary to decipher the existing information on interest rates and wages. Trends in capital accumulation at least become apparent, even though statistics on overall levels of capital relative to labor are not as solid as one might wish. The evidence points to France becoming more capital-abundant, although it never reached the levels of the Dutch capital-labor ratio.

France as a Challenger

Because France was a powerful state less sensitive to domestic political competition, the accumulation of capital encouraged the French state to undertake a political challenge against the Dutch. As capital was accumulated, France became an economic competitor of the Netherlands. As an absolutist, Louis wanted to expand France's economic activities without lessening his control or undercutting his revenues. Capital-intensive sectors within France would have rising incentives to disrupt any rents as capital accumulated; the problem Louis faced was to maintain the rents without unduly restricting employment of capital.

As a first measure, foreign participation in the French economy had to be eliminated. Like other ambivalent powers, France had earlier relied on Dutch trade and capital; Louis's first conflict with the Dutch was to end or at least restrict Dutch penetration of the French economy. Eventually, leading an expanding closed economic subsystem would place Louis in direct conflict with the Netherlands. Rather than compete with the Dutch in open trade, Louis could maximize his gains by increasing the size of the area in which he sanctioned rents. He therefore used the state's increased revenues and greater control of domestic economic activity to expand France's borders.

Colbert again was the wizard behind French policy. In 1659 he had imposed a 50-sou-per-ton duty on the entry and departure of ships. But, just as the English Cockayne project had proven that getting rid of the Dutch was easier said than done, French domestic resources could not fill the economic demand once met by Dutch ships. In the Cockayne project, ending Dutch control of the cloth trade required domestic capital, technology, and skilled workers to be employed to finish the cloth; when the necessary capital and inputs were not cheaply available in England, the project failed to be interna-

83. Extensive discussions of the problems related to capital hoarding and hiding can be found in Part 2 of Julian Dent's *Crisis in France*.

tionally competitive and could not buy up all the unfinished cloth the Dutch had previously purchased. Unemployment and economic downturn resulted. In France, this story was repeated with the shipping duties. The duties drove away Dutch carriers, but with only five or six hundred ships, the French merchant marine was not nearly large enough to replace the Dutch; within three years the resulting economic problems led the state to charge dues on departures only and to reduce those on salt exports by half.[84] These changes took the sting out of the duties for the Dutch, since they were particularly interested in the export of salt, which they used in the packing and processing of herring or reexported to the Baltic to help balance the exports of Baltic grain.

Other commercial tariffs were established in 1664 and 1667.[85] Besides a protective tariff system, the monarchy's powers and revenues were used to support several mercantilist ventures to counter Dutch competition. The state created these companies to capture domestic rents. Chartered companies were formed, shipyards subsidized, and new industries in clothmaking, glassblowing, tapestry weaving, and iron production begun with state guidance.[86] Not only did these companies receive financial support from the monarchy, they were given monopolistic privileges to ensure that the returns on the king's investments were high.

The trading companies Colbert helped establish were heavily influenced by Dutch example. Unlike Scandinavian trading companies formed with Dutch financial backing, the French companies raised their own capital. But Colbert knew how to use that capital wisely. The French East India Company (Compagnie des Indes Orientales) set up in 1664 sent out its first expedition under the guidance of Francois Caron, who had worked for the VOC in Japan; the expedition's fleet was partially outfitted in the Netherlands. The Amsterdam house of Coymans was used as agent.[87] But, unlike the Dutch or English East India companies, the French company was established by the state and not by commercial interests: the company was controlled by politicians, not merchants. Because of this political control and the resulting continual squabbling over monopoly rents, the company's financial history is full of manipulation, stock jobbing, and government subsidies, which suggests that the company

84. Van Houtte, *Economic History of the Low Countries*, p. 276.
85. McKay and Scott, *Rise of the Great Powers*, pp. 24–25.
86. Anderson, *Lineages of the Absolutist State*, p. 103.
87. Barbour, *Capitalism in Amsterdam*, pp. 132–133.

did not make a profit between 1663 and 1793, even when the costs of defense and military support given by the state are not included.[88]

From Mercantilism to Political Challenge

The implementation of mercantilist policies was only the first step toward challenge of Dutch liberal hegemony. The final step was taken in 1672 when France, with England as an ally, attempted to eliminate the Dutch through political incorporation in the French kingdom. The aims of French mercantilism were to suppress Dutch competition, and the French military assault was merely a more direct means toward this end. By taking over the Netherlands and its trading system, the French state's revenues would soar, since its chief international economic competition would end and the area under state control would be widened and enriched. As Colbert advised Louis, "the Dutch have no right to seize all trade," and "if [Louis XIV] should subject the provinces constituting the Netherlands, their commerce becoming the possession of his majesty's subjects, no advantage could be left to be desired."[89]

The use of war by absolute monarchs, as Louis's wars with the Dutch show, flows directly from the rent-seeking nature of the absolutist state. Rather than emulate the Dutch economic system, and perhaps open the French domestic market in order to compete more effectively with the Dutch, Louis looked at the existing Dutch economic system as something to appropriate and exact revenues from. This zero-sum logic meant that Louis saw the Dutch-led open international subsystem as similar to other physical objects to be taken or denied by force.[90]

The incentives to challenge the Dutch were heightened as the French economy accumulated capital, for this raised economic competition between the two countries. Dutch competition meant that relative returns to capital would fall with economic growth and increasing capital abundance; the best way to maintain high relative returns to capital while capital increased in abundance was to continue to sanction rents, which at a minimum required controlling the extent of competition with the Dutch. With a large army at his disposal, Louis saw that he could maximize the state's revenues, not by simply ending

---

88. Attman, *Bullion Flow*, pp. 54–55.

89. Wilson, *Economic History and the Historian*, p. 29; Colbert quoted in McKay and Scott, *Rise of the Great Powers*, p. 25, and in Anderson, *Lineages of the Absolutist State*, pp. 36–37; also, Packard, *Commercial Revolution*, p. 67.

90. Anderson, *Lineages of the Absolutist State*, pp. 36–37.

Dutch competition, but by bringing the Dutch economic system under his control. In 1672, French armies moved against the United Provinces.

The wars the French waged against the Dutch in order to appropriate their economic system for the French king follow the pattern predicted in Chapter 1. As the expansionary challenger, France could be expected to build a minimum-winning coalition; in fact, France fought most of the wars alone. As an expansionary power, France could be expected to apply a bold, offensive strategy. As the defending liberal leader, the Dutch should construct a broader alliance from the large group of potential allies to defend the status quo and then use this broader alliance to win the war of challenge through a strategy of attrition.

In the first war between Louis's France and the Dutch Republic (1672–1678), Louis was in fact able to draw England in as an ally, although he did not really expect, or want, much English help. If England played a vital role in defeating the Netherlands, the English would ask for part of the spoils. For the French, this would endanger the whole point of the war. This same problem for the French would arise in other wars against the Dutch; indeed, it is an inherent problem for expansionary challengers, since it would be self-defeating to fight a war to seize the land and possessions of another country, only to share them with others. As expansionary powers, the challengers' problems are increased, for countries that would otherwise be ambivalent toward the liberal hegemon may see the challenger as a threat to themselves and thus turn to the liberal leader for protection. In Louis's case, Anglo-French relations showed that being a French ally meant running the risk France would dominate the relationship; this was an even greater risk for smaller continental powers. Since the 1672 war against the Dutch was one of Louis's first expansionary wars, few other states saw France as a threat. Louis's actions would create those fears soon enough, though.

The Dutch entered the 1672 war with no immediate allies. All the other major European powers were either ambivalent (Spain, Austria, Prussia, Sweden, and Denmark) or on the verge of challenge too (England). The pivotal change would occur in England, with the Glorious Revolution of 1688 changing that country into an economic competitor but political supporter of Dutch leadership. Before 1688, though, the Dutch had to convince the ambivalent powers to come to their aid; these powers did not particularly want to rescue the Netherlands, but they soon developed a fear of France and an appetite for Dutch subsidies. Until then, the United Provinces fought alone.

When Louis attacked in 1672, he brought an army 100,000 strong against Dutch forces only a fourth that size. The French army was well organized and equipped, whereas the Dutch were generally unprepared for combat. The expansionary power, taking the offensive, selected the time and the place for the initial onslaught. These advantages gave the French overwhelming local superiority, which they used to its fullest, attacking out of the east (from the electorate of Cologne) rather than from the south as expected. French forces outflanked and cut off Dutch forces concentrated in the south, facing France, thus allowing the French to overrun three of the Republic's seven provinces in a single fortnight. The French army advanced so quickly it outran its supply lines.[91]

The French army was only kept from overrunning the province of Holland itself, which would have brought about Dutch capitulation, because the Dutch flooded vast expanses of the countryside to form the famous "water barrier." Although this act is appreciated today as one of great heroism and tactical genius, it was in fact an act of desperation, a last-ditch effort to stop the French after the army had failed to achieve that end. Surviving Dutch forces were either beseiged in isolated fortresses or pinned along the coast of the province of Holland. Although the key political and economic centers (Amsterdam and The Hague) were still in Dutch hands, the Dutch were in dire straits.

The Dutch Response to the French Challenge

In their predicament, Dutch political leaders attempted to negotiate a peace treaty with Louis. Through intermediaries, they let it be known that they were willing to make grand concessions; but Louis, predicting total victory, turned down any offers of a limited victory.[92] French goals were total victory and nothing less, unlike the limited aims of England in the earlier Anglo-Dutch wars.

This left the Dutch with no choice but to rise to the French challenge, which they did. The domestic system was mobilized for war. The provinces of Zeeland and Holland selected William, Prince of Orange, to be the first stadhouder in thirty years; he was soon named captain-general and admiral-general by the States-General. Public hostility toward the republican leaders who had failed to prevent the war, and who had resisted the return to a stadhoudership, resulted in lynchings of republican leaders (the brothers de Witt). The water barrier gave the Dutch time to reorganize and retrain the

---

91. Baxter, *William III*, p. 71; McKay and Scott, *Rise of the Great Powers*, pp. 28–29; Paul Sonnino, "Louis XIV and the Dutch War," in *Louis XIV and Europe*, ed. R. M. Hatton (New York: Macmillan, 1976), p. 158.

92. McKay and Scott, *Rise of the Great Powers*, pp. 29–30.

army. The Dutch also raised more money to enlarge and reequip the army. William quickly proved to be a capable leader and a good motivator.

Internationally, the time bought by the water barrier was used beneficially. Domestic pressure in England forced Charles to end his alliance with France. Dutch diplomats convinced the rulers of other states that, if the Netherlands fell, they would be Louis's next victims. Subsidies and the lure of seizing French territory made this argument more convincing for the ambivalent powers, and eventually Austria, Spain, and Prussia became Dutch allies. Though the Dutch could not command others to join their alliance, their battle with France developed into a wider conflict.

The new Dutch army counterattacked across the water barrier, and the new allies deployed their armies to threaten French territory. The situation was reversed. Instead of having his enemy cornered, Louis found his own forces overextended and threatened. The French were forced to pull back as pressure built on several fronts at once. When peace was finally agreed on in 1678/79, it was a considerable victory for the Dutch; not only had they retained their independence, Louis was forced to make concessions by lowering the commercial tariffs that had been aimed at crippling the Dutch economic system. The importance of the Dutch as a central partner in the coalition against France can be seen in the peace proposals, all of which included provisions for William's personal gain. France received some gains, getting the Franche-Comte and an improved border in Artois and Flanders.[93]

The first Franco-Dutch war fits our notion of a major war in several, but not all, ways. As witnessed by French war aims, one of the central goals was to allow one country to expand a closed economy at the expense of the open economic subsystem. The war spread to include most of the major powers in the system. What it lacked was the awesome destructiveness of major wars. This last characteristic of the major wars of challenge would appear as a larger number of countries became involved in Louis's next two wars against the Dutch. The war from 1672 to 1678 was only the prelude to a political challenge that would culminate in the War of the Spanish Succession.

Prince William and other Dutch statesmen knew that the 1672–1678 war was only the first round. The Dutch state spent much time and energy preparing for another war after 1678. In the Holy Roman Empire, the Dutch helped orchestrate Austria's formation of the League of Augsburg. Although the Dutch were not signatories to this alliance, their diplomats were in close contact with the German princes and the Austrian government during the nego-

93. Ibid., p. 34; Baxter, *William III*, pp. 129, 159; Anderson, *Lineages of the Absolutist State*, p. 103.

tiations. Austria was inspired to form the alliance because it saw its leadership of the Holy Roman Empire threatened by France; the German princes viewed French expansion as a threat to their independence, a threat that became very real after the French attack on the Netherlands.[94] Traditionally, the German princes had looked to Austria to protect their independence from outside forces, so the League of Augsburg was merely the latest manifestation of an older relationship. Yet the Dutch role in constructing this alliance should not be underestimated.

The Special Role of William III

The key success of Dutch diplomacy came with the solidification of an alliance with England, after William became not only stadhouder of the Republic but also king of England. The significance of dynastic linkages in this period exemplifies contextual factors that are not systematically included in the model presented here. Such linkages are relevant for an understanding of how the alliance between the struggling liberal leader and the only emerging supporter developed, and they also help explain what the expansionary challenger was aspiring to achieve—for the major war would be fought over Louis's attempts to link the French and Spanish thrones. Still, these dynastic linkages are omitted from the model because they are less relevant for later cases. Moreover, the fact that such links existed did not solely determine how alliances were set up, and the liberal leadership model actually explains why William III was able to enforce his own dynastic claims in the first place.

It is necessary to tell this story in some detail, in order to explain why William's dual role should be viewed as the culmination of closer ties between England and the United Provinces rather than as their cause. As a starting point, England had withdrawn from the alliance with France against the Dutch in 1674, when Parliament exerted pressure on Charles and the split between the crown and Parliament was widening. Charles and the royal court supported absolutism, France, and the Catholic religion. Reflecting the interests of domestic social-economic groups more generally as well as its own institutional interests, Parliament opposed all three. Meanwhile, William had wed Charles's daughter Mary, giving him claim to the English throne, but his claim was behind that of Charles's brother, James. Whereas Charles was se-

---

94. McKay and Scott, *Rise of the Great Powers*, p. 44; David J. Hill, *A History of Diplomacy in the International Development of Europe*, Vol. 3: *The Diplomacy of the Age of Absolutism* (New York: Howard Fertig, 1967; reprint of 1914 edition), p. 108.

cretly a Catholic, James practiced Catholicism openly. Therefore, Parliament saw James as a poor choice for king. But, since James was not healthy and it was widely believed that Charles would outlive him, there was little concern. When Charles died first, it set off the political problems that led to the Glorious Revolution.

With Charles's death, James became king. Parliament accepted this, not because they had no choice, but because it was still widely believed that James would not reign long, since his health had not improved. His chances of producing a healthy heir were still considered quite slim. Though Parliament accepted him as king, it hoped that natural forces would improve the situation soon enough.

When James II had a child, and a son no less, prospects for the future were radically altered. The supporters of Parliament suggested that James and his supporters had faked his wife's pregnancy, producing an heir out of nowhere, or switched a sickly or stillborn child with a healthy son. Either way, the extension of the lineage created a future with Catholic, absolutist kings aspiring to the French model, which was naturally not palatable for Parliament. This new heir preceded William in the succession to the throne.[95]

William's claims to the English crown were weaker than James's, but after Charles died William had kept in close contact with several English politicians to monitor the situation. William knew that he had to prevent future Anglo-French alliances to protect the Netherlands, and the surest way to do that was to become English king himself.[96] When James II produced a healthy heir, William's agents and the leaders of Parliament began to consider the possibility of William expressing his wife's claim to the throne. To stake his weaker claim, though, William would need force; Parliament watched helplessly while James tried to revamp the English army under Catholic officers in order to make it more loyal to himself. When the English opposition finally asked William to come to England, he had to rely on a Dutch fleet and a Dutch army of 15,000 men.[97]

William could raise these forces only because he had the support of the States-General, which voted him a loan of 600,000 pounds. The States-General was also acutely aware of the danger of a future alliance between France and England against the United Provinces. The pattern of French activity in the

95. Geoffrey Symcox, "Louis XIV and the Outbreak of the Nine Years War," in *Louis XIV and Europe*, ed. Hatton, p. 191.

96. Baxter, *William III*, pp. 228, 234; also, see the speech William made on his return to the Netherlands, in Hill, *History of Diplomacy*, 3:230.

97. Henry Horwitz, *Parliament, Policy, and Politics in the Reign of William III* (Manchester: Manchester University Press, 1977), p. 5.

late 1680s was ominously like that before the 1672 onslaught: French diplomatic overtures to James II were known to the Dutch political leadership, and French tariffs were reestablished in 1687. Louis also banned the importation of Dutch salted herring, as a supposed health measure, although this was in fact the usage of what is now known as a nontariff barrier to trade.[98]

By the summer of 1688, Dutch trade with France had been reduced by one-fourth and had even fallen below levels of trade achieved during the previous war. The falling levels of trade meant that the Dutch had less to lose by adopting a policy openly hostile to France. The possibility of a Franco-English alliance forced them to act decisively. This was a risk for the States-General, since supporting the stadhouder's personal power could very well diminish the States-General's own power, but supporting William was chosen as the best way to protect the country.[99] In other words, the strategic situation influenced the state's decision to support William's dynastic claims.

Other factors less relevant for later cases came into play in this period. Religious conflicts had raised tensions between France and the United Provinces. In 1685, Louis revoked the Edict of Nantes and began harrassing Protestants in France, including Dutch and English merchants. Many of those who fled the persecution came to the Netherlands, which heightened Dutch perceptions of the threat Louis posed to Dutch ideas and Dutch interests as well as to the open international subsystem.[100] Both English and Dutch governments depicted the ensuing wars against France as religious conflicts—Protestantism versus Catholicism. But religious differences are a poor overall explanation for the alliance against France: as much as England and the Netherlands lauded themselves as the champions of Protestantism, they were quick to turn a blind eye to any criticism of their numerous Catholic allies.[101]

William's arrival in England, the dissipation of James's support, and his departure to France can only be explained through the interests of the Parliament of England and the States-General of the Netherlands. William did not inherit the crown, he came with an army and took it away from James. The army that made this possible and the fleet that carried the army to England

---

98. Wilson, *Anglo-Dutch Commerce*, p. 91; Hill, *History of Diplomacy*, 3:209, 219; Symcox, "Louis XIV," p. 191; Baxter, *William III*, p. 211.

99. Carter, *Neutrality or Commitment*, p. 25; Baxter, *William III*, p. 211.

100. Symcox, "Louis XIV," p. 184; Thomas J. Schaeper, *The French Council of Commerce, 1700–1715: A Study of Mercantilism after Colbert* (Columbus: Ohio State University Press, 1983), p. 58; Williams, *Ancien Regime*, p. 50.

101. R. M. Hatton, "Louis XIV and his Fellow Monarchs," in *Louis XIV and Europe*, ed. Hatton, p. 26, notes that the Austrians were suppressing some of their Protestant minorities during those same war years.

were provided by the States-General. This is called a revolution rather than an invasion because so many Englishmen supported William's move. William's dual leadership resulted from the shared interests of England and the Netherlands.

Both legislatures kept a tight rein on William. In fact, the final steps in the transition to Parliament's supremacy in England were undoubtedly smoothed by the fact that Parliament did not trust William fully and exacted control over him. William was ready to accept such control, for he was experienced as a ruler limited by laws and a representative political body. From his experience as stadhouder he knew how to work inside and along with rather than against such republican institutions.

The first sign of this control over the king was the failure of Parliament to grant William revenues for life automatically, as was the custom; this was a serious alteration in the traditional relationship between Parliament and the crown. The monarch was now subordinate to the laws of Parliament. In their coronation oath, William and Mary swore to rule "according to the statutes in parliament agreed on and the laws and customs" of the kingdom. William exercised his right to veto bills of Parliament only five times before 1696, and each subsequently became law; after 1696, William did not exercise his veto power again.[102] William's international experience and personal contacts built up during his years as stadhouder, his continued dual powers, the short sittings of Parliament, and the English tradition of giving the king a free hand in foreign affairs surely gave him wide leeway in foreign policy in the early years. Yet Parliament was wary of this and in the Act of Settlement (1701) placed the first legal limits on the royal control of foreign policy by providing that Englishmen were not to be involved in a non-English war by a foreign king. After this bill was passed, William was always careful to consult Parliament on foreign policy.[103] Even as king, he could not bring Englishmen to follow policies they did not support.

Of course, as stadhouder William relied on the States-General for the funds to carry out Dutch policy. Although his personal appeals now carried tremendous weight, he could not simply do as he pleased. A good example of his limited powers was in the coordination of military policies. As king and stadhouder, he was commander of both countries' military forces; since Wil-

---

102. This is the key factor behind my classification of the English state as more sensitive to domestic political competition after 1688, since the Glorious Revolution marks the point the representative legislature established real control over the monarchy; see Baxter, *William III*, pp. 269–270; Horwitz, *Parliament, Policy and Politics*, pp. 85, 314; Hill, *Century of Revolution*, p. 277.
103. Horwitz, *Parliament, Policy, and Politics*, p. 314; Hill, *Century of Revolution*, pp. 278–279.

liam's personal powers were greatest in this area, we should expect the greatest coordination of Dutch and English policies here. But, in fact, problems often arose over naval obligations and the supply of English forces on the continent.

Escalating Wars with France

The second war between France and the United Provinces began before the French intended. Louis's actions leading up to 1688 suggest that he had long-term plans for conquering the Netherlands. But, in 1688, England moved into the Dutch camp, when William became king. Instead of attacking the Netherlands, Louis decided to strengthen his position on the continent first. In the electorate of Cologne, a new ruler was to be selected; Louis put forth his own candidate. When that candidate lost, Louis moved his armies into Germany to enforce his selection. By confronting only a few minor German principalities directly, he hoped to intimidate others and achieve by bluff what he had failed to achieve by diplomacy. Instead, he activated the League of Augsburg and brought about a general war.

The alliances facing France had been carefully constructed over the previous decade. Although England and the Netherlands were not technically allied with the League of Augsburg, as soon as the League declared war on France the English and Dutch governments followed suit. Louis was caught off guard, and alone. France tried to support the Ottoman Turks, who were involved in a war against Austria, but this alliance was never formalized and was never significant. The French army was also caught by surprise and unprepared: officers had recently decided to reorganize their forces and improve their weaponry (by replacing muskets with flintlocks and introducing the plug bayonet), but the outbreak of war prevented these policies' implementation until 1697.[104]

Since this was more of a preventive war instigated by the liberal leader's alliance rather than a war of challenge, Louis's armies were unable to strike an early, offensive blow. Instead, a war of attrition began immediately on land. At sea, the French navy launched an offensive stroke and won control of the sea in the first battles, but it was unable to keep large fleets at sea. The naval war then too dissolved into a struggle of attrition as the French adopted a *guerre de course* (commerce raiding).[105] The French hoped that moving from a fleet

---

104. Symcox, "Louis XIV," pp. 187–188.
105. Symcox, *The Crisis of French Seapower, 1688–1697: From the Guerre d'Escadre to the*

strategy to commerce raiding would more effectively harm the Dutch-led open trading subsystem.

The alliance now brought together against France in the War of the League of Augsburg successfully implemented the attrition strategy. One historian described this as "the most relentless economic war of the mercantilist era." An embargo on French trade, only contemplated in the previous war with France, was used with telling effect. France was defeated not on the battlefield but through economic pressure. Consistent with the expectations derived from the model presented earlier, the alliance patterns led to each side following a particular strategy, with the liberal leader's alliance winning through attrition. This strategy worked by breaking the French economy, thereby preventing Louis from achieving any of his war aims. Between 1693 and 1694, revenue from taxation fell, and, since the state could only borrow at ever higher rates of interest, expenditures also fell.[106]

Although the war appeared to end in stalemate, the Treaty of Ryswick (1697) that ended it shows a Dutch victory. The previous duty on ship tonnage was removed from Dutch-flagged ships only. Further advantages were given in the treaty, including a guarantee that Dutch merchants in France would enjoy the same rights as Frenchmen, a reduction of the tariff placed on Dutch goods in 1667, and an agreement by France to respect the Dutch principle of "free ships, free goods" during future wars.[107] In other words, the Dutch got most of what they wanted—a return to economic penetration of France and the reduction of French economic barriers vis-à-vis Dutch capital and the open international economy.

The peace lasted less than four years. When the king of Spain died in 1701, Louis took the opportunity to bring Spain within his dynastic lands. The resultant war, fought over the threat of so much power concentrated in Louis's hands, was also another chance for Louis to attack the Netherlands and England. The alliances were similar to those of the previous war, with France fighting virtually alone and with England and the Netherlands at the core of a wider alliance. England and the Netherlands again provided the bulk of the forces in the war and much of the finances for the operations of the allies.[108]

Guerre de Course (The Hague: Martinus Nijhoff, 1974), p. 4; Kennedy, *Rise and Fall of British Naval Mastery*, p. 76.

106. Israel, *Dutch Primacy in World Trade*, p. 343; Baxter, *William III*, pp. 289–290; Symcox, *Crisis of French Seapower*, p. 146.

107. Schaeper, *French Council of Commerce*, pp. 63–64, 108–109.

108. McKay and Scott, *Rise of the Great Powers*, p. 59. See Hill, *History of Diplomacy*, 3:233, for the measures of troops pledged to the alliance against France; the Netherlands pledged 15,000 more men than any other country.

Unfortunately for France, this meant that the war evolved much as the previous one had.

The French navy did not try an offensive gambit but immediately undertook commerce raiding. In particular, the French goverment licensed privateers to wreak havoc on the Dutch merchant and fishing fleets. The war on land also picked up where the last had ended, with even larger armies engaged in a series of inconclusive engagements.[109] The French did not do any better this time, although Spain did become a Bourbon land.

I classify this War of the Spanish Succession (1701–1713) as a major war because it involved all but two of the major European powers and combat deaths reached a level of more than 10,000 per million European population.[110] It was the first war since the Thirty Years' War to reach such levels. It also culminated the wars Louis fought to destroy Dutch liberal leadership, which had begun with commercial rivalry and the mercantilism of France in the 1660s.

Was the French Challenge Successful?

As a war of challenge, the War of the Spanish Succession was partly successful. The French did end liberal international leadership by the Netherlands. After 1713 the Dutch Republic could not mobilize the resources to live up to the role of a major power: its aspirations of wider liberal hegemony were frustrated, and it even lost its ability to hold open trade in the Mediterranean and Baltic. At the same time, France never clearly won the wars and was unable to expand a closed economic subsystem. England, which might have benefited if it had been prepared for liberal international leadership after the wars, also paid a heavy price for victory and lacked the incentives for bearing the costs of leadership. After 1713 the system lacked a liberal leader and therefore devolved into competition between several closed economic subsystems.

Dutch costs were high. In the 1672–1678 war, much of the fighting had occurred on Dutch territory, and the use of the water barrier brought great physical destruction in the Netherlands itself. The later two wars against France did not bring as much destruction within Dutch borders, but they damaged the international trading system, which has been described as the

---

109. For a recent discussion of the strategies of the countries in the war, see John B. Hattendorf, "Alliance, Encirclement, and Attrition," in *Grand Strategies in War and Peace*, ed. Paul Kennedy (New Haven: Yale University Press, 1991).

110. Levy, *War in the Modern Great Power System*, tab. 4.1 (pp. 88–91).

lifeblood of the Dutch Republic. The political economic system the Dutch relied on in the seventeenth century, says Charles Wilson, was "uniquely profitable, rational and commercially efficient" but "also uniquely vulnerable, exposed and extended."[111]

The limited liberal international subsystem the Dutch had been able to establish placed Dutch assets at sea and in foreign lands, where they were continually at risk. The role of liberal leadership can be summarized as protecting those overseas economic interests, and expansionary powers often damage those interests. The carrying trade, the centerpiece of the whole Dutch system, was based on the ability of the huge merchant fleet to ply the waters of Europe. The ships traveled between foreign ports, and in each port Dutch merchants resided as local agents or factors. In wartime the merchant fleet became an easy target for privateers, and the merchants living abroad became potential hostages. The Dutch herring fleet, one of the few domestic industries of the Netherlands, was particularly ravaged by French privateers in the War of the Spanish Succession.[112] When seized, merchantmen and fishing vessels were often not ransomed but added to rival fleets.

As much as the wars disrupted the Dutch economy, this was not the reason for the end of Dutch liberal leadership. The United Provinces remained the most capital-rich country in Europe, and representative institutions in the Netherlands were saved. Accordingly, Dutch interests remained in having an open domestic economy and in liberalizing trade, in order to increase consumption of capital internationally. Yet the wars against France made it clear that the Dutch state could no longer mobilize the power necessary to provide effective order and protection to the open international subsystem.

The Dutch government had had one of the highest levels of public debt before the conflicts with France began, but the war effort made these figures soar. Public debt went from 30 million guilders in 1688 to 148 million guilders in 1713, forcing tax rates up accordingly. For instance, the province of Holland was forced to pay some 70 percent of its revenues to service its debts. Taxes rose to extremely high levels to pay for yesterday's victory, not to arm the fleet needed for tomorrow's battles. During the War of the League of Augsburg, the United Provinces had sent out about one hundred warships each year, with crews numbering in the tens of thousands; by the 1780s the Netherlands could only raise a fleet of seventeen ships and 3,000 men. William Thompson and Karen Rasler claim that Dutch naval capabilities declined from

---

111. Wilson, *Dutch Republic*, p. 40.

112. C. R. Boxer, "The Dutch Economic Decline," in *The Economic Decline of Empires*, ed. C. M. Cipolla (London: Methuen, 1970), p. 242.

41 percent of the global powers' total in 1652 to 29 percent in 1713, *before* relative economic decline began.[113]

Several reasons for this change in position can be argued. The costs of warfare increased, and the Dutch had trouble keeping up. Likewise, the size of the competitors in the system had grown, whereas the population of the Netherlands had started to decline after 1713 (thereby keeping the capital-labor ratio fairly high). With the large public debt, the state simply could no longer provide international protection to its citizens.

Since the French challenge occurred before Dutch liberal leadership was particularly successful, and therefore before the Netherlands' capital abundance was reduced through international economic links, the war had what must be seen as an unexpected impact. The challenge occurred as Dutch labor-intensive industries were just starting to lose competitiveness. Thus the end of Dutch attempts at liberal leadership and the resulting closure of the international economy may have actually *slowed* Dutch economic decline by limiting the very processes that encouraged economic competition. By the same token, the capital-intensive sectors were unable to make the same profits they had earned earlier. The dilemma for the Dutch was how to respond to the various demands of domestic groups when they had so little international political power.

The French, too, came out of the wars poorer. The French military establishment, groomed during the early years of Louis's reign, was mostly wrecked by 1713. The large population of France and French military tradition enabled the army to recover after a short period. But, just as the Dutch state had gone deeply into debt, so had the French. The war of attrition had served to destroy the capital accumulation of the previous decades. Debts would plague the French government until the Revolution of 1789. War debts and their repudiation would wreck French moneylenders for many years to come. France came out of the war of challenge as a powerful autocratic state, but without the relative capital abundance of the prewar period. France therefore stayed imperial, but it would be ambivalent to any future liberal international leaders rather than a political challenger.

England (which became Britain with the union with Scotland), was truly a

---

113. Wilson, *Dutch Republic,* p. 233; Williams, *Ancien Regime,* pp. 52–54. Also see William R. Thompson and Karen Rasler, "Global Wars, Public Debts, and the Long Cycle," *World Politics* 35 (July 1983): 494, for these last figures, although it is not entirely clear how these percentages were derived, since the inclusion of different powers in the base figure can vary the percentage quite dramatically.

major power in 1713. Not only did Britain have colonies scattered around the world, but for the first time since the Hundred Years' War English troops were significant in a war on the European continent. The English navy left the wars the strongest in the world. During the War of the Spanish Succession, Britain came to dominate the alliance with the Dutch; Britain provided more naval warships, and the duke of Marlborough, the British captain-general, commanded joint Anglo-Dutch land forces.[114] The Treaty of Utrecht handed over the strategic ports of Gibralter, Minorca, and Hudson's Bay to Britain. Britain ended the major war a much stronger country than before the French challenge had begun.

The British state was also more republican after 1688 and the Glorious Revolution. William's Dutch political traditions influenced British traditions. If the British had continued to accumulate capital during the wars, and if Britain had ended the War of the Spanish Succession as a capital-rich major power ruled by republican institutions, a transition of liberal leadership might have occurred. In fact, the wars increased capital consumption in Britain, and the capital-labor ratio fell. Capital had to be imported from the Netherlands to continue the war effort.

According to Gregory King, Britain invested some 6 percent of national income in 1688, a very prosperous year. But the next decade of war lowered both the savings rate and national income, so that capital accumulation actually declined in the 1690s. King estimated that the stock of productive capital (exclusive of buildings) actually fell 10 percent during the wars against France.[115] Britain would certainly have had a lower capital-labor ratio in 1700 than in 1688, because the population had risen at this same time.

Money to finance the war effort had to be brought in from the Netherlands, making Britain a major international debtor. Before the outbreak of the War of the Spanish Succession, the English government owed the Dutch States-General almost £1,000,000, and there were many loans from private Dutch investors to the English government on top of this. Of a total war debt of £14,000,000–15,000,000 in 1713, two-thirds were owed to Dutch investors.[116]

Instead of becoming the next prospective liberal leader, Britain came out of

114. For comparative figures on force sizes, see Parker and Smith, "Introduction," in *General Crisis*, ed. Parker and Smith, p. 14; McKay and Scott, *Rise of the Great Powers*, pp. 46, 59; Hill, *History of Diplomacy*, 3:322.

115. Phyllis Deane and W. A. Cole, *British Economic Growth, 1688–1959* (Cambridge: Cambridge University Press, 1962), p. 260; Deane, "Capital Formation," p. 97.

116. Wilson, *Anglo-Dutch Commerce*, p. 95; Wilson, *Economic History and the Historian*, pp. 36, 57–58.

the war of challenge between France and the Netherlands as a capital-poor, republican, powerful country—a perfect supporter of liberal leadership but not willing to lead an open subsystem on its own since the interest of British capital was in domestic investment. Without some other state in the system to act as the leader to support, Britain adopted a policy of mercantilism.

THREE

Rival Mercantilism,
a New Prospective Liberal Leader,
and Challenge, 1713–1815

After 1713, no single country held the necessary combination of interests and capabilities to lead an open international economic subsystem. The major countries were only ambivalent powers or potential supporters that lacked a liberalizing leader, and so the system broke down into several closed, rival mercantile empires. The model I present still creates testable propositions about specific countries' policies for this period, which can be used to construct a picture of the emerging international system. Britain and France both pursued mercantilism but employed different styles of policy, reflecting the domestic nature of each state. Meanwhile, the Dutch continued to have the interests to act as a liberal leader, but they now lacked the capabilities to attempt to lead even a limited open economic subsystem.

Composition of the System after 1713

The Netherlands came out of the War of the Spanish Succession a capital-rich country ruled by republican institutions, but it no longer controlled the resources to be a major power. Still, Dutch policy continued to be shaped by Dutch capital. Policy changes resulted from an inability to provide order and protection to the economic subsystem after the war.

The Dutch state was in a particularly difficult position to serve the interest of either the capital-intensive or labor-intensive sectors. Labor's wages were relatively high, perhaps as much as two to three times as high as in Belgium, Switzerland, or England,[1] so labor-intensive sectors were not competitive in-

---

1. Jan de Vries, "Holland: Commentary," in *Failed Transitions to Modern Industrial Society: Renaissance Italy and Seventeenth-Century Holland,* ed. Frederick Krantz and Paul M. Hohenberg (Montreal: Interuniversity Centre for European Studies, 1975), pp. 55–56.

ternationally, especially once other markets were blocked by tariffs. Capital-intensive sectors were still competitive internationally, but they faced the highest tariff walls. The state would have preferred to use power to force down barriers to trade, but now it was too weak to expect this policy to succeed. Another option was to close off the Dutch market, but this too would have created problems.

According to the dynamic argument on hegemonic decline, successful liberal leadership results in domestic difficulties with the labor-intensive sectors as they come under increasing foreign competition; later, fixed capital comes under increasing competition as capital becomes more diffuse in the international system. Since Dutch leadership was challenged and ended before economic decline set in, the economic problems the Dutch faced in the early eighteenth century were not from declining competitiveness of capital-intensive sectors but rather from difficulties in employing their comparative advantage in capital as other states closed off the international economic system. Capital was stuck in the Netherlands, where it was underemployed in comparison to the returns it could earn elsewhere. As other states developed extensive mercantilistic policies, they amassed capital and increased their competition in capital-intensive sectors, but this took fifty years or more to develop.

Britain lacked one key ingredient for liberal leadership as well. The Dutch had the interests, but they needed international power; the British had the power, but they lacked the high capital abundance to create the incentives to lead an open international economic subsystem. As a strong, republican power, lacking relatively abundant capital, Britain would have been a perfect supporter of a liberal leader. Without such a leader to support, Britain developed its own mercantile empire instead. The overall model can still be tested; the French and British styles of mercantilism can be compared to illustrate the differences in the sorts of rents sanctioned by republican and autocratic states.

Without the abundance of capital to encourage the British to organize international trade, and with international debts to pay, the British were quite willing to make sure capital was invested where it was needed—at home. At the end of the seventeenth century, domestic sectors expressed interest for the state's policies of encouraging the exports of capital goods and services (and indirectly free trade) and of assisting in the defense of the open international political economy led by the Dutch.[2] The war reduced Britain's relative capital abundance, and in its aftermath it was clear Britain would have to be the leader of any open international subsystem. Britain's foreign policies changed

2. See George L. Cherry, "The Development of the English Free Trade Movement in Parliament, 1689–1702," *Journal of Modern History* 25 (June 1953): 103–119.

after the War of the Spanish Succession, and this break is identifiable in the interests expressed in Parliament. The owners of capital, who had wanted policies supporting Dutch liberal leadership in the 1680s and 1690s, reversed their positions and were now content with the returns they received on domestically invested capital. The owners of capital should in fact fear foreign competition.

Britain's mercantilism exemplifies the policies of a supporter that lacks a liberalizing leader. The British exhibited a "republican" style of mercantilism, with a closed economy that retains a high degree of competition at the domestic level. In other words, the return to closure meant greater rents for national factors *in the aggregate*. Rents were still sanctioned versus external competitors, but policies did not discriminate among firms within the sector. For instance, the Navigation Acts did not establish any one company with a monopoly of all shipping; these laws gave all British shippers an advantage. This is consistent with the model and contrasts with the mercantilist policies of an autocratic state, as the examples below show. For the most part, within the British political realm all British producers could compete for the rents created by mercantilism. In an autocratic state, the domestic interventions in the market would create preferences for one producer over others.

Mercantilism by a republican state amounts to holding a captive market, which makes sense only as long as the country relatively lacks capital; for once capital is abundant its returns can be raised by employing it outside the economy. If the closed economic system is maintained and returns to capital are kept high, capital is eventually accumulated and relative capital abundance achieved. Interests in maintaining a closed international economic subsystem then shift in favor of openness, where the newly accumulated capital can be more gainfully employed. In other words, the state's successful mercantilism ultimately create interests desiring the dismantling of mercantilism.

This is precisely what happened to Britain in the eighteenth century. By plotting trends in capital accumulation and noting when the rate of capital formation accelerated dramatically, one can see the expected change in domestic economic interests, then the articulation of these new interests in Parliament, and eventually a different foreign economic policy and an end to mercantilism. But, before reviewing this history, it is necessary to consider some of the details of British mercantilism, the basis for its success in accumulating capital, and the importance of Britain's relations with colonies and other states.

The other great mercantile power of the eighteenth century, France, ended the War of the Spanish Succession with less capital abundance than before, a stable monarchy, and military power that needed a respite to rebuild. As a powerful autocracy lacking highly abundant capital, France should be expected to pursue mercantilistic policies, but in the style of an autocratic state. Not only should the national economy be closed off from foreign competition, but the internal market should be manipulated and distorted as one French producer is given preferences over other French producers. This difference should be quite visible in the mercantile policies of Britain and France in the eighteenth century.[3]

Whereas the shift to capital abundance in a powerful republican state leads to the end of mercantile policies, a similar shift in a powerful autocratic state merely creates the pressures for expansion associated with challenges. Capital accumulation in France could only be expected to create market pressures lowering relative returns to capital there, so simply maintaining capital's relative returns would require intensifying domestic rents or expanding the area within which rents were sanctioned.

The main difference between this period and the previous one is the absence of a liberal leader. Only the Dutch wanted freer trade, but their state was too weak to provide the necessary leadership. The eighteenth century was a period dominated by rival mercantile empires, as the most powerful nation-states battled for control of economic activity and areas in which to sanction rents. The only other major divergences from this pattern were Britain's policies, which maintained an open economy domestically. Although the system was characterized by conflict, none of the wars exhibited both the systemwide scope and the ferocity of wars of challenge.

The Netherlands: Tough Choices in Decline

The Netherlands faced a difficult situation in the decades between 1713 and 1790. It still had an open domestic economy and, as a republic with capital more abundant than in any other country, wanted to continue the liberalized trade system as a method of exporting capital and capital-intensive services. But now the state lacked the power to protect and provide order to the open international economic subsystem. The ineffectiveness of foreign economic policy led to disruptive domestic politics, for the state had difficulty meeting the demands of any of its constituents.

3. This same point is supported by the work of Hilton Root; see "The Redistributive Role of Government: Economic Regulation in Old Régime France and England," *Comparative Studies in Society and History* 33 (April 1991): 338–369.

Dutch Sectoral Interests

The Netherlands' international economic links were not totally destroyed by the French challenge. Until the 1790s, there was not an absolute decline in trade and shipping, and foreign investment and financial activities actually grew; only in manufacturing was there positive decline and collapse. The Netherlands continued to be a major source of international investment, as it is today. Since no other country was as abundant in capital as the Netherlands in this period, Dutch activity in the capital-intensive sectors was still competitive and difficult to replace. Certainly when major war ended in 1714, no other country had the merchant ships or ready money the Dutch could offer. In the 1720s, Dutch ships still carried more trade between England and France than did English ships. Until 1750, two-thirds of Finnish timber was carried away in Dutch ships; before, Holland had been the main market for these exports, but by 1770 London could make that claim.[4] Dutch trade was eventually hurt by the maritime legislation of several countries, but the large Dutch merchant fleet was not immediately replaceable.

Although the carrying business remained intact in the short run, mercantile legislation more quickly cut into the entrepôt function Amsterdam and the other Dutch ports had provided. The laws that forced direct shipment of goods from source country to final market upset the entrepôt role. The decline in stapling activities was not counterbalanced by domestic industrial development, which was the real reason for Dutch economic decline.[5] Eventually, the navigation controls passed in other countries also reduced the demand for Dutch shipping. In the Baltic, where the Dutch had once carried the majority of imports of salt, wine, cloth, and herring and the majority of exports of timber, grain, and iron, competition from other countries' ships grew until the Dutch no longer had the largest fleet engaged there. Their share of the total number of ships passing through the Sound and paying tolls to

4. Joel Mokyr, *Industrialization in the Low Countries, 1795–1850* (New Haven: Yale University Press, 1976), p. 2; Derek McKay and H. M. Scott, *The Rise of the Great Powers, 1648–1815* (New York: Longman, 1983), p. 100; J. A. van Houtte, *An Economic History of the Low Countries, 800–1800* (London: Weidenfeld & Nicolson, 1977), p. 272.

5. Charles H. Wilson, "The Economic Decline of the Netherlands," in *Essays in Economic History*, ed. E. M. Carus-Wilson (London: Edward Arnold, 1954), p. 256. Fernand Braudel, *The Perspective of the World* (New York: Harper & Row, 1984), p. 246, suggests that Britain was able to string economic hegemony out longer because of the Industrial Revolution. B. H. Slicher van Bath, "The Economic Situation in the Dutch Republic during the Seventeenth Century," in *Dutch Capitalism and World Capitalism / Capitalisme hollandais et capitalism mondial*, ed. Maurice Aymard (New York: Cambridge University Press, 1982), p. 33, sees the lack of raw materials and the high cost of labor as the reasons for the Dutch failure to create new industries.

Denmark fell from around half in the 1660s to closer to a quarter in the 1770s. Between 1700 and 1790, the overall volume of the Netherlands' foreign trade fell almost a fifth, while in that same period British exports rose in volume four times and those of France doubled.[6]

Direct shipments between other countries did not necessarily end the role of Dutch capital in international trade, though, even as Dutch shipping was increasingly excluded. As the commercial sector ceased growing, earnings from invisibles almost certainly rose. The Dutch still financed and insured trade, and Amsterdam remained the center of the international payments system until late in the eighteenth century.[7] Amsterdam's continued clearing-house function can be noted in the payment of Russian trade and customs. Before 1763, no official exchange rate was quoted between English pounds and Russian roubles, for all international payments between the two countries went through Amsterdam. And Russian customs could be paid only in Dutch guilders until late in the eighteenth century.[8] The new emphasis on financial services was easy to develop given the structure of Dutch commerce. Traders continued to handle the financial affairs as they always had, but they no longer brought the goods through Dutch territory. The merchants slowly became creditors and then rentiers. Bankers in the Netherlands did not really notice the difference; the shift did not decrease the accumulation of profits or savings.

As the Dutch found capital's international uses continually cut back by the legislation of other countries, Dutch capitalists turned to ever riskier investments. New areas of investment were explored, such as the development of a whaling fleet, and more was sunk in the trading companies; but the high risks involved made much of this investment unprofitable. Although whaling required only cheap unskilled labor, the size of the ships and the length of the voyages called for large capital outlays.[9] The ultimate problem was that markets for the goods produced could not be guaranteed.

The strength of the economy remained in capital-intensive services. Before

6. Van Houtte, *Economic History of the Low Countries*, pp. 271–273; Alice Carter, *The Dutch Republic in Europe in the Seven Years War* (New York: Macmillan, 1971), p. 130; Angus Maddison, *Phases of Capitalist Development* (New York: Oxford University Press, 1982), p. 33.

7. Charles H. Wilson, *Economic History and the Historian: Collected Essays* (New York: Praeger, 1969), p. 117, and *Anglo-Dutch Commerce and Finance in the Eighteenth Century* (Cambridge: Cambridge University Press, 1941; reprint 1966), p. 17, quoting a contemporary; Jan de Vries, *The Economy of Europe in an Age of Crisis, 1600–1750* (New York: Cambridge University Press, 1976), p. 123.

8. Wilson, *Economic History and the Historian*, p. 59; Violet Barbour, *Capitalism in Amsterdam in the Seventeenth Century* (Ann Arbor: University of Michigan Press, 1963), p. 48.

9. Van Houtte, *Economic History of the Low Countries*, p. 253.

the 1790s, Dutch finance and insurance in international trade was as great as that of any other country; in 1790, Dutch foreign investment probably amounted to some 800 million guilders, at a time when national income was only about 250 million guilders.[10] As returns to investment within the Netherlands stayed low, investment increasingly went abroad.

One new major source of capital employment, and certainly a risky one, was the practice of making loans to foreign governments. Repayment, of course, was where the risk lay. But in a period of increasing closure of the international economy, this was one of the few ways to make money on that change—by loaning money to the very agents of closure. The loans to Britain during the wars against France had already established a financial bond, which by the 1780s had developed so strongly that perhaps one-third of all Dutch investment (and more than two-thirds of the foreign loans) went to Britain.[11] By the 1740s, demand for capital inside the Netherlands had fallen enough, and the risks had lowered enough, that capital was loaned to foreign governments in ever larger amounts. In the wars of the 1750s and 1760s, loans were extended to almost all major powers.

The Labor-Intensive Sectors

The decline of the entrepôt function had a major impact not only on Dutch capital but also on labor. This function had naturally aided industrialization. As the entrepôt role declined, so did industrialization. Once fewer goods passed through Dutch markets, the prices of inputs rose. For example, the decline of sugar refining forced the state to adopt subsidies for imports of raw sugar in the 1770s and 1780s in order to stay competitive. Also, foreign competition now matched Dutch technical competence in shipbuilding and textiles.[12]

As the argument on the economic decline of liberal leaders predicts, the combination of the continued high cost of labor in the domestic economy and the emergence of cheaper capital in other countries makes the liberal leader's economy less competitive. And as Jan de Vries argues, the high ratio of capital to labor in the early seventeenth century made Dutch wages rise to become

10. Maddison, *Phases of Capitalist Development*, p. 33; Sidney Homer, *A History of Interest Rates* (New Brunswick: Rutgers University Press, 1963), pp. 175–176.

11. Braudel, *Perspective of the World*, pp. 245, 267, citing van de Spiegel's estimate of 1782. James C. Riley, *International Government Finance and the Amsterdam Capital Market, 1740–1815* (New York: Cambridge University Press, 1980), p. 16, argues that this may be overestimation.

12. Van Houtte, *Economic History of the Low Countries*, p. 256; Wilson, *Economic History and the Historian*, p. 33.

perhaps the highest in Europe, because labor was more productive there than elsewhere at that time. Since wages were relatively high, the sectors that did well were those in which labor was not the key input; demand for labor fell after 1675. The labor market reflected high unemployment while simultaneously attracting immigrants with relatively high wages.[13]

The high taxes necessary to pay off the war debts were yet another problem. The public debt had risen from about one million guilders in 1579 to some 140 million guilders in 1655, and then to more than 400 million guilders in the 1750s. Tax rates rose accordingly to service this huge debt. Dutch taxes predominantly took the form of excise taxes, and several historians have argued that this was one cause of the high wages.[14]

New Constraints on Dutch Foreign Policy

The Dutch state faced a predicament. Labor's returns were relatively high, making labor-intensive sectors uncompetitive. Capital was abundant and relatively cheap, but the state could not find ways to keep capital safely employed on the international market. For the state's own interests, the first priority was in lowering costs; although the Netherlands was involved in several wars in the 1720s and 1740s, it did its best to avoid the obligations of major power politics. As Grand Pensionary van de Spiegel wrote in 1782, war was a luxury the Netherlands could no longer afford.[15] The provincial government of Holland

13. Jan de Vries, "An Inquiry into the Behaviour of Wages in the Dutch Republic and the Southern Netherlands from 1580 to 1800," in *Dutch Capitalism and World Capitalism*, ed. Aymard, pp. 48–50. If monetary factors alone had been driving the decline in competitiveness, sectors would have been hit evenly; see Wilson, *Economic History and the Historian*, p. 122, and Carter, *Dutch Republic in Europe*, p. 132.

14. Carter, *Dutch Republic in Europe*, pp. 131–132; De Vries, *Economy of Europe in an Age of Crisis*, p. 203. In *The Ancien Regime in Europe: Government and Society in the Major States, 1648–1789* (New York: Harper & Row, 1970), pp. 53–54, E. N. Williams cites somewhat lower figures on the debt. For a discussion of the various forms taxes took, see K. W. Swart, "Holland's Bourgeoisie and the Retarded Industrialization of the Netherlands," in *Failed Transitions*, ed. Krantz and Hohenberg, p. 45; also H. R. C. Wright, *Free Trade and Protection in the Netherlands, 1816–1830* (Cambridge: Cambridge University Press, 1955), p. 78. But as de Vries has pointed out ("Holland: Commentary," p. 56), excise taxes cause a proportional increase in the prices of goods only insofar as demand is inelastic and supply is completely elastic, and rising goods prices only raises money wages if the prevailing wage is at subsistence levels, neither of which applied to the Netherlands at this time. According to Joel Mokyr, taxes were probably only about 10 percent of wages for Dutch labor; see Mokyr, "Industrial Growth and Stagnation in the Low Countries, 1800–1850," Ph.D. diss., Yale University, 1974. Taxes may have kept wages high and stimulated the investment of capital in foreign countries, but taxes alone do not explain why Dutch labor was so expensive.

15. Wilson, *Economic History and the Historian*, p. 124. Wilson draws a parallel to Britain's

was now paying well over half its revenues to service debts, and no new taxable industries were emerging.

By abandoning power politics after 1713 and adopting a policy of neutrality, the state hoped to cut costs but still benefit from trade, especially when wartime might boost international demand and lead to relaxation of other states' mercantile regulations. Whereas Dutch diplomats had been at the center of important international alliances in the seventeenth century, in the eighteenth century Dutch statesmen spent most of their time steering clear of international obligations.[16]

Economic policies could still be designed to please the owners of capital in their pursuit of the international market for the services of capital, as when the value of currency was kept high. The exchange rate was relatively stable between 1700 and 1775. This policy kept capital flowing overseas, but it also prevented other policies that might have offset the problems linked with uncompetitive manufactures and the high cost of labor.

Pressure from labor-intensive sectors of the economy to adopt protective measures developed in the 1730s and voiced itself in a political movement called the Economic-Patriots. The groups who supported this movement sought commercial and industrial revival through protection from international competition. They also accused capitalists of unpatriotically investing abroad when they should have been investing at home. They supported the stadhouder in order to centralize political authority and better their chances for achieving protection. When the stadhouder did propose changes in economic policy in 1751, merchants feared an attack on their social position.[17]

In fact, the stadhouder's proposal for a "limited Porto Franco" made quite a lot of sense. Most of the duties then existing were for fiscal purposes; if those were ended but replaced with purely protective measures, industry could be protected, the state's revenues could be maintained, and commerce would still have basically free trade. These movements combined in the pressure for changing the level of tariffs as laid down in the *plakaaten* (regulations). The

---

decline in the twentieth century by noting how apparent van de Spiegel's point is for "an Englishman living in 1962."

16. Alice Carter's books on eighteenth-century Dutch diplomacy brilliantly display the Dutch approach to foreign affairs given these constraints: *Dutch Republic in Europe*, pp. 2–3, and *Neutrality or Commitment* (London: Edward Arnold, 1975), p. 79. Also see McKay and Scott, *Rise of the Great Powers*, p. 100; Arthur McCandless Wilson, *French Foreign Policy during the Administration of Cardinal Fleury, 1726–1743* (Cambridge: Harvard University Press, 1936), pp. 129–130; Riley, *International Government Finance*, p. 78; Wilson, "Economic Decline," pp. 256–257.

17. Wilson, *Economic History and the Historian*, p. 43; Carter, *Dutch Republic in Europe*, p. 131; Wright, *Free Trade*, pp. 59–60.

plakaat of 1725 had established moderate tariff levels to support the continuance of the entrepôt function. This *plakaat* had been a compromise between commercial interests, which wanted low tariffs, and domestic agricultural and industry, both of which supported higher tariffs.[18] Dutch capitalists, who had relied for many years on international trade, naturally opposed raising the *plakaat* as a threat to their own competitiveness and as a spark to retaliation. They feared that a higher *plakaat* would merely make a bad situation worse.

Although no sweeping changes occurred, protectionist measures began to creep up in an ad hoc manner. Certain industries prohibited the export of tools in 1749. Some types of skilled workers were prohibited from emigrating in 1751. Subsidies began to be given to fisheries at the local (municipal) level in 1754, and these were later established at the provincial level.[19] Although the amount of legislation was not as high as in other countries, protection became much more common.

The natural outcome of the Dutch predicament was economic decline for all but the most capital-intensive sectors of the economy, and even these would eventually feel the pinch. By supporting the entrepôt position and keeping the currency high to support the position of international services, the Netherlands prevented the development of a domestic export industry; the failure to develop domestic industry meant that Dutch capital was better invested in foreign lands. The Dutch Republic was the first modern country to experience the economic decline of a liberal leader its capital continually invested abroad as the domestic economy became less competitive.

France: Mercantile Expansion and Failure

As a powerful autocracy with capital in less abundance than its economic competitors, France searched for opportunities to expand rents. It developed a closed imperial subsystem with a domestic market that did not foster open competition. Successful mercantilism would have resulted in capital accumulation and pressure to intensify rents. The evidence of capital accumulation in France in the period in question indicates a trend toward greater capital abundance in the 1730s and 1740s which, however, was stifled by the large government debts of the Seven Years' War. This pattern is broadly confirmed

18. Wilson, *Anglo-Dutch Commerce*, p. 21; Van Houtte, *Economic History of the Low Countries*, p. 293.

19. Van Houtte, *Economic History of the Low Countries*, pp. 287–288; C. R. Boxer, "The Dutch Economic Decline," in *The Economic Decline of Empires*, ed. C. M. Cipolla (London: Methuen, 1970), p. 244.

by nominal and real interest rates charted from 1720 until 1769. France's relative position in capital abundance can also be seen in the inflow of foreign capital whenever large government loans were undertaken. For instance, in the 1750s, investors could claim a premium of almost 3 percent by buying French rather than Dutch paper (a point not lost on wealthy Dutch investors).[20]

The French domestic political economy matched relative capital scarcity with the propensity of the absolutist state to sanction rents. Although there is some evidence that trade within France itself was loosened up in the 1720s and 1730s, the overall picture of the economy remains one of regulations and monopolies. The most prominent examples of economic activity in France in this period are the development of monopolistic banks (such as Law's System) and the repeated efforts to establish trading companies such as the Compagnie des Indes, which had a monopoly in the beaver skin trade. Both were backed by the state.[21]

France still took almost every opportunity to expand its empire.[22] In 1733 it became involved in the War of the Polish Succession, and when the War of the Austrian Succession (1740–1748) was started by Prussia in a bid to steal away Austrian territory, France again tried to snatch away neighbors' territory. These limited wars are exactly the kind one would expect in an international system that lacks a liberal leader and is largely populated by countries dedicated to forms of mercantilism. Although these wars involved many countries, not one exhibited the intensity of major wars.

French military power slowly recovered with time. In 1740 a school for naval construction was established at Paris, and spies were sent out to learn the secrets of British and Dutch shipbuilding; an improvement in the technical quality of French warships resulted. At the same time, the number of warships in the French navy also rose. In 1740, France had only forty-one ships of the line, whereas Britain was reckoned to have more than one hun-

---

20. James C. Riley, *The Seven Years War and the Old Regime in France: The Economic and Financial Toll* (Princeton: Princeton University Press, 1986), pp. 31–32, 89–91, 171, 187. Riley also notes (pp. 142–143) that three-fifths of the financing of the French war effort in the Seven Years' War came from credit.

21. Wilson, *French Foreign Policy*, pp. 66–67, 301–302.

22. Initially, France was still drained from the wars with Britain and the Netherlands; see Riley, *Seven Years War*, pp. 14–15. The best way to prevent further exhaustive wars was for France to become an uneasy ally with the two maritime powers. This Triple Alliance was formed in 1717, and in fact France and Britain remained allied until 1731. French weakness shows in two ways: Britain held all the initiative in the alliance (causing France to be described as "the unwilling handmaiden of English policy"), and France was unable to assemble the financial resources to maintain an army large enough to defend itself (the real reason France needed an alliance). Also see Wilson, *French Foreign Policy*, pp. 7, 29, 102.

dred. By 1756 the respective numbers were forty-five and sixty, and the absolute size of the French fleet continued to grow.[23]

The revived French military was pitched against Britain again in the Seven Years' War (1756–1763), which was not only a European war but also a global battle for empire which France lost. French colonies in Canada and India were seized by British troops. And, as noted above, the war proved a tremendous drain on the finances of the whole French economy. France eventually sought revenge by helping the Americans win their war of independence from Britain. This aid to the colonies also marked a rebounding of French military strength, overcoming the poor showing French forces had made in the Seven Years' War.

Whereas the Dutch state faced a dilemma in selecting policy, the French state had a clear choice. Domestic rents were sanctioned, mercantilism continued, and international power was used to support rents through mercantilism. Yet French mercantilism was not very successful. In the words of Fernand Braudel:

> Should one really forget the missed opportunities even before 1789? In 1713, at the end of the War of the Spanish Succession, France was deprived of free access to the silver of Latin America. In 1722, with the failure of Law's System, she was deprived until 1776 of a central bank. In 1762, even before the Treaty of Paris, France had already lost Canada and for all practical purposes India as well.[24]

The French bid to take and hold an intercontinental empire was essentially thwarted during the wars with Britain.

The continued sanctioning of rents and the arbitrariness of state policy hindered capital formation in France.[25] Some important chances for success in French mercantilism were lost because of arbitrary state actions: for instance, when France held the *asiento* (the lucrative right to the slave trade to Spanish America) in 1701, it proved unprofitable, partly because of disruption caused by war, but partly because the crown continually raided the company's capital, thereby discouraging investment. This was hardly an isolated example.[26]

---

23. Wilson, *French Foreign Policy*, pp. 75, 78; Riley, *Seven Years War*, p. 81.

24. Braudel, *Perspective of the World*, p. 50.

25. For some specific examples of the crown's arbitrariness, see Hilton Root, "Tying the King's Hands: Credible Commitments and Royal Fiscal Policy during the Old Regime," *Rationality and Society* 1 (October 1989): 240–258.

26. Barry Baysinger, Robert B. Ekelund, and Robert D. Tollison, "Mercantilism as a Rent-

As France entered the 1780s, it faced a high level of debt from the continual imperial wars. At the same time, slow but evident capital accumulation was beginning to erode the relative returns to capital. For the state and the owners of capital to continue to receive inflated gains (or have the potential to increase them), the state-sanctioned rents held by the capital-intensive sectors within France would need to be intensified. This combination of internal problems and the failure to solve them through external policy (i.e., successful expansion) were the ingredients for the Revolution of 1789.

Britain: Successful Mercantilism and Its Impact

In contrast to French mercantilism, British mercantilism protected a relatively open domestic economy from international competition. Britain came out of the War of the Spanish Succession no longer relatively rich in capital and in debt to the Dutch. As Charles Wilson eloquently stated, "With the borrowed profits from Holland's Golden Age, Britain gambled on an imperial future, and gambled successfully."[27]

With the alteration in economic interests caused by the war, pressure developed to return to policies of mercantilism. These interests first manifested themselves in the Tory party that came to power in the House of Commons under Queen Anne. The Tories tended to be protectionist, whereas the Whigs were generally interested in promoting trade. This new constellation of interests reacted against the negotiations for freer trade with Spain and France in the Treaty of Utrecht (something that would have been considered an important goal when the War of the Spanish Succession started). The trade agreement was soundly rejected in Parliament.[28]

Britain Reemphasizes Mercantilism

As the political balance shifted in Parliament, British foreign economic policy also moved. Mercantilist legislation was brought into place. But this legislation differed from earlier British mercantilism and the mercantilism of France in that it attempted neutrality among domestic economic actors: legis-

---

Seeking Society," in *Toward a Theory of the Rent-Seeking Society,* ed. James N. Buchanan, Robert D. Tollison, and Gordon Tullock (College Station: Texas A&M University Press, 1980), p. 265; Wilson, *French Foreign Policy,* pp. 45–46.

27. Wilson, *Economic History and the Historian,* p. 60.

28. John Carswell, *From Revolution to Revolution: England, 1688–1776* (London: Routledge & Kegan Paul, 1973), pp. 40–41, 72.

lation might favor British shippers, but not one shipper over another. Along these lines, the West India merchants (who were not organized into a trading company) successfully got restrictions on foreign competition in the Molasses Act of 1733 and the Sugar Act of 1739. Still, the great trading companies had trouble with enforcement, even when each might claim a legal monopoly: for instance, the Royal Africa Company continually protested the actions of the South Sea Company, and the Russia Company developed overland trade with Persia that competed with the Levant and East India companies. Each company could only fight its domestic competitors in Parliament, where those companies were also well supported.[29] In this way, Britain was the center of the largest free-trading area, but that area was deliberately separated from the outside.

Unlike the policies of a liberal leader, which are designed to foster the involvement of capital in economic relations with foreign markets, British legislation strove to prevent foreign investment. In striking comparison to the Dutch, who had proven to be formidable investors in almost every other country's East India company, eighteenth-century British policies effectively blocked the use of British capital, British men, and British ships in the service of competing foreign companies.[30]

English mercantilist writers continued to argue in the eighteenth century that internal free trade supported by external controls was desirable. This seeming contradiction in theory followed from the combination of domestic and international political economic environments, not just from the domestic institutional one, as Robert Ekelund and Robert Tollison claim. The latter argue that state-sanctioned rents are more likely to increase in number and importance in nondemocracies than in democracies.[31] If they were correct, the break toward free trade in Britain would have come in 1688, and it would be a clean break. In fact, there were fluctuations in the liberalization of trade after Parliament became the dominant institution in 1688. These fluctuations can

29. Harry T. Dickinson, *Walpole and the Whig Supremacy* (London: English Universities Press, 1973), pp. 110–111; Jeremy Black, *British Foreign Policy in the Age of Walpole* (Edinburgh: John Donald, 1985), pp. 94–95.

30. Black, *British Foreign Policy,* p. 98.

31. Robert B. Ekelund and Robert D. Tollison, *Mercantilism as a Rent-Seeking Society* (College Station: Texas A&M University Press, 1981), p. 11. Ekelund and Tollison suggest seeing A. F. Chalk, "Natural Law and the Rise of Economic Individualism in England," *Journal of Political Economy* 59 (1951): 330–347, and W. D. Grampp "The Liberal Element in English Mercantilism," *Quarterly Journal of Economics* 66 (1952): 465–501. This discussion of the mix of British tariffs also fits some of the recent work of John Vincent Nye, though Nye's main point is that British tariffs were higher than French ones in the nineteenth century; see his "The Myth of Free Trade Britain and Fortress France: Tariffs and Trade in the Nineteenth Century," *Journal of Economic History* 51 (March 1991): 23–46.

be understood only by examining both Britain's domestic political situation and its international economic position.

The model presented here expects British mercantilism, but in a style significantly different from French mercantilism in content. The contrast between British and French mercantilism comes from the greater representative basis of British government.[32] The East India Company's monopoly was opened to competition in 1698. The old and new companies were eventually united in a single monopoly, but it is significant to note that the new monopoly was subject to parliamentary rather than royal review. After 1688, the rights of the Merchant Adventurers and the Royal African Company were changed; attacks on other companies came again in the 1740s and 1750s.[33]

At the same time domestic competition was fostered, barriers to international competition rose. In 1721/22, Robert Walpole reformed tariffs to ensure that British manufactures could be exported free of duty, and overall customs were consolidated and simplified. In 1723 all Great Britain's customs were placed under one commission. In 1725 excise officers were given extensive powers, and rewards for catching smugglers were raised to improve enforcement. Perhaps most important, the book of rates was updated. The old book had been established in 1660; any types of good introduced after that time paid duties based on their sworn value; that is, importers had to state the new items' value in order to establish new duties. Since it is safe to assume that importers routinely understated the value of these new items to avoid taxes, the creation of a second book covering new items (in 1724) closed one of the major loopholes allowing lowly taxed imports into Britain. During all these changes, no import duty on a finished good that would compete with British manufactures was ever dropped.[34]

Walpole's tariff reforms were quite successful in the beginning. Revenue rose £120,000 per annum without damaging reexports. The excise scheme was based on the concept that reexports were not charged as much duty as goods to be consumed at home, with the use of bonded warehouses to control the distinction between imports and reexports. This system worked well on coffee and chocolate because these were not widely consumed at the time; with tea, the East India Company held a monopoly, so it was only too willing to comply with greater controls, since this helped eliminate interlopers on the tea

32. Root's works on the mercantilism of Britain and France give historical support for this argument.

33. Carswell, *From Revolution to Revolution,* pp. 39, 42; W. E. Minchinton, "Editor's Introduction," in *The Growth of English Overseas Trade in the Seventeenth and Eighteenth Centuries* (London: Methuen, 1969), pp. 12–13.

34. Norris A. Brisco, *The Economic Policy of Robert Walpole* (New York: AMS Press, 1967), pp. 131–141.

trade and did not cut into the company's sales. When Walpole sought to extend controls to wine and tobacco, where there were many merchants and competition for a large market was fierce (i.e., where many merchants were cheating on duties), opposition was vociferous, and he had to back down.[35]

Government finance was changed in other ways. Britain learned how to mobilize national capital for the state by copying Dutch bond-raising techniques. Parliament had consistently blocked attempts to set up a central bank before 1688, because it feared the crown could then get money without Parliament's approval. Once Parliament was made responsible for the national debt in 1693, Dutch investors trusted that English government debts would be repaid. Parliament then offered annuities based on the example of Dutch government annuities. Although this enabled Britain's government to tap into Dutch capital to win wars, it also put the state deeply into debt.

Britain did more than copy Dutch institutions, it managed to adapt and perfect them. The Bank of England, for instance, was an indirect descendant of the Bank of Amsterdam, but the British bank had better tools to intervene in markets. In the crisis of 1773 the Bank's intervention enabled the London market to remain stable, whereas Dutch financial markets crashed because there was no responsible institution capable of stabilizing that market. The British treasury's control over tax collection led to centralized bookkeeping, which made the British system much more efficient than the melange of Dutch taxes.[36]

The international financial links developed during the wars against France were still important in the middle of the eighteenth century. The families of Dutch financiers who had come to England during William III's reign continued to be important socially and economically. Many contemporaries believed that Dutch capital was indispensable for the British government from the end of the War of the Spanish Succession until 1780 and perhaps even later. One Frenchman, Luzac, in a treatise entitled *La richesse de la Hollande* (1778), attacked this financial arrangement as "the artificial power of England." He argued that Britain was able to play the role of a major power only because the Dutch loaned them so much capital.[37]

35. Dickinson, *Walpole and the Whig Supremacy*, p. 96; Paul Langford, *The Excise Crises: Society and Politics in the Age of Walpole* (Oxford: Clarendon Press, 1975), pp. 60–61.

36. Wilson, *Economic History and the Historian*, p. 39; Braudel, *Perspective of the World*, pp. 271–273; Riley, *International Government Finance*, pp. 5, 70–71, 104; Larry Neal, *The Rise of Financial Capitalism: International Capital Markets in the Age of Reason* (New York: Cambridge University Press, 1990), esp. chap. 8.

37. By 1723 the prices of British funds were quoted on the Amsterdam market, and when the South Seas Bubble burst on the London market in 1720 Dutch speculators were among those who

Yet the British were able to break free of the Dutch middlemen and develop their own trading network over the course of the eighteenth century. Important to Britain's rise as a commercial power was the shifting content of trade as colonial goods climbed in importance. In 1700 the Netherlands was still Britain's largest export market, but by then Britain was importing more from the colonies. As a source of goods, Holland fell to tenth place by 1760.[38]

The volume of Britain's trade grew incredibly. The official value of exports in 1760 was twice that of 1700 and nearly eight times the figure for 1660. The British merchant fleet grew in size and efficiency too. Between 1702 and 1788, the merchant fleet's tonnage increased more than threefold. At this same time, the English East India Company became more dominant than the VOC in the Indian Ocean. The Dutch reaction to this was, not surprisingly, to invest in ever larger numbers in the English company.[39]

The Impact of Successful Mercantilism

Britain was successful in continually expanding her empire. Military success in the middle of the eighteenth century brought Canada and much of India into the realm. As Britain's economic control expanded, the variety of goods produced within its far-ranging empire increased. Slaves from West Africa, rum and sugar from the Caribbean, tobacco and cotton from the American colonies, fur and naval stores from Canada, and textiles from India were traded within the closed imperial economy. This increased London's importance as an entrepôt. The exotic commodities from the empire enabled British merchants to develop trade within Europe.[40] Just as important, these areas were all markets too. Given that Britain did not have capital as abundant as the Netherlands, investments in shipping, trade, and capital-intensive produc-

---

lost money. See Wilson, *Anglo-Dutch Commerce*, pp. 70–71, 75, 78, and Riley, *International Government Finance*, p. 85.

38. Wilson, *England's Apprenticeship, 1603–1763* (New York: St. Martin's, 1965), pp. 271–272.

39. W. A. Cole, "Factors in Demand, 1700–1780," and Donald N. McCloskey and R. P. Thomas, "Overseas Trade and Empire 1700–1860," in *The Economic History of Britain since 1700*, Vol. 1: *1700–1860*, ed. Donald N. McCloskey and Roderick Floud (New York: Cambridge University Press, 1981), pp. 38, 92; Wilson, *Economic History and the Historian*, p. 162; K. N. Chaudhuri, *Trade and Civilisation in the Indian Ocean: An Economic History from the Rise of Islam to 1750* (New York: Cambridge University Press, 1985), p. 86; Holden Furber, *Rival Empires of Trade in the Orient, 1600–1800* (Minneapolis: University of Minnesota Press, 1976), p. 103.

40. Geoffrey Parker, "The Emergence of Modern Finance in Europe, 1500–1730," in *The Fontana Economic History of Europe: The Sixteenth and Seventeenth Centuries*, ed. C. M. Cipolla (Glasgow: Collins/Fontana, 1974), p. 552.

tion found higher returns than if Dutch shippers had been allowed to compete.

In comparison to France, Britain employed mercantilism to success. The British were able to expand their empire, chiefly by frustrating the French in the pursuit of the same goals. But the very success of the closed system produced two rather different events. In the American colonies, higher capital abundance began to show in the New England colonies, which wanted to spread trade beyond the boundaries of the empire. These interests clashed with Britain's mercantile policies. Without political recourse to the British state to change policies, illegal activites such as smuggling became big business. New England became the hotbed for independence. Revolts against taxation without representation, any new taxes, and British foreign economic policy show the depth of the disagreement many Americans felt toward British mercantilism, though these were certainly not the only issues. Americans believed, correctly, that these policies benefited British rather than American capitalists.

The American war of independence ended in American victory, thanks to French help. The American states then achieved free trade among themselves after the development of the federal government with the Constitution's ratification in 1787. After opening the domestic economy, the United States would initially follow policies exhibiting a similar interest in liberalizing trade internationally.

The other result of successful mercantilism was that capital accumulation increased in Britain too. The new accumulation of capital was noticeable in the wave of investments in economic infrastructure (canals, toll roads, buildings, and enclosures) of the 1750s–1770s; the same is true for agriculture, for if (as Phyllis Deane and W.A. Cole suggest) parliamentary enclosures are used as a proxy for increased investment, the acreage enclosed in the years between 1761 and 1792 was seven times that of the preceding three decades. In the 1780s and 1790s, capital accumulation grew at an even faster rate. Before the 1780s capital accumulation was slow (probably below 5 percent of national income), but it then increased as a proportion of national income.[41]

---

41. Phyllis Deane and W. A. Cole, *British Economic Growth, 1688–1959: Trends and Structure* (Cambridge: Cambridge University Press, 1962), pp. 18–20, 261–264. N. F. R. Crafts gives reduced figures for gross domestic investment as a proportion of gross national product, though there is still an increase between 1760 and 1801; see *British Economic Growth during the Industrial Revolution* (Oxford: Clarendon Press, 1985), p. 73. Crafts argues that Deane and Cole overestimated some of their figures in order to rethink the processes of the Industrial Revolution; he also argues that the changes took much longer to develop before reaching the threshold of industrialization. He notes (p. 31) that the large increase Deane and Cole found between 1780 and 1801

This accumulation should have increased the capital-labor ratio, and we would expect owners of capital to become more interested in ending mercantilism as the relative returns to capital began to decline. Particularly after the rate of capital formation increased, we expect the owners of capital to begin lobbying for a change in Britain's foreign economic policies in Parliament. This shift is identifiable first with the earl of Shelburne's ministry, but it is much more apparent in the administration of William Pitt after 1784. The new domestic economic interests worked through Parliament to change Britain's foreign economic policy. Despite the difficulties created by American independence, and with international enemies everywhere, Britain made its first efforts to liberalize the international economy in the 1780s.

These feeble first steps at liberal leadership would stumble first on the French Revolution and then on the fact that France had also accumulated capital over the previous fifty years. Just as Britain became a prospective liberal leader, France was moving into a position to launch an expansionary challenge. The next major war would begin before the new liberal leader had effectively established an open international political economic subsystem.

Britain as a Prospective Liberal Leader in the 1780s

Britain had entered the 1780s as an increasingly capital-rich, powerful country with a representative state set on establishing an open international economy, but there were no significant willing partners to be found. All the strongest powers were ambivalent to British attempts at liberal leadership. Revolutionary France was quickly engulfed in war. The only potential supporters or peaceful economic competitors were weak states such as the United States and the Netherlands, and these two countries were still smarting from recent wars with Britain.

Britain's capital-labor ratio changed in the final two decades of the eighteenth century as capital was accumulated at an even faster rate. The first large wave of investments to come out of this cheaper capital was between 1783 and 1792. Between 1790 and 1810, money wages in Great Britain rose by an estimated 75 percent, a definite sign of the changing ratio of capital to labor (though prices, too, rose sharply during these twenty years). Between 1780 and 1800, the rate of capital formation jumped from below 5 percent of na-

---

(when compared to 1760–1780) is partially due to their reliance on trade figures that show an increase after the American war of independence ended. This expansion of trade is of interest for our purposes.

tional income to 7 percent, so that the rate of capital accumulation was moving faster than national income.[42] The volume of trade increased as the interest rate fell, and London came to replace Amsterdam as the most important international financial center. Changes in the state's foreign policies could be expected soon.

The Shelburne ministry of the early 1780s exhibited some of the first movements toward liberal leadership. Although the first order of business was to end war with France and the American colonies and restore some stability to government finances, the strengthening of trade by revising commercial restrictions and abandoning the mercantile system were also goals for this government—for the best domestic investment opportunities were rapidly disappearing. Shelburne spoke on proposals for recognizing American independence in 1782:

> Whilst we are delivered from the vast expense of maintaining and protecting the Colonies, our commercial intercourse with them will still be productive of many advantages . . . and possibly, if America, as may rationally be expected, should rapidly increase in populousness and cultivation, the benefits of our trade with her may be greater than ever. . . . The system of monopolies and little restrictions in trade, begins to be exploded in the world, and will justly every day more and more out of fashion.[43]

Clearly Shelburne was arguing that movement away from "democratic" mercantilism (an open domestic economy closed to foreign competition) toward policies of liberal leadership (supporting an open international economy) would be more beneficial for Britain, for international investment opportunities would not be affected (and would probably even rise) and costs to the state might fall.

When Pitt and his supporters won the election of 1784, unseating some 160 opposition members and practically sweeping the London area, it signaled the triumph of the capital-intensive sectors most interested in expanding trade at the expense of mercantilism—the domestic shift driving policies toward lead-

---

42. Francois Crouzet, "Capital Formation in Great Britain during the Industrial Revolution," in *Capital Formation in the Industrial Revolution*, ed. Crouzet (London: Methuen, 1972), p. 207; Deane and Cole, *British Economic Growth*, pp. 24, 263–264. See C. H. Lee, *The British Economy since 1700: A Macroeconomic Perspective* (New York: Cambridge University Press, 1986), p. 50, for a discussion of the more recent sets of data produced by C. H. Feinstein and N. F. R. Crafts (these also place the rapid upturn in capital formation in the last two decades of the century).

43. Robin Reilly, *Pitt the Younger, 1759–1806* (London: Cassell, 1978), pp. 71–73.

ing international liberalization. A good example of the supporters for the new policies is the General Chamber of Manufacturers, founded in March 1785, whose first chairman was Josiah Wedgwood, a passionate exponent of freer trade with Europe.[44]

Britain's overtures to the ambivalent countries were mostly failures. Although Pitt conducted commercial negotiations with Spain, Portugal, France, Prussia, Russia, the Netherlands, Poland, the Kingdom of the Two Sicilies, and Morocco, his only successes were with France and Morocco, primarily because Britain was not willing to relent on the Navigation Acts. These controls were particularly an obstacle in talks with the United States. Negotiations with Britain's great rival of the eighteenth century, France, led to the Anglo-French Commercial Treaty of 1786 (also known as the Eden Treaty). This treaty lowered customs duties to 10–15 percent of the value of goods and abolished prohibitions on some imports. The treaty was an attempt to minimize the trade barriers on the goods each country exported. Tariffs were lowered on French exports to Britain such as oil, wine, and vinegar, and British exports such as textiles also received lower tariffs. The only British industry that feared French competition, silk production, was protected with a total ban on French imports.[45] This treaty was the most successful deal Britain completed in its efforts to liberalize economic relations in the 1780s.

At the same time, Pitt took unilateral steps toward freeing trade. One of his first actions after the 1784 election was to reduce the duties on tea (which averaged 119 percent) to a uniform 25 percent of value—which doubled the amount going through customs as less tea was smuggled and thus raised both the profits of the East India Company and government revenues. The positive impact of these reductions led to the lowering of customs on other items such as wine, spirits, and tobacco.[46] The higher rate of capital formation also moved Britain from an international debtor to the tune of £20 million in 1760 into an international creditor of £10 million in 1800—and this despite the higher level of domestic investments during this same period.[47]

The eruption of continental revolutions put a temporary halt to British attempts to create an open international economic subsystem within Europe.

44. Eric J. Evans, *The Forging of the Modern State: Early Industrial Britain, 1783–1870* (New York: Longman, 1983), pp. 31–32.

45. Eli F. Heckscher, *The Continental System: An Economic Interpretation* (Oxford: Clarendon Press, 1922), p. 20; Reilly, *Pitt the Younger*, pp. 114–115, 173.

46. Reilly, *Pitt the Younger*, pp. 109–110.

47. C. H. Feinstein, "Capital Formation in Great Britain," in *The Cambridge Economic History of Europe*, ed. Peter Mathias and M. M. Postan (Cambridge: Cambridge University Press, 1978), 8.1:71.

Even then, Britain had no interest in attacking revolutionary France. The British government called charges that it was harassing France through secret intrigues in 1792 absurd, proclaiming that "a commercial people stands only to gain by the freedom of all those who surround it."[48] Britain entered the wars with France reluctantly and would rather have opened trade than continued mercantilism in another war. In fact, a representative regime in France could be expected to be a supporter or, at worst, a peaceful economic competitor to British liberal leadership, and therefore it could be accommodated rather easily in a British-led open economic subsystem.

The Napoleonic Wars: France as an Expansionary Challenger

France entered the 1780s with growing capital abundance, international power, and autocratic government institutions. But the failure of the state to continue to find ways to expand externally and maintain rising returns to capital meant that domestic rents had to be intensified at home. The state tried to intensify the rents it sanctioned and thereby drove away political support from consumers, peasants, and other small producers. Most notably, the inability to create free trade in grain internally kept this important foodstuff in short supply and at high prices.[49] At the same time, the state could not raise returns to capital high enough or quickly enough to placate the large owners of capital. Potential reforms to loosen up investment opportunities were too little and too late.

The state's support eventually crumbled away in the revolution. The state's inability to raise its own funds forced it to call a parlement in 1789, the first in over 150 years. Although all social groups were unhappy with the state's policies, they could not agree on what should replace the existing system; yet all allied to dismantle the old structure of government.

The new leaders who seized power in the revolution also could not satisfy all these groups at once. The Constituent Assembly initially established during

48. John H. Rose, *William Pitt and the Great War* (Westport, Conn.: Greenwood, 1971; reprint of 1911), p. 44. Rose concludes that these were the words of Pitt; he notes that they recall Adam Smith's phrase in *The Wealth of Nations*: "A nation that would enrich itself by trade is certainly most likely to do so when its neighbours are all rich, industrious, and commercial nations."

49. In "Politiques frumentaires et violence collective en Europe au XVIIIe siècle," *Annales E.S.C.* 45 (January-February 1990): 167–189, Hilton Root examines the specific problems with grain, and he points out (p. 177) that the threat of famine persisted because of insufficient means of transport and market imperfections often due to local regulations.

the revolution removed all internal customs duties, suppressed guilds and other restrictions on manufactures, and destroyed some monopolies.[50] This alienated the beneficiaries of the old system of governmental controls. The advantages of a more open domestic economy were not quickly realized, though, so consumers and small producers were not placated either. Any chance of a stable democracy being established was lessened by the fact that some major social groups were turned into enemies while a new base of support was hard to find.

In the early years of the revolution, the most obvious political split was between the Jacobins, who represented the urban center of Paris and supported a broad-based, pyramidal government structure with centralized regulation of food supplies, prices, and wages, and the Girondins, who represented the provinces and supported decentralization as a better safeguard for private property.[51] The Jacobins proved to be more ruthless and effectively purged the Girondins from leadership. The emerging revolutionary government lost most of its democratic character and began to centralize power and sanction rents.

The Terror and the breakdown into factional fighting gave France's neighbors the opportunity, and the excuse, for invading that country in hopes of expanding their imperial territories. For Britain, the revolutionary wars may have been defensive, but for Prussia and Austria these were opportunities to expand. Claiming to protect either the institution of monarchy or specific dynastic interests, both Prussia and Austria sent armies against France. The French leadership generally welcomed war: the various factions expected Britain to stay out of any fighting, revolutionary groups thought war would help radicalize the populace, and royalists thought war would show the need for a strong executive that only a monarchy could provide.[52]

Britain's prime minister, Pitt, chose first to follow a policy of strict neutrality with the revolutionary government. As France was about to go to war with Austria in 1792, Charles-Maurice de Talleyrand, France's representative in Britain, wrote Antoine-Nicolas Delessart, the French foreign minister who was sizing up the European situation, to say "Your best ground is England." When Britain finally went to war with France, it was over French attempts to conquer the Netherlands—a violation of a British alliance, and perceived as a

50. Stuart Andrews, *Eighteenth-Century Europe: The 1680s to 1815* (London: Longmans, Green, 1965), p. 288.

51. Ibid., pp. 298–299.

52. Agatha Ramm, *Europe in the Nineteenth Century, 1789–1905* (New York: Longman, 1984), p. 37. These expectations proved true, although not quite as intended.

direct threat to Britain's security. Pitt justified the war to Parliament as the only way to attain peace, which was essential for trade; France anticipated Britain's moves and declared war on Britain first.[53]

The rise of the Directory and then Napoleon to political predominance in France led to changes in that country's relations with Britain. France became an expansionary challenger against Britain's initial attempts at liberal leadership. As a challenger, Napoleonic France wanted to avoid Britain's leadership and create a closed international political economic subsystem. Pitt saw this as a challenge to "the Public Law of Europe."[54] Napoleon's imperial wars were not only as widespread as the wars of the French Revolution, they were also characterized by the offensive nature of Napoleon's strategies, a higher level of destructiveness, and the adoption of a rigid policy of economic warfare as France attempted to take as much of the international economy as possible into a closed system.[55] These are all distinguishing features of a war of challenge.

Alliances of the Napoleonic Wars

The alliance patterns of the Napoleonic Wars fit those expected by the model. In a system with a prospective liberal leader, an expansionary political challenger, and all other major powers ambivalent toward the aspiring liberal hegemon, the ability of the liberal to construct a durable alliance is undermined by the challenger's ability to attract ambivalent countries. This may be one reason the Napoleonic Wars lasted so long. France had been virtually alone in the wars of the revolution. In the Napoleonic Wars, France was able to bully or bribe some of the ambivalent states into becoming allies. Successful wars also enabled Napoleon to create several satellites, which were also allies. But French desires to create a closed economic system that it would dominate at the expense of others was a great disincentive for allies to support France's efforts.

Britain, in contrast, had several potential allies among France's neighbors who feared French expansion. But these countries were almost all from the ambivalent category: as bandwagoners, they were always willing to switch sides

---

53. Rose, *William Pitt*, pp. 29, 43, 117; Ramm, *Europe in the Nineteenth Century*, p. 43.

54. McKay and Scott, *Rise of the Great Powers*, p. 303.

55. In terms of battle deaths per million European population (Levy's severity factor), the Napoleonic Wars were almost three times worse than the preceding revolutionary wars. See Jack S. Levy, *War in the Modern Great Power System, 1495–1975* (Lexington: University Press of Kentucky, 1983), tab. 4.1 (p. 90).

or make a separate peace if they could do so to their own advantage.[56] For instance, in the second coalition arrayed against France, Britain was allied with Russia and Austria in an attempt to encircle and attack France from all sides, but the Austrians used their forces to consolidate gains in Italy and then attempted to take Belgium (hoping to exchange it for Bavaria when arranging a separate peace with France). In the process, Austria removed support for Russian forces in Germany and Switzerland, where they were defeated. Furthermore, the collapse of every coalition left Britain with the prospect of France concentrating her efforts on her navy and gaining control over the fleets of other European powers—the great fear of the wars with France from the previous century. Indeed, Napoleon himself had written in October 1797, "Let us concentrate our energies on the navy and annihilate England. That done Europe is at our feet."[57]

Britain followed the typical strategy of a liberal leader in a war of challenge: as a capital-rich nation with a state sensitive to domestic political competition, it used its capital and capital-intensive industries to its advantage. These tendencies were exhibited in several ways: (1) Britain always chose a slower strategy of attrition, of wearing France down with economic resources rather than going for a quick strike; (2) Britain always tried to combine her financial and industrial assets with those of another country's manpower assets, so that British troops did not bear the brunt of the fighting; and (3) when British troops did fight, they used capital-intensive rather than manpower-intensive tactics—in other words, British military tactics stressed firepower.

The British government could borrow vast sums because of financial improvements and innovations made before the wars. Pitt's reforms of government finances enabled Britain to raise vast sums for the war effort.[58] Britain also had the capital to attract ambivalent powers into alliances. Since ambivalent powers did not particularly agree with British preferences concerning the nature of the international system but did have economies complementary to Britain's, economic incentives to join alliances were usually more effective than appeals to wider political goals. Without subsidies, several countries could not have opposed France. Prussia, for instance, went to war in 1813 with almost all her men armed with British-bought, British-made guns. The quality of such weapons was so recognized by the Russians that they used

56. Paul Kennedy, *The Rise and Fall of British Naval Mastery* (London: Lane, 1976), p. 133.

57. Napoleon's comment is as quoted in Andrews, *Eighteenth-Century Europe*, p. 328. Also see Piers Mackesy, *War without Victory: The Downfall of Pitt, 1799–1802* (Oxford: Clarendon Press, 1984), pp. 4, 122.

58. Kennedy, *Rise and Fall of British Naval Mastery*, p. 121.

them to reward their troops who exhibited bravery under fire. Uprisings against the revolutionary and later Napoleonic governments were continually supported with both British money and materiel.

Though Britain was able to pull together many allies, these coalitions were extremely fluid. In the six coalitions that fought against France between 1793 and 1814, Britain was a member of all six, Austria was a member of five, Russia was a member of four, and Prussia, Sweden, and Portugal were members of three. In the War of the Third Coalition (1805), France faced Britain, Austria, the Netherlands, Sweden, Russia, and Prussia. France continued the war against Russia and Prussia in 1806–1807 and invaded Spain and Portugal (1807–1814), where large formations of British troops once again entered direct combat. France fought Austria alone in 1809 and then launched the attack on Russia in 1812, dragging along several client states. (As a good ambivalent power watching out for its own interests, Prussia jumped sides.) Finally, Britain brought a wide range of powers (Russia, Prussia, Austria, Portugal, and Sweden) to bear in the War of Liberation (1813–1814) to depose Napoleon.

Military Strategies of the Napoleonic Wars

Because of their war aims and the size of their forces, French leaders selected an offensive strategy. To conquer new territories French troops had to attack. Napoleon himself is best known as a master of maneuver. He first won fame in the campaigns in Italy by using the old adage "divide and conquer." By creating local advantages in numbers through maneuver, France was able to deploy smaller armies to win a series of battles and conquer neighboring territory. British military doctrine, in contrast, stressed attrition and the use of allies. But Britain's allies were not particularly dependable. Almost all the wars followed the same pattern: war on the continent would lead to a British army landing there; then the coalition would collapse, the British army would have to be withdrawn, and the war would be carried out by naval means.

In battles, the British used superior firepower for success. Whereas French tactics emphasized infantry in columns or heavy cavalry for crashing through the enemy's lines, British tactics dispersed troops widely to gain greater firepower. British troops were often deployed in lines only two deep, whereas all other armies deployed their troops in lines three or more deep.

In the naval war, the French tried to gather a fleet to challenge British control of the high seas, but this fleet was destroyed in battle at Trafalgar. Superior tactics, gunnery, and leadership gave British fleets advantages in mêlées, and they used such tactics to destroy a great number of French ships in fleet confrontations. Destruction of the enemy fleet was the prime goal of British naval tactics. As on land, the British used capital-intensive tactics (such as superior firepower) to win battles. One example is the superiority of British gunnery, seen in the deployment of large numbers of light cannon called carronades. Not only did the British develop new weapons such as these, but they built up their fleet to massive proportions—increasing the number of ships of the line from 135 in 1793 to 202 in 1802 and raising naval personnel from around 16,000 to some 135,000 over that same time period.[59] With better tactics and more economic support, the British navy took control of the seas.

After the defeat of the French main fleet at Trafalgar, France adopted a more concerted commerce-raiding strategy. Even before Trafalgar, French frigates had begun to implement such a strategy. After Trafalgar, the French admirals really had no choice, so the naval pattern of the war conforms to our expectations: Britain tried to protect trade by controlling the seas, while France merely sought to deny Britain that control. Britain's naval strength also blocked any possibility of a French invasion, as in 1803 to 1805, when a French army was poised across the English Channel. This strong defensive position gave Britain the opportunity to pursue the attrition strategy. The navy was also important for this strategy in a direct sense, since it was critical for Britain's assault on Napoleon's economic policies. France had tried to bar British goods from Europe, and Britain's response was to flood European markets with exports to undercut French sales.

Economic Warfare and the Continental System

In November 1806, Napoleon announced the creation of the Continental System, built on trade controls established in 1793. The earlier restrictions had had little effect; between 1792 and 1800, the percentage of British exports headed for France and the Netherlands had fallen only slightly.[60] But from 1806 on, France and her client states would trade only with each other. Napoleon hoped to use political control of the continent to make French commerce dominant there. As one historian has written, "the Continental System was, in Mowat's phrase, 'a blockade of the French Empire by itself.' But exclusion of British goods was not Napoleon's only aim: he wanted to

---

59. Ibid., pp. 126–127; also McKay and Scott, *Rise of the Great Powers*, p. 306.

60. Frederick L. Nussbaum, *Commercial Policy in the French Revolution: A Study of the Career of G. J. A. Ducher* (Washington, D.C.: American Historical Association, 1923), p. i; Heckscher, *Continental System*, p. 42.

capture European markets for French goods."[61] The specific controls established underline the French goals. Napoleon's decree of November 1806 forbade trade or any intercourse with Britain and called for the arrest of all Britons in the French-controlled areas as well as the seizure of all British property. Also, any ship doing business with the British Empire was liable to seizure. Clearly, the hope was to displace Britain as the dominant economic country. As Napoleon told a merchant, "You and I, we are fighting a good war against the English; you through your work, I with arms. You are doing the better."[62]

Napoleon hoped that France, as the most capital-abundant country in a closed subsystem, would dominate the European market in capital-intensive goods and services. In this sense, the aims of the Contintental System harkened back to those of Louis XIV. The main principle was *la France avant tout* in what has been described as an "Uncommon Market." The rules of the Continental System were aimed not only at blocking Britain's trade with the continent and asserting French economic dominance but also at preempting the rise of other economic competitors.

Although the system was reorganized in 1810, it retained the same goals. In a massive coordinated program, Napoleon's government used prohibitions and tariffs, commercial treaties, loans and subsidies, and other means of suasion. The assumption was that trade could be structured so that France would exchange manufactured goods and agricultural products for primary materials on a preferential basis. Napoleon pushed for all the countries in France's orbit to adopt the same tariff structure, tried to use navigation controls and licensing to give French financiers the edge over competitors in Europe, and supported other related efforts to increase France's industrial advantages over other contintental countries.

French military might was used to close off Europe, either through direct action or by bullying other states to close themselves off. Evidence suggests that these were indeed prosperous times for France. But the costs to France were in terms of allies and the war effort, for the French satellites suffered under the restrictions without receiving any benefits.[63] Instead of turning conquered or dominated countries into allies in the war against Britain, the Con-

---

61. Frank Edgar Melvin, *Napoleon's Navigation System: A Study of Trade Control during the Continental Blockade* (New York: D. Appleton [University of Pennsylvania], 1919), p. 224; Clive Trebilcock, *The Industrialization of the Continental Powers, 1780–1914* (New York: Longman, 1981), p. 129. Quotation from Andrews, *Eighteenth-Century Europe*, p. 333.

62. Quoted in Geoffrey Ellis, *Napoleon's Continental Blockade: The Case of Alsace* (Oxford: Clarendon Press, 1981), p. 120.

63. Ramm, *Europe in the Nineteenth Century*, p. 109.

tinental System created resentment against French domination. The difference in interests between France and her satellites created numerous problems concerning enforcement of the Continental System. Sharp protests and an embargo by France were used to pressure Dutch authorities to undertake better policing in 1809.[64] Napoleon was even forced to remove his own brother as king of the Netherlands and to transfer coastal areas from the kingdom of Westphalia to France in order to enhance the enforcement of the Continental System.

British control of the sea exacerbated these problems. Smuggling and stapling bases, such as on Helgoland, penetrated the Continental System, allowing British goods to reach the groups on the continent that were resisting French domination. The British also established a license system to manipulate trade, but these licenses could be bought and sold and were exchanged openly in countries at war with Britain, including France. British attempts to control trade did not rest on barring trade but rather on redirecting it through British ports. Britain also used force to open some states to British goods. In 1807 a fleet was sent to Copenhagen to force Denmark out of the Continental System. The position of the weaker states was precarious, for retribution could come from either side. Some states tried to walk the fine line between British and French policies. For example, in 1811 a Swedish governor complied with French commands by seizing oxen intended for the English fleet, but the Swede wisely took the precaution of warning the English admiral beforehand.[65]

The Continental System failed to achieve overall French aims for several reasons. First, successfully blocking British goods from European markets created a greater demand for capital-intensive goods, which did in fact benefit French industries. What was lacking was an increased demand for capital-intensive goods in parts of the Continental System outside France. Second, the failure of the fleet strategy left merchantmen unguarded, so France could not get supplies from colonial areas or America except through British ports. Neutral carriers were not numerous enough to replace British ships, and the Royal Navy could block any other sources. Bottlenecks in production appeared once items normally received in trade could no longer be imported. Some substitutes were found: beet sugar was produced, chicory replaced coffee, new pastel and madder-worst dyes were used, and cotton was grown in southern Italy. New processes of iron, steel, and soda production were also developed.[66]

64. Melvin, *Napoleon's Navigation System*, p. 143.

65. Heckscher, *Continental System*, pp. 160, 207–208.

66. Ellis, *Napoleon's Continental Blockade*, pp. 127, 151, 232. For more details see Heckscher, *Continental System*, chap. 2 in pt. 4.

Loopholes in the trade restrictions abounded, and countries that cheated earned handsome profits. The Prussian government actively traded forbidden goods through a special office in 1811 and 1812. Even French officials could be (and often were) bribed to look the other way, allowing illicit trade in the occupied or satellite states.

France could not produce some things because access to raw materials was limited among the Continental System's members. Licenses were issued to exempt certain imports from the Berlin and Milan decrees. For instance, wool coats for the French army had to be imported from Britain. Some trade also flowed the other direction: France allowed licensed trade in grain with Britain. For many, this seems a rather foolish policy, since Britain had had difficulties producing enough to feed itself. Shortages had occurred in 1795, 1800, and 1812, but these were actually offset by very small amounts of imports.[67]

Britain applied the attrition strategy effectively through economic penetration and selective blockade, but these same policies brought about an interesting side effect in Europe's relations with the United States. As another representative government, America should have accepted British liberal leadership. At first it seemed that the two countries shared interests, but as Britain's war strategy demanded closing Europe to non-British trade the interests of the two countries diverged.

America's Relations with Europe during the Napoleonic Wars

Despite its victory in the war for independence, the United States did not have strong international power. The American military budget and number of men in uniform were both small in comparison to European figures for the 1790s. The United States was governed by a republican state and, depending on how one includes slaves and land in the measurement of capital, could be considered richer in capital than many European countries. But three-fourths of the money invested in the first central bank of the United States (1809) was from foreign sources, and after the war of independence the government was deeply indebted to the Dutch.[68] If one considers the United States capital-rich at this time, it should have been a free rider on British leadership (if not a peaceful economic challenger); if the United States was capital-poor, it should

67. Heckscher, *Continental System*, pp. 38, 214–215, 322, 338–340; Melvin, *Napoleon's Navigation System*, pp. 88–89.

68. Jeffry A. Frieden, *Banking on the World: The Politics of American International Finance* (New York: Harper & Row, 1987), p. 16.

have been a supporter. In either case, American interests should have been linked more closely to those of Britain than to those of any other major country in the international system.

On the assumption that it was capital-abundant, the United States should have been Britain's economic competitor within a British-led liberal subsystem. This expectation fits with the essence of American foreign policy goals in this period as they were succinctly stated by George Washington in his farewell address and then reiterated by Thomas Jefferson in his first inaugural speech: the United States wanted to extend commercial relations and avoid international political entanglements. It had a large merchant marine, which was profitable enough not only to balance out America's trade, reduce its foreign debt, and attract foreign capital but even to allow the export of specie to the Orient.[69] American interests were similar to Britain's in that both should want to maintain or even expand an open international subsystem.

As colonies, America had been Britain's best market for manufactured goods. After independence, Britain's Navigation Acts hurt American shipping, particularly by prohibiting direct trade between the United States and the West Indies. America then established protective tariffs to use as a lever against Britain's position.[70]

The United States did not join the British alliance against France because it hoped to remain neutral and keep the costs to the state low while maintaining high returns through free trade, which it wanted Britain to protect—a true free rider position. In consequence, an Anglo-American treaty was negotiated in 1794 (though not ratified in the Senate until 1796). This treaty opened some markets to American shipping, and trade between the United States and the West Indies boomed; by 1800 a quarter of British exports were going to the United States. The United States also hoped to maintain trade with France, which was usually in the Americans' favor since France imported coffee, sugar, and tobbaco from the West. French shipping lost this trade after Trafalgar, and the Americans hoped to take it over.[71]

Initially, America had warm relations with France. Many American political leaders offered advice to the revolutionaries privately. But during the revolutionary wars the French navy had seized other countries' ships on the high seas. The United States maintained that it was a neutral power and would

69. James A. Field, Jr., "1789–1820: All Economists, All Diplomats," in *Economics and World Power*, ed. William H. Becker and Samuel F. Wells, Jr. (New York: Columbia University Press, 1984), p. 6.

70. Evans, *Forging of the Modern State*, pp. 29, 32–33.

71. Ibid., pp. 33–34; Melvin, *Napoleon's Navigation System*, p. 177; Heckscher, *Continental System*, p. 101; Ellis, *Napoleon's Continental Blockade*, p. 20.

trade with whomever it wished. To protect American merchantmen, U.S. frigates fought a series of engagements against French vessels in an undeclared war from 1798 to 1800.[72] Tensions again ran high after the Milan decree of 1807, when neutral ships in French ports were seized. Yet, at the same time, Anglo-American relations deteriorated. British retaliations against the Continental System meant that both Britain and France were stopping ships on the high seas; between 1803 and 1812, France captured more than five hundred American ships, but Britain seized upward of a thousand more.[73]

A prominent flaw in the American diplomatic stance was that Britain lost interest in establishing a liberal subsystem during the Napoleonic Wars. First, liberalized trade was not in Britain's interests for prosecuting the attrition strategy against France. Britain did not want certain types of materiel to reach France, since these could aid the French war effort. Second, Britain would break the Continental System for its own benefit, not for any other country's. Since the expressed goal of the Continental System was to make France the predominant economic producer on the European continent, Britain was not willing to prevent this only to hand that leadership over to another country. This attitude was heightened by a decline in the British capital-labor ratio during the first decade of the nineteenth century. Capital accumulation declined, and at the same time capital consumption and exports (in the form of subsidies to allies) increased. Overall capital abundance declined. New investment was limited between 1803 and 1815 as capital became relatively more expensive.[74]

Britain's war expenditures played a large part in this consumption of capital. The national debt soared from close to £ 300 million in 1793 to well over £ 800 million in 1815. Eli Heckscher gives slightly different figures, claiming that the debt was only £ 230 million in 1793 and then £ 507 million in 1802 (compared to a £ 587 million funded debt on the eve of World War I). During the period of most intense warfare, from 1801 to 1815, Britain's government borrowing averaged £ 20.7 million annually, compared to an annual £ 1.3 million for the period from 1815 to 1830.[75] Meanwhile, labor's wages did not fall as able-bodied men were removed from the labor pool and placed in uniform. Britain's military effort took from 5–10 percent of the labor force

72. Ellis, *Napoleon's Continental Blockade*, p. 20.

73. Melvin, *Napoleon's Navigation System*, pp. 70–71; Gordon K. Tull and P. McG. Bulwer, *Britain and the World in the Nineteenth Century* (London: Blandford, 1966), p. 148.

74. Crouzet, "Capital Formation in Great Britain," p. 209.

75. Kennedy, *Rise and Fall of British Naval Mastery*, p. 141; Heckscher, *Continental System*, p. 61; Glenn R. Hueckel, *The Napoleonic Wars and Their Impact on Factor Returns and Output Growth in England, 1793–1815* (New York: Garland, 1985), pp. 36–38.

off the domestic market during the Napoleonic Wars. Real wages in Britain went up considerably in the years 1800–1824.[76]

Foreign competition looked much fiercer by 1810 than it had in 1800. And now the state had a massive war machine at its behest with which to impose a British monopoly of production, which is exactly what it did. Before the wars with France, Britain had moved significantly away from mercantilism and led a movement to liberalize international economic relations; but once Napoleon's wars of challenge began, Britain's ratio of factor endowments was altered, and the country was driven back toward mercantilist policies. The state began to award monopolies again, to improve infrastructure, reassert London as an entrepôt, and raise new revenues. For example, the West India Dock Act of 1799 compelled all vessels coming from or going to the West Indies to use the new dock for the next twenty-one years.[77]

These policies were obviously not in the interest of the United States, whose ships were now being harrassed by British warships as well as by French and British protective legislation. The Continental System and Britain's response led the United States to adopt the Embargo Act of 1807, which prevented any exports from the United States and prohibited any American ship from entering foreign ports. This policy inflicted tremendous difficulties on many Americans, so it was repealed and replaced by the Non-Intercourse Act of 1809, which specifically prohibited trade with Britain and France.[78]

The issues of free seas and free trade finally pitted the United States against Britain in the War of 1812. Both supporters and opponents of freer trade in America wanted war with Britain: those interested in a more open trading system desired war over freedom of the seas; those who supported American economic closure saw an opportunity for expansion to the west and into Canada at Britain's expense.[79] The United States was clearly too weak to go against British wishes, even as that country was locked in the wars with France in Europe. Americans tend to think of the war as ending in a draw, although almost the entire war was fought on American soil or in American coastal waters. Although neither side won a clear-cut, decisive victory, Britain made clear its resolve in closing the international political economic system.

---

76. Hueckel, *Napoleonic Wars*, p. xliii. Deane and Cole, *British Economic Growth*, pp. 25–26, suggest that real wages rose by perhaps a quarter.

77. Sydney Checkland, *British Public Policy, 1776–1939: An Economic, Social, and Political Perspective* (New York: Cambridge University Press, 1983), p. 15.

78. Frank W. Taussig, *The Tariff History of the United States* (New York: Putnam's Sons, 1931), p. 16; Tull and Bulwer, *Britain and the World*, pp. 148–149.

79. Tull and Bulwer, *Britain and the World*, pp. 149–150.

The Effects of Challenge on Prospective British Liberal Leadership

The second war of challenge against a liberal leader also ended in the challenger's defeat. Victory against France would come only after the defeat of Napoleon in Russia and the steady drain of French men and materiel in Spain. As the argument here anticipates, the prospective liberal leader had used attrition to withstand a challenge.

Britain had achieved its goal in both the Napoleonic Wars and the War of 1812, but the long wars against France stunted economic growth. In particular, the rate of capital formation had fallen. Deane and Cole claim that capital formation as a percentage of national income fell in the years 1800–1815 and would not reach high rates again until the dislocations of the war had been overcome some fifteen or twenty years later. This situation was worsened by the demobilization of the military forces, which shifted the capital-labor ratio further. Some 400,000 men reentered the domestic economy after 1815.[80] The net result was to encourage the support of mercantilism, as domestic capital's relative returns were once again high and capital was strongly demanded in Britain itself. Labor's wages were falling, and the state was looking for ways to cut costs, for it was again deeply in debt. Leadership of an open international political economic subsystem was no longer attractive.

The Napoleonic challenge to prospective British liberal leadership prevented the immediate establishment of an open international political economy, but once again France had lost a war aimed at establishing itself as the dominant country in a closed economic subsystem. France no longer had capital as relatively abundant as Britain. It would recover as a major power but, more important, its domestic system would change constantly in the next century as part of the legacy of the revolution and Napoleon. The impact of these domestic changes, plus the eventual emergence of Britain as a more successful liberal leader, shaped European relations for some time to come.

80. Deane and Cole, *British Economic Growth*, pp. 262–263; Hueckel, *Napoleonic Wars*, p. 43.

FOUR

Emergence and Decline of British Liberal Leadership, 1815–1918

After the Napoleonic Wars, Europe had relative peace for almost half a century, and then economic relations between the major powers expanded dramatically. This period, called the *pax Britannica*, provided the initial basis for hegemonic stability theory. Yet, closer examination of this case has called standard theories of hegemony into question. Difficulties emerge with purely structural models of hegemony because Britain moved into a position of naval dominance at the end of the Napoleonic Wars yet did not act as a liberalizing leader for several decades. This is not, however, a problem for the model presented here, which focuses on more than the distribution of military power: Britain would slowly reemerge as a prospective liberal leader, acting in the absence of any expansionary challengers, only after relative capital abundance returned in the 1830s and 1840s. Economic or political rivals arose only later, after British liberal leadership was well established.

Still others have been critical of hegemonic leadership models by arguing that the trade expansion of the nineteenth century was not British-led. These arguments, put forth most forcefully by Timothy McKeown and John Vincent Nye, stress that British tariffs did not move to levels dramatically lower than those of other states (notably in comparison with France or the Zollverein) and that Britain was not the only country interested in trade expansion.[1] In

---

1. John Vincent Nye, "Revisionist Tariff History and the Theory of Hegemonic Stability," *Politics and Society* 19 (June 1991): 209–232; Timothy J. McKeown, "Hegemonic Stability Theory and Nineteenth-Century Tariff Levels in Europe," *International Organization* 37 (Winter 1983): 73–92. Nye's arguments are based on trade-weighted tariff levels, that is, tariff revenues as a percentage of total import values; thus he considers the high tariffs Britain left on a small number

this chapter's application of the earlier theoretical arguments, the fact that countries shared an interest in liberalizing trade (though one in particular might have gained more from that liberalization) is consistent with expectations. Moreover, each country's liberalizations covered specific goods that reflected the sorts of complementary concessions we would expect when a liberal leader is negotiating with its followers and other ambivalent powers. Nye shows that Britain actually retained several tariffs that effectively protected agriculture from foreign competition. As I suggested in Chapter 1, true free trade (total elimination of protection) is not a rational policy, even for the state whose economy stands to gain the most from trade expansion. By examining the interests of both the liberal leader and other states sectorally, we can put Britain's leadership in the liberal international subsystem of the nineteenth century in perspective. That said, I would still argue that Britain led the liberalization of the international economy after the 1840s.

Britain and the Pace of Liberal Leadership

Contrary to traditional views on the Napoleonic Wars and the establishment of British hegemony, I argue that these wars were important because they temporarily *broke* Britain's interests in constructing an open international political economy; the wars brought on a decline in the trend toward capital abundance, which lessened British capital's need for foreign outlets. Between 1790 and 1820 (unlike the three decades before 1790), capital stock per man-hour in Britain did not change dramatically.[2] The Napoleonic Wars slowed capital accumulation and hastened capital consumption.

Capital accumulation would not accelerate until the 1830s, and this is reflected in the pace of foreign investment. Britain's capital exports reached a large proportion of national product only in the 1850s. From the 1770s to the 1820s, foreign investment was perhaps 1 percent of national product; from the

---

of goods for revenue purposes in the same vein as tariffs other states used to reduce trade across the board, although he has made efforts to guard against any overstatements. See, too, Patrick K. O'Brien and Geoffrey A. Pigman, "Free Trade, British Hegemony, and the International Economic Order in the Nineteenth Century," *Review of International Studies* 18 (April 1992): 89–113; they argue that Britain provided some sort of leadership, but they seem more convinced that this leadership was ideological.

2. Angus Maddison, *Phases of Capitalist Development* (New York: Oxford University Press, 1982), pp. 37–38. This sort of pattern is seen in Phyllis Deane and W. A. Cole, *British Economic Growth, 1688–1959: Trends and Structure* (Cambridge: Cambridge University Press, 1962), though N. F. R. Crafts has provided new estimates of gross domestic investment to suggest that one of the more rapid periods of increased investment was between 1811 and 1821; see *British Economic Growth during the Industrial Revolution* (Oxford: Clarendon Press, 1985), tab. 4.1 (p. 73).

1820s until the 1840s, this rate may have risen to 2 percent. In the 1850s the rate climbed to 3.3 percent, in the 1860s to 3.8 percent, and then from the 1870s to 1914 to 5.2 percent.[3] The commercial reforms of the 1820s were often geared to attracting foreign capital and goods to Britain, not to making Britain "the workshop of the world."[4]

As noted above, the period between 1815 and the middle of the 1840s is perplexing for standard realist theories of hegemony, since Britain failed to act hegemonically immediately after 1815. For instance, McKeown chides Robert Gilpin for marking the peak of British hegemony as 1849, when Gilpin's arguments rest on British naval supremacy, the defeat of France, and the settlement in Vienna—all present some thirty years earlier. McKeown argues that British hegemony really dates from 1849 to 1880, because there are no signs of success before 1849 and after 1880 challengers to Britain's political and economic leadership emerged. If anything, he adds, Britain turned away from a hegemonic role after 1815, as protection actually increased then. He points to the Reciprocity of Duties Act passed in 1823 as a reversal of earlier policies designed to open trade.[5]

In the argument presented here, there is no lag as in other models' depiction of the early part of the nineteenth century. Once British capital formation accelerated in the 1830s, the capital-labor ratio would again rise, and interests would be created and expressed for policies of liberal leadership. Phyllis Deane and W. A. Cole believe that British capital formation fell after 1803 and did not pick up again until the 1830s, when it accelerated dramatically. In the 1840s the railway boom pushed capital formation upward toward a tenth of national income. Similarly, the 1840s were a period of rapid rise in capital investment and the application of new technology in agriculture. As a result of these changes in the capital-labor ratio, real wages moved up an estimated 40 percent between 1824 and 1850, the largest increase in any twenty-five-year period in Britain between 1800 and 1914.[6]

3. Michael Edelstein, *Overseas Investment in the Age of High Imperialism: The United Kingdom, 1850–1914* (New York: Columbia University Press, 1982), p. 3.

4. Boyd Hilton, *Corn, Cash, Commerce: The Economic Policies of the Tory Governments, 1815–1830* (New York: Oxford University Press, 1977), p. 63.

5. McKeown, "Hegemonic Stability Theory," pp. 75–76, 81–82. McKeown's points about the dating of a hegemonic cycle suffer their own problems; specifically, why should the emergence of rivals be seen as the end of hegemony, especially if leadership is still effective? Also see Hilton, *Corn, Cash, Commerce*, p. 176.

6. Deane and Cole, *British Economic Growth*, pp. 25–26, 261–264; Francois Crouzet, "Editor's Introduction," and "Capital Formation in Great Britain during the Industrial Revolution," in *Capital Formation in the Industrial Revolution*, ed. Crouzet (London: Methuen, 1972), pp. 14–15, 211; Rondo Cameron, "England, 1750–1844," in *Banking in the Early Stages of Industrialization: A Study in Comparative Economic History*, ed. Cameron, Olga Crisp, Hugh T. Patrick, and Richard

This capital formation increased competitive pressures in capital services within Britain, to which the government responded. In 1825 the Bubble Act of 1720 was repealed, once again allowing the formation of large joint-stock companies. The establishment of companies was further eased in 1837, when the Letters Patent Act gave authority to an agent of the crown to grant powers of incorporation. Previously incorporation could be gained only through an act of Parliament.[7]

Changes in the banking sector also reflected this greater capital accumulation, as domestic competition in capital services increased markedly. In 1709 the government had conceded a virtual monopoly on large-scale operations to the Bank of England by prohibiting any other banking concern from having more than six partners, guaranteeing the Bank of England predominance in domestic banking. Between 1826 and 1844, legislation changed the banking structure dramatically. The 1826 Bank Act ended the six-partner limit except within a 65-mile radius of London and allowed the Bank of England to operate branches outside London. Another bank act in 1833 made Bank of England notes legal tender throughout England (except at the Bank itself, where gold was legal tender) and removed the 65-mile barrier to other large banks (although all banks new to London were not to issue their own notes). The 1844 Bank Charter Act prohibited all new banks from issuing notes and subjected the Bank of England's note issues to a code of control, which included a ratio limiting issues to the gold supporting it.[8] These rules would soon make sterling one of the most attractive currencies to hold internationally.

As capital formation increased, domestic investment rates grew. This was the construction boom linked to the Industrial Revolution, which had been delayed by the wars against Napoleon. The Industrial Revolution took off again with the railway boom of the 1830s. As capital investment created returns, more capital was accumulated, and domestic competition increased, causing the owners of capital to look for new areas of investment. Capital was accumulated at a faster rate than safe investments could be found.[9] Trade and international services were again attractive areas.

Tilly (New York: Oxford University Press, 1967), pp. 17–18; E. J. Hobsbawm, *The Age of Revolution, 1789–1848* (New York: New American Library, 1962), p. 48.

7. Sydney Checkland, *British Public Policy, 1776–1939: An Economic, Social, and Political Perspective* (New York: Cambridge University Press, 1983), pp. 73–74; Trevor May, *An Economic and Social History of Britain, 1760–1970* (New York: Longman, 1987), p. 175.

8. Checkland, *British Public Policy*, pp. 21, 69–70; Cameron, "England, 1750–1844," p. 20; May, *Economic and Social History*, p. 177.

9. Hobsbawm, *Age of Revolution*, p. 45.

The Political Shift Caused by Capital Abundance

The new international interests wanted the state to ensure order to the international system and help open it for their economic benefit, particularly to help in the increased employment of capital in the international economy. The greatest barrier these new interests confronted was not shortcomings in British power but domestic opposition to changing foreign economic policy. This domestic struggle was fought *after* the Parliamentary Reform Act of 1832. The importance of this act is not simply that it redistributed political power; rather, the old coalition of Whigs and their allies fell apart after the attainment of parliamentary reform, the issue that had bound these various interests together. Now a new range of political options was available, especially since the Whig government in power had a fiscal deficit and no widely acceptable program for ending it. The Tories were able to unseat the Whigs only by offering an alternative program, not by gaining support solely from the newly enfranchised areas. Tory support came from England and the rural areas that were the party's traditional base, and they made gains in the cities and ports (places of capital accumulation and trade, not the newly industrialized areas).[10] Thus, the passage of the Reform Act of 1832 does not itself explain the domestic political shift related to the advent of liberal leadership. Instead, profound changes in the economy explain the political shift related to Britain's adoption of policies of liberal leadership, since this shift was supported not only by the newly represented areas but by a wide variety of sectors.

The change to a foreign policy of liberal leadership was still difficult: sectors that had earlier been shielded from foreign competition had to give up protection for bargaining against other states' trade barriers. There had been some earlier moves toward freer trade, but not until 1841 was a broad reduction in duties (on raw materials to 5 percent, on manufactures to 20 percent) achieved. These and further reductions in 1845 (including the prohibition of duties on some 450 items) were made possible by the reintroduction of the income tax, which replaced the state's lost tariff revenues.[11]

10. Eric J. Evans, *The Forging of the Modern State: Early Industrial Britain, 1783–1870* (New York: Longman, 1983), pp. 247–249.

11. In 1813 the East India Company's monopoly in India had been attacked, the Navigation Laws were relaxed in 1822 and 1825, the reciprocity treaties were begun in 1823, in 1824 artisans were no longer prohibited from emigrating, and in 1825/26 the tariff schedules were codified and slightly reduced; see May, *Economic and Social History*, pp. 183–185. The point about the reintroduction of the income tax was made earlier in Arthur A. Stein, "The Hegemon's Dilemma: Great Britain, the United States, and the International Economic Order," *International Organization* 38 (Spring 1984): 355–386.

Also, domestic reforms were aimed at lowering wages relative to the returns to capital, another indication of the change in the capital-labor ratio. Wages could fall only if the cost of living could be brought down; the repeal of the Corn Laws would act to lower food costs, therefore lowering the "floor" for wages, and could also be used to encourage greater amounts of international trade. As the Liberals described the policy, cheap food would benefit both capital and labor.[12]

The repeal of the Corn Laws is a well-known example of unilateral trade liberalization, when Britain opened its own markets. It was a Tory prime minister, leader of the party that had previously been the defender of agricultural protection, who repealed the Corn Laws—not simply because of party political and international pressure but also because the Tories themselves were split over the efficacy of protection.[13] The need for this protection was eroding among its supporters, and instead a demand for extensive growth in the employment of capital was increasingly expressed.

The movement toward repeal followed the same pattern as that of capital accumulation. In 1828 the Corn Laws were changed from an absolute prohibition on the import of grain when prices fell to a sliding scale of duties. Under the government of Sir Robert Peel, half of this sliding scale was removed in 1842, and then in 1846 the Corn Laws were finally repealed. The repeal lowered wages (by lowering the costs of the goods labor consumed) and encouraged the import of agricultural goods, which required such capital services as shipping and international insurance. It was a unilateral step toward trade specialization. In other matters, the economy was opened. Areas of activity that had been reserved politically were challenged, as when the monopoly of the East India Company in the China trade was abolished in 1834.[14]

The new policies were driven by the deep changes in the British economy brought about by growing capital abundance, so changes of the political party in control of Parliament did not result in changes in policy. Peel's actions split his party (already divided over other issues), but after his government fell in 1846 the following Whig administrations continued the movement toward liberal leadership and the opening of trade. In 1849 the Navigation Acts were repealed. By 1860 the number of articles liable to duty had been reduced to 48

12. Hobsbawm, *Age of Revolution*, pp. 41–42; David P. Calleo and Benjamin M. Rowland, *America and the World Political Economy* (Bloomington: Indiana University Press, 1973), pp. 24–25.
13. Evans, *Forging of the Modern State*, p. 269.
14. May, *Economic and Social History*, pp. 102–103.

(compared to 1,146 in 1840), and all but twelve of these were revenue duties placed on luxury items.[15]

Britain Adopts a Foreign Policy of Liberal Leadership

The British state moved to build a liberal economic subsystem. Besides positive inducements to get other states to join an open system (such as unilateral tariff reductions), the British also used force to open some states to British trade. In Africa and Asia, British military force imposed concessions on several small states. In Latin America, Britain protected the independence of the states created from Spain's decaying empire in order to keep these areas open to British trade.[16] Even large sovereign states were not exempt from having concessions forced on them. In the Opium War against China (1839–1842) and again in the Second Anglo-Chinese War (1856–1860), Britain forced the Chinese government to accept exports from India. Countries such as India and Egypt actually underwent deindustrialization through the economic specialization enforced on them.

British liberal international leadership centered on the country's relative capital abundance. Britain became the center of international capital services. London was the financial center of the world's economy, and the London market's entrepôt role also flourished. At this early stage, the capital abundance of Britain had not eroded labor's returns much. In fact capital abundance meant capital investment in machinery, which helped make the production of capital-intensive goods competitive. Because Britain's economic position was fairly unique, the gains from specialization for international trade lasted for a long time. For several decades after 1846, Britain became the "workshop of the world." Except for the most labor-intensive sectors, the material returns to labor stayed high as both capital and labor benefited from the increased economic activity of the growing international market.

Just because Britain was acting as a liberal leader, it did not relinquish its empire. To expect the liberal leader to give up areas of control for nothing would require a view that the leadership was altruistic. The argument presented here is based on interest maximization. Britain would have been willing to give up the closed economic nature of the empire in order to stimulate

15. Ibid., pp. 184–185. John Vincent Nye, in "Revision Tariff History," argues that these tariffs were actually designed to continue protection of British agriculture.

16. Stein, "Hegemon's Dilemma." Also, Duncan Snidal, "The Limits of Hegemonic Stability Theory," *International Organization* 39 (Autumn 1985): 579–614. For a comment on Latin America, see Evans, *Forging of the Modern State*, p. 199.

trade, but it is important to remember that stimulating the trade between third parties was a significant way to increase the returns to the financial and international service sectors. Additions to the empire might well occur, not necessarily where investment was targeted or markets were available, but where threats to the international market or international order were seen. This is the essence of liberal leadership as opposed to expansive imperialism.[17] Market penetration does not require formal rule—and such direct rule would be more costly, as John Gallagher and Ronald Robinson note in their argument on informal imperialism. Direct rule would be needed only if a market was threatened.[18]

Examine Britain's relations with China or India. It was much more cost-effective for the British state to effect economic penetration without actually taking formal control. In India, it gradually became necessary for the government to take control of most of the subcontinent. It is significant that the state was willing to do this only after the Sepoy mutiny. In China, the British state did not take over responsibilities until the East India Company's monopoly was ended and trade relations were disrupted. When the British government finally dealt directly with China (resulting in the Treaty of Nanking in August 1842), it was the first Western country to sign a treaty with the Chinese.

At other times, strategic threats to the open subsystem were perceived and acted on. To protect the Indian subcontinent, Britain invaded Afghanistan twice. Egypt was brought under formal control to protect the Suez Canal. One reason for the Boer Wars was to protect shipping lanes around the Cape of Good Hope from possible German influence.

Models of hegemony that suggest that the leading state acts out of altruism misinterpret British imperialism, for the British empire was not tightly closed off from other countries' exports. Again, this openness is consistent with the model presented here, even if it was not motivated by trade concessions from other countries. Maintaining the relative economic openness of the empire could only stimulate trade, which would increase the demand for capital-intensive services. If one instead takes the view that the empire was justifiable only as a special place reserved for British capital investment, then the openness of the British empire was in fact either stupid or altruistic, neither of which are persuasive explanations.

17. See the works of John Gallagher and Ronald Robinson, specifically "The Imperialism of Free Trade," *Economic History Review* 6 (1953): 1–15. I refer to liberal leadership of a subsystem of sovereign states, whereas imperialism is direct rule and political incorporation.

18. To verify this point, research concerning the timing and choice of Britain's imperial acquisitions after 1840 should find significant differences from the imperial conquests of other countries or, for that matter, from Britain's own imperial conquests before 1780.

Unlike other theories of hegemony, the argument here stresses that the success of British liberal leadership in the nineteenth century depended a great deal on the other states in the system. Until the rise of Germany and the United States at the end of the century, there were no serious economic or political rivals. This lack of rivalry reflects not only the distribution of power but also the *interests* of the other states, since no country worked to challenge Britain's position.[19] Britain was constructing an economically open international subsystem, using the combination of the previously acquired empire, British capital abundance, British military might, and the British market as tools.

France in the Nineteenth Century

The French economy after the Napoleonic Wars grew slowly. The reason for France's poor economic performance (only considered poor when compared with Britain's rapid industrialization) has become a major question among economic historians. British and French trade had been at roughly the same level in 1780, but by 1848 British trade was twice the volume of the French.[20]

Many explanations of France's slower growth argue that either the savings rate was not high or savings were poorly distributed to finance economic growth. For the concerns of the model presented here, French rates of capital formation are most interesting. Rates for the period 1810–1900 show a smooth and gradual increase of capital formation as a share of national product, with a slight ripple of loss after the defeat in the Franco-Prussian War of 1871. Capital formation as a percentage of national income may even have declined after 1875.[21]

According to Angus Maddison, in terms of nonresidential fixed capital stock per employee France was one of the highest ranked nation-states by 1913. But Maddison does not carry comparable figures on France back very far. If one extrapolates back from the available figures, we can compare France to Britain, Germany, and the United States. France appears to have been one

19. Paul Kennedy makes this point about the Royal Navy's dominant position, stating that "their rivals simply did not wish to spend the time and energy necessary to curb it." *The Rise and Fall of British Naval Mastery* (London: Lane, 1976), p. 157.

20. Hobsbawm, *Age of Revolution*, p. 51.

21. Maurice Lévy-Leboyer, "Capital Investment and Economic Growth in France, 1820–1930," in *The Cambridge Economic History of Europe*, ed. Peter Mathias and M. M. Postan (Cambridge: Cambridge University Press, 1978), 7.1:233–234, 239.

of the capital-rich countries early in the century, then it fell away as Britain accumulated relatively more capital. France did not reattain relatively high levels again until the 1880s, at the earliest. Savings were the prime factor behind this pattern; between 1871 and 1911, the French saved some 10 percent of national income, compared to 12–15 percent in Britain and 15–20 percent in Germany.[22] This picture is loosely confirmed by the rise and fall of French interest rates and the periodization of French exports of capital: as soon as Frenchmen began to accumulate capital, they invested it abroad.[23]

If capital accumulation in France moved in a smooth pattern, the changes in the domestic political structure certainly did not. Between 1815 and 1914, France had two monarchies, imperial rule, and two republics. This should provide ample ground for testing arguments about other categories of countries besides the liberal leader, to show how the domestic political system matters in foreign economic relations. Before 1880, France was relatively capital-poor, though certainly not weak. Changes in government should have moved France back and forth from ambivalence to support of British liberal leadership. Although there is overlap in the expected actions of ambivalent powers and supporters, there is still room for testing the model in this case.

By the time Britain began acting as a liberal leader in the early 1840s, the July Monarchy was in power in France. This government was committed to limited constitutionalism. Domestic political liberalization pulled France away from ambivalence and closer to support for British leadership. Although talks to establish a comprehensive tariff reduction between the two countries failed, French tariffs on some 120 items (including coal and iron goods, prime British exports) were reduced. Tariffs between France and Britain were further reduced in the 1840s.[24] The founding of the Second Republic in 1848 should have moved France even closer to Britain, but in fact there is little evidence that support for British leadership grew stronger in the short time before Napoleon III took office.

With this reversion to personal rule, France should have become more ambivalent. Yet its expression of ambivalence was to draw closer to Britain in economic affairs in order to give France a free hand militarily. This stance included the deal struck in the Cobden-Chevalier treaty. Napoleon agreed to a commercial treaty lowering French tariffs on British goods, even though Rich-

22. Maddison, *Phases of Capitalist Development*, p. 54; for the later figures, see Clive Treb-ilcock, *The Industrialization of the Continental Powers, 1780–1914* (New York: Longman, 1981), p. 173.

23. Hobsbawm, *Age of Revolution*, p. 178.

24. John A. C. Conybeare, *Trade Wars: The Theory and Practice of International Commercial Rivalry* (New York: Columbia University Press, 1987), p. 139.

ard Cobden himself believed that the French public did not support such a treaty—and indeed the opinion of the manufacturers and moneyed classes in France had swung against the emperor.[25]

The Third Republic (formed after defeat in the Franco-Prussian War discredited Napoleon) was a perfect supporter of British liberal leadership. A republic with significant military power but lacking capital in the same relative abundance as Britain, it looked to that country to provide the leadership in the liberal subsystem. As a supporter, France protected its own industry in the tariffs of 1892 and 1910.[26] Though the Third Republic was never deeply capital-poor and even exported capital to countries with even lower capital-labor ratios, it was also never in a position to compete with Britain and was soon passed by both the United States and Germany in terms of capital abundance.

The Political and Economic Rise of the United States

Before the Civil War, the United States was arguably capital-rich and republican, but not internationally powerful. It should, by the model, have been a free rider on British liberal leadership. Despite the fact that Britain and the United States had fought a war as late as 1815, the latter was the country most receptive to the prospective liberal leader. In the 1830s the United States was one of the first countries to liberalize its economic relations with Britain.

Britain's actions clearly pleased some American interests. For the New England states, with their capital abundance and interest in international trade, closeness to Britain meant access to Britain's economy and empire. Britain's return to mercantilism had led the United States to retaliate by raising tariffs in 1816 and again in the 1820s. The 1816 tariff was aimed at protecting textiles and the iron industry. Merchants and southern planters had united to defeat a tariff in 1820 but then failed to defeat the combination of northeastern manufacturers and western farmers in 1824. American prohibitions on trade with British colonies passed in 1818 hurt British shippers, who in turn put pressure on Parliament. The result was a reduction in the level of protection afforded by the British Navigation Acts and the reciprocal opening of American ports in 1825.[27]

25. Agatha Ramm, *Europe in the Nineteenth Century, 1789–1905* (New York: Longman, 1984), p. 245.

26. Michael Tracy, "Agriculture in Western Europe: The Great Depression, 1880–1900," in *Agriculture in Western Europe* (New York: Praeger, 1964), 98–111.

27. Gordon K. Tull and P. McG. Bulwer, *Britain and the World in the Nineteenth Century*

The agricultural areas of the South and West were the easiest to induce to join the open international subsystem by developing a market in Britain. These groups consistently argued for a lower tariff between 1820 and 1860. The southern states had already developed markets in tobbaco and cotton. This made the South a ready follower of British free trade; the North began opposing free trade as a threat to nascent industrialization. The West, which grew foodstuffs, could have gone either way;[28] Britain made this possible by repealing the Corn Laws.

From 1816 until 1832, before Britain was a true leader, American tariffs had generally risen. From 1833 until 1842 Britain was accommodated; then from 1842 to 1846 American tariffs rose again. But the duties set by Congress in 1846 and 1857 were actually supposed to support freer trade. The Elgin Treaty of 1854 helped open trade between the United States and Canada by creating reciprocal free trade in some goods and liberalizing fishing and navigation rights.[29]

The United States as a Supporter

Britain's increased capital accumulation altered the relative position of the United States; the rate of capital accumulation of the latter could not keep pace with Britain's. Although the United States might look like a free rider early on, as Britain increased her capital accumulation American capital abundance declined relatively and the United States became a supporter of British liberal international leadership.

If the United States is considered a supporter rather than a free rider, the economic sectors the United States should have protected would be those that were capital-intensive and therefore especially sensitive to British competition, just as in Britain the sectors protected should have been the most labor-intensive. This sectoral split manifested itself regionally. The division of the country

---

(London: Blandford, 1966), p. 153; James A. Field, Jr., "1789–1820: All Economists, All Diplomats," and Kinley J. Brauer, "1821–1860: Economics and the Diplomacy of American Expansionism," in *Economics and World Power: An Assessment of American Diplomacy since 1789,* ed. William H. Becker and Samuel F. Wells, Jr. (New York: Columbia University Press, 1984), pp. 40–41, 80; Benjamin H. Williams, *Economic Foreign Policy of the United States* (New York: McGraw-Hill, 1929), p. 248.

28. Brauer, "1821–1860: Economics," pp. 82–83; Hobsbawm, *Age of Revolution,* p. 179; Scott James and David A. Lake, "The Second Face of Hegemony: Britain and the American Walker Tariff of 1846," *International Organization* 43 (Winter 1989): 1–29.

29. James and Lake, "Second Face of Hegemony," Frank W. Taussig, *The Tariff History of the United States* (New York: Putnam's Sons, 1931), p. 156; Evans, *Forging of the Modern State,* p. 273. Also, Brauer, "1821–1860: Economics," p. 104.

that ultimately led to the Civil War was exacerbated because the North was capital-abundant and industrializing and the South was poorer in capital and staying agricultural. The North was developing in competition with Britain, whereas the South was growing in complement to Britain. The North was becoming an economic challenger; the South was remaining a supporter. This led to deep differences between the states on tariff policies. In the North, the capital-intensive industries wanted protection from British trade, and shipping and railroad interests wanted lower tariffs.[30] These differences over tariffs were tied to more emotionally charged regional issues, slavery being the most prominent. The changing relative factor endowment provides an economic logic behind the politics of both the tariffs and slavery.[31]

During the Civil War, Britain found its interest tied more closely to the Confederacy. Although British aid to the South was never very strong, Confederate cruisers were allowed to dock in Britain, and the Confederacy purchased some of its war materiel there. Tensions between the federal government and Britain ran high on several occasions, but in each case war was avoided.

After the North won the war, the slaves were emancipated. This act can be seen as clearly lowering the capital-labor ratio. At the same time, the war acted as a stimulus to American industry. With southern opposition silenced, higher tariffs were established during and after the war to protect capital-intensive industries from British competition, as we would expect in a supporter of the liberal leader. These changes, along with the extension of the frontier, merely tempered America's economic rise in capital abundance, by consuming the capital on hand and acquiring more labor in the form of immigrants.

The Economic Rise of the United States

The United States was growing economically at this time, and accumulating capital, but Britain remained relatively more capital-abundant and was still dominant in capital-intensive sectors. In the first four decades of the nineteenth century, the percentage of net U.S. national product invested was around 6–7 percent and may have risen to 12 percent just before the Civil War; it was 18–20 percent by the end of the century. Between 1840 and 1900, the price index of capital goods in America fell, as did the interest rate (rela-

30. Peter J. Buckley and Brian R. Roberts, *European Direct Investment in the U.S.A. before World War I* (New York: St. Martin's, 1982), p. 25.
31. Ronald Rogowski, "Political Cleavages and Changing Exposure to Trade," *American Political Science Review* 81 (December 1987): 1130–1131.

tive to wages).[32] As the cost of capital fell with higher accumulation, producers substituted capital for labor.

In 1880, British exports of iron, steel, machinery, and textiles were much greater than American exports; in 1883, Britain supplied more than a third of the entire world trade in manufactures, whereas U.S. exports were still a marginal amount of the total. By 1899, American manufactured exports were still less than 10 percent of the world total. American shares in foreign investment and international shipping were also still quite small—but growing as the United States accumulated capital. America became capital-rich by accumulating capital domestically and by importing capital from Britain. After 1890, American domestic investment rates passed those of Britain, and the United States soon had the highest level of labor productivity in the international system.[33]

Americans began repurchasing stock from foreign investors at the turn of the century, as evidence on the ownership of stocks in American railways shows. Britain's share of foreign investment in the United States fell as other countries also invested there. America became an international investor too. In 1914 the United States had loaned some $2.5 million to Canada, Mexico, Cuba, and other neighboring countries, though it still owed $4.5–5 million to European countries.[34]

The United States as a Free Rider

The economic competition from America was clearly recognized in Britain. J. A. Hobson, writing in the *Fortnightly* in 1902, claimed, "We have reason to fear, less perhaps of Germany, though her competition will be serious, than from America. . . . Still behind us, she is coming up with a pace which is really formidable."[35] But a significant point to emphasize is that the United States could rise within the British-led international economic subsystem without resorting to political confrontation. The shift in the American position from

---

32. Lance E. Davis and Robert E. Gallman, "Capital Formation in the U.S. during the Nineteenth Century," in *Cambridge Economic History of Europe*, ed. Mathias and Postan, 7.2:1, 25–26.

33. David M. Pletcher, "1861–1898: Economic Growth and Diplomatic Adjustment," in *Economics and World Power*, ed. Becker and Wells, p. 121; Maddison, *Phases of Capitalist Development*, pp. 29, 39.

34. Buckley and Roberts, *European Direct Investment*, pp. 12–13; Williams, *Economic Foreign Policy*, pp. 16–17.

35. Ross J. S. Hoffman, *Great Britain and the German Trade Rivalry, 1875–1914* (New York: Russell & Russell, 1964; reprint of 1933), p. 260.

supporter to economic challenger created British anxiety about its own future economic role, but not about its continued political position.

A. F. K. Organski argues that the United States did not truly challenge Britain because it did not want to be a leader; that it grew without threatening Britain; that it accepted the rules of Britain's subsystem; and that Britain had no way of preventing this growth.[36] But clearly Organski's first and third points are merely descriptions of the lack of an American challenge, not explanations of that behavior. The second point is contestable, since trade rivalry did exist, Canada had to be defended, and there was friction over U.S. involvement in South America and the Pacific. Finally, Britain could have done much to slow America's economic rise—by blocking British investment there or establishing a tariff discriminating against American goods. The model presented here can account for the limited friction, explain why that competition took place within a given set of rules, and explain why Britain did not take steps to prevent America's economic rise.

As a capital-rich country with a republican state, America chose to free ride on British liberal leadership. As Paul Kennedy has shown, American economic growth was one of the largest fundamental changes in the distribution of power in the international system, but at the same time the United States had no real military establishment.[37] This fact emphasizes the difficulty of measuring power. Specifically, if power is measured in terms of potential, the United States was a major power by the 1890s; but since economic competitors accept the policies of the liberal leader and eschew the political burdens of protecting the open international subsystem in favor of letting the leader continue to carry out those tasks, the economic challenger has an incentive (i.e., savings by the state) to remain a free rider as long as possible and leave its potential power undeveloped.

Eventually the sheer size of America's military grew, and, as the military was used to exert international pressures, U.S. relations with Britain became more important. British military leaders seemed unable to confront the possibility of war between the United States and Britain, because of the potential for disaster for both sides in such a conflict. Backing down in the face of American expansion in Alaska, Panama, and elsewhere was actually a relief for most British naval officers. This thinking was officially recognized with the aban-

36. A. F. K. Organski, "The Power Transition," in *World Politics* (New York: Knopf, 1968), pp. 362–363.
37. Paul Kennedy, "The First World War and the International Power System," *International Security* 9 (Summer 1984): 23.

donment of the Two-Power Standard, in which Britain ruled out the United States as a potential enemy.[38]

Britain and the United States had agreed in the Clayton-Bulwer treaty of 1850 that neither country would build a canal in Panama exclusive of the other, nor would they limit the navigation rights of other powers in such a canal or fortify it. In 1900/01 the United States almost unilaterally ended the Clayton-Bulwer treaty, getting Britain to concede to an American-built, American-operated, and de facto fortified canal.[39] In the Venezuelan crisis of 1895, the United States invoked the Monroe Doctrine to limit the actions of Britain in strong and belligerent tones. At the time, because of the need for British naval forces in European waters, Britain had no choice but to rely on U.S. forces in South American waters, even though the U.S. Navy was still untried in 1895. The same story holds for the Pacific. In the Samoan crisis, the United States stood squarely with Britain against Germany. In 1898 the United States annexed Hawaii as a security measure to preempt a similar move by other countries (such as Germany or more likely Japan). Germany went to Britain for assistance in blocking such a move, but Britain refused to do anything, thereby allowing the annexation to proceed.[40]

In the Spanish-American War, Britain supported the United States indirectly. This war showed the asymmetric benefits accruing to the United States in this situation. Essentially, British interests were for a more orderly Cuba, so American and British interests coincided. Britain's promise not to intervene was also a promise to prevent the intervention of other major powers, causing Lionel Gelber to remark that "the United States in any case now profited from an Anglo-American alliance without its costs." Britain did *not* get an alliance; the United States could derive the benefits of British protection without actually guaranteeing anything in return. As Teddy Roosevelt himself said in 1898, "I am glad there seems to be so friendly a feeling between the two countries, though I don't believe that we ought to have an alliance."[41]

The Venezuelan crisis of 1902 served as a great impetus to the construction of a larger American navy. The Venezuelan government of Cipriano Castro was allowing (if not instigating) the violation of contracts with and the disruption of debt payments to foreigners. In February 1901, four British ships were

---

38. Kennedy, *Rise and Fall of British Naval Mastery*, pp. 211–212, 229. The Two-Power Standard refers to the British practice of maintaining a fleet as strong as the next two most powerful fleets combined.

39. Lionel Gelber, *The Rise of the Anglo-American Friendship: A Study in World Politics, 1898–1906* (Hamden, Conn.: Archon Books, 1966; reprint of 1938), pp. 40, 51, 56–57, 100–101.

40. Kennedy, *Rise and Fall of British Naval Mastery*, p. 211; Gelber, *Rise of the Anglo-American Friendship*, pp. 2–3, 26–27.

41. Gelber, *Rise of the Anglo-American Friendship*, pp. 17–18, 22–23.

seized; these actions led Britain and Germany to install a blockade. When the United States questioned the European powers' use of force and threatened to apply the Monroe Doctrine, British prime minister Arthur Balfour not only did not object but in fact wished that the United States would take over the burden of handling international problems in South America. This was not done officially until the Roosevelt Corollary to the Monroe Doctrine was established in 1904.[42] The United States now claimed the exclusive right to exercise international police powers in the Western Hemisphere.

The United States as a Peaceful Economic Competitor

In 1907 the Great White Fleet toured the world and demonstrated America's new ability to project power around the globe. Although this act was largely symbolic, the tour, coming on the heels of the American victory over Spain, heralded the arrival of a new major power in the international system.

With the Open Door Policy in China, the United States began arguing for more open economic relations. Britain had asked for American support for an opening of China in 1898, which the United States had at first refused. When Britain, too, started to close off a portion of China as its own, the United States reacted with the Open Door notes issued in 1899. These notes asked the major powers to declare equality of commercial treatment in their spheres of influence, with the Chinese government itself to operate tariffs equally across all spheres, along with further limitations on preferential treatment within the spheres. Because the Open Door Policy shaped American positions elsewhere, its adoption and support should be seen as a turning point in America's overt support for an open international system.[43]

In the years when America was accumulating capital and catching up to Britain, it could have some protection at home and still trade abroad under the protection of Britain's liberal leadership. But this situation changed after 1897. David Lake dates the time when relative labor productivity in the United States passed Britain's as 1897. This catching up in capital abundance is also represented in the destination of American exports: in 1888, 52 percent of American exports went to the United Kingdom and its colonies, but this

42. H. H. Herwig and D. F. Trask, "Naval Operations Plans between Germany and the U.S.A., 1898–1913: A Study of Strategic Planning in the Age of Imperialism," in *The War Plans of the Great Powers, 1880–1914*, ed. Paul Kennedy (London: Allen & Unwin, 1979), p. 55; Gelber, *Rise of the Anglo-American Friendship*, pp. 109, 118; Jeffry A. Frieden, *Banking on the World: The Politics of American International Finance* (New York: Harper & Row, 1987), pp. 20–21.

43. David A. Lake, "International Economic Structures and American Foreign Economic Policy, 1887–1934," *World Politics* 35 (1983): 530–531; Gelber, *Rise of the Anglo-American Friendship*, pp. 77–78; Calleo and Rowland, *America and the World Political Economy*, p. 33.

figure fell to 46 percent in 1897 and to 26 percent in 1912 (as more was exported to economically advanced countries and to South America).[44]

As Lake's analysis of American tariffs shows, the United States was willing to drop protection of capital-intensive sectors as these became more competitive after capital accumulation increased. This would be the final sign of America's shift to economic challenge of British leadership. In fact, the McKinley Tariff of 1890 protected industry *and* agriculture.[45] This and the Wilson-Gorman Tariff of 1894 were attempts to establish special relations with Latin America by lowering duties on some raw materials. The guiding principle of the McKinley Tariff was to place duties on goods the United States produced but to allow in goods not produced domestically free of duty; thus the rates on dutiable goods rose, but the number of items on the free list was expanded, so that the overall rate of duties on all imports fell from 29.9 to 23.7 percent. The Wilson-Gorman Tariff lowered the rates on the dutiable goods list, so that overall rates fell from 23.7 to 20.5 percent.[46]

The Dingley Tariff of 1897 is significant in that the United States finally offered reciprocal reductions in duties to economically advanced countries. The United States was now trying to expand its markets in Europe. As part of this strategy, however, it raised tariffs on dutiable imports and reduced the free list as a negotiating lever, so that the overall tariff rate went from 20.5 to 26.2 percent. This strategy worked in the sense that some concessions were made by both Germany and France.[47]

The Payne-Aldrich Tariff of 1909 continued this trend by accepting the principle of nondiscrimination, and the Underwood Tariff of 1913 drastically lowered tariff rates and clearly embraced the principle of free trade. By expanding the free list and lowering the rates on dutiable goods, the overall tariff rate was lowered from 26.2 to 20 percent. By 1910, President Taft was able to remark that the United States faced no undue discrimination from any other country, so all goods imported into the United States received the minimum schedule of duties. The Underwood Tariff reduced the tariffs on dutiable goods substantially and further increased the percentage of goods allowed in free of duty, so that the overall average rate of duty fell from 20 to 8.8 percent.[48]

The emphasis of protection went from industry in the 1880s, to industry and agriculture in the 1890s and 1900s, to agriculture only, to little protection

44. David A. Lake, *Power, Protection, and Free Trade: International Sources of U.S. Commercial Strategy, 1887–1939* (Ithaca: Cornell University Press, 1988), pp. 91–92, 119–121.
45. Tracy, "Agriculture in Western Europe."
46. Lake, *Power, Protection, and Free Trade*, pp. 6–7, 99–101, 106–107.
47. Ibid., pp. 6–7, 125, 129–130.
48. Ibid., pp. 6–7, 131, 133–135, 154–155.

for any sectors in 1913. If one assumes that agricultural goods are relatively more labor-intensive than manufactures, this pattern of change exactly parallels the shift of the United States out of the category of supporter and into the category of peaceful economic competitor.

America's military position also reflected the changes in America's relationship with the international system. In 1890 the only American war plans were for a conflict between the United States and Britian (which reflects America's defensive posture, since Britain was the only country able to attack it). By 1900 military planners were drawing up contingencies that placed Britain and the United States in one coalition and Germany in the other (thereby reflecting America's new ability to project power, as well as the shared interests of the United States and Britain). As one historian notes, "American naval strategists would not soon forget that at every disputed point in the Pacific, Germany contested the American wishes during 1898 and 1899 while England seemed invariably to favor the United States." Before the end of Theodore Roosevelt's administration, army planners too had already focused their energies on strategies for fighting the most likely enemy—Germany.[49]

By 1914 the United States was capital-abundant, republican, and potentially powerful. But, as the second state in this category, it let Britain bear the burdens of maintaining and defending the open subsystem. The U.S. military remained relatively undeveloped.

Britain's View of Others in the System: Russia and Japan

Russian Expansion

As early as the 1840s, Britain had perceived Russia as the most likely challenger to British liberal leadership. Russia's imperial expansion was seen as a threat to Britain's liberalized trading system and the British empire. In 1854, Britain had led a coalition of major powers against Russia in the Crimean War. France was the first country to join this alliance, and Austria was later added. Some leaders in the British government (particularly Lord Palmerston) even considered expanding the war into a world war so as to prevent a Russian challenge permanently.[50]

This is an example of misidentifying the expansive challenger. The British

---

49. Quotation from Paul Kennedy, *The Samoan Tangle: A Study in Anglo-German-American Relations, 1878–1900* (New York: Barnes & Noble, 1974), p. 292. William H. Becker, "1899–1920: America Adjusts to World Power," in *Economics and World Power*, ed. Becker and Wells, p. 206.
50. See Winfried Baumgart, *The Peace of Paris, 1856* (Santa Barbara, Calif.: ABC-Clio, 1981).

interests threatened by Russian expansion into the Black Sea area were not worth a large-scale war. Furthermore, the benefits to Russia were not of a grand scale. Like the wars of the middle of the eighteenth century, the Crimean War involved a great number of the major powers but was fought with limited intensity for limited goals. Certainly Britain had reasons to fear eventual Russian imperial expansion, but there was never a real attempt by Russia to challenge the rules of the open international political economy Britain led. Russia posed a threat to Britain's empire, but it was not being driven to expand. More important, Russia could also be accommodated within Britain's open international economic subsystem.

Russia had failed to accumulate capital to the point of relative capital richness, and thus it never rivaled Britain economically. In terms of the model, Britain perceived Russia as the emerging challenger, but in fact Russia was still ambivalent. Russian state power had been used over other domestic actors to build cartels and sanction other forms of rents along German lines (which we see in the next section). But, whereas Germany could do this and invest heavily from domestic sources, Russia had to rely on foreign funds for investments. Russian industry and capital accumulation never caught up with that of the Western powers. As evidence of its position as an ambivalent power, Russian tariffs continually protected capital-intensive sectors. The tariff of 1891 placed heavy duties on imported manufactures and on exported raw materials.[51]

Even after the Crimean War, Britain feared a domino effect from Russian expansion in Asia and even sent troops into Afghanistan twice out of fear that the Russians might ultimately threaten India. As Palmerston stated in 1840,

It seems pretty clear that, sooner or later, the Cossack and the Sepoy, the man from the Baltic and he from the British Islands will meet in the centre of Asia. It should be our business to take care that the meeting should take place as far off from our Indian possessions as may be convenient and advantageous to us. But the meeting will not be avoided by our staying at home to receive the visit.[52]

Using this logic, Whitehall sent British troops into Afghanistan on several occasions. Despite failures and setbacks, the British remained preoccupied with the Russian threat, and these fears were amplified in 1885 when Russian forces seized part of the Afghan frontier. This, combined with the threat that

---

51. Ramm, *Europe in the Nineteenth Century,* p. 347.
52. Ibid., p. 324.

Russian railways would enable large troop movements into the area rapidly, led Britain to intimidate Russia into shifting her expansionist interests elsewhere.

Unfortunately for Britain, Russia shifted her energies to China and Manchuria, which were also sensitive strategic spots for Britain. Britain failed to woo support from other European countries to block the possible Russian seizure of large parts of northern China, and the United States did not give any practical support beyond the issuance of the Open Door notes. This situation pushed Britain into an alliance with Japan. Britain hoped to use Japan as a possible counter to Russian strength in Asia. Clearly, the Japanese were an effective counterweight to Russia in Asia, as the Russo-Japanese War showed. In terms of British strategy, Britain could lower its naval commitment in Asia and reconcentrate the fleet in European waters, but it failed to achieve the broader goal of keeping China open; Russian expansion was checked, but by Japanese imperial expansion.

A turnabout in Anglo-Russian relations would come about because of France. France had turned to Russia as a balance against German strength; and since both were directly threatened by German expansion, an alliance was easily formed. France then made many cheap loans to the Russians, in order to strengthen the alliance and the Russian military. As Britain and France moved closer together, Russia was brought in as a third party.

Japan's Rise as a Major Power

The United States had been opening trade connections on its own in the nineteenth century. One of the most famous was the opening of Japan. The Oriental state was suddenly thrust onto the modern international scene. Under the guidance of Westerners, Japan embarked on a major economic growth program in the late 1800s to restructure and modernize the domestic economy. As late as 1872, more than four-fifths of the population was still involved in agriculture and forestry. Both agriculture and industry used old, labor-intensive production techniques.[53]

Economic development and centralization of political power increased the state's resources, and military power was built up. Before 1914, Japan was a major power, developing economically but still relatively labor-abundant, and it was only beginning to experiment with representative government. By the

53. Henry Rosovsky, *Capital Formation in Japan, 1868–1940* (New York: Free Press of Glencoe, 1961), p. 59; Kazushi Ohkawa and Henry Rosovsky, "Capital Formation in Japan," in *Cambridge Economic History of Europe*, ed. Mathias and Postan, 7.2:138.

model, then, it should be ambivalent toward British liberal leadership. This ambivalence shows up in Japan's China policy. Japan was interested in imperial expansion. As the leader of the liberal subsystem, Britain opposed this. Since Japan wanted British technology and capital and Britain needed regional military support, an alliance was arranged, even though neither party wholeheartedly supported the policies of the other.

Since Britain understood Russia to be the emerging challenger and sensed Russian threats to Turkey, Persia, India, and China, it was faced with the difficult possibility of responding with force in all these areas. Unable to commit militarily in so many places at once, Britain looked for regional allies to help bear the burden. Japan was a willing ally and in fact the Anglo-Japanese defense arrangements were extended to cover India. The long-term consequences of Britain's alliances would only appear as a liability much later; in the short term, the alliance with Japan allowed Britain to reconcentrate military forces (most important, naval power) in Europe. This was crucial in the short run, for the real challenger had finally emerged—Germany.

Germany's Rise as the Political Challenger

Before 1870, Germany comprised several small and large states, of which Prussia was the largest. Under the leadership of Prussian diplomacy, the Zollverein (customs union) was created. After the end of the Napoleonic Wars, access to the French market ended just as British goods began to flood in; with no country willing to lead a free trade system, Austria, Russia, and the Netherlands, as well as Britain, had raised tariffs. The ability of Prussia to levy duties on goods in transit enabled it to persuade neighboring states to join in a tariff union. As a capital-poor area with an autocratic state, this Prussian-led economic zone could be expected to be ambivalent toward British liberal international leadership.

Despite the hopes of some Germans, who wanted the Zollverein to be an attack on British trade, a low tariff was adopted and labor-intensive items were exported for capital-intensive ones, as one would expect from an ambivalent power. For instance, iron manufacturers were not protected at all until 1844, and even then the level of protection was probably too low to do much good. McKeown argues that manufactures did begin to receive higher tariff protection in the 1840s as British exports grew, again conforming to our picture of an ambivalent power. The first steps toward faster rates of capital accumulation were made in the late 1840s and 1850s, signaled by the formation of the first industrial investment banks.[54] These banks were able to mobilize large amounts of capital at a time when the overall German economy was still characterized by a lower capital-labor ratio than in Britain.

The Impact of German Unification

Victorious wars against Denmark, Austria, and then France made Prussia the dominant state in Germany. Military success created political success. The German Empire that was established in 1871 took on a distinctly autocratic Prussian flavor. The Prussian king became emperor. The kaiser had direct control of the imperial army and navy, and the chancellor had no real voice in military strategy decisions. The Reichstag could not appoint ministries or force ministers to resign; these powers resided with the emperor, acting on the advice of the chancellor. Imperial officials fulfilled their duties for and reported to the imperial chancellor, who was not responsible to the parliament. Military budgets were nominally under the control of the Reichstag, but budget votes were not annual (they occurred every seven years between 1874 and 1893 and every five years after 1893).[55] Although the empire had a federal structure, and this allowed for political variations at the lower levels of government, the national system can be categorized as autocratic.

After 1870, Germany was a powerful country with an autocratic state. According to the model, then, it should fall under the category of either ambivalent power or expansive political challenger. Initially, Germany was not capital-abundant, so it should have been ambivalent toward British liberal leadership. According to Maddison, Germany had little over half the British level of gross fixed nonresidential capital stock per employee in 1870.[56] As Germany caught up in terms of capital accumulation in the 1870s–1890s, it became an expansive power challenging the liberal leader. In domestic affairs, the German state fostered monopolies in industry and gave monopoly rights to Prussian agriculture when capital was relatively scarce. The concentration of investible capital in the largest few banks led to cartelization in industry.[57]

As an ambivalent power, Germany should have protected the capital-intensive sectors that were receiving state-sanctioned rents; the shift toward capital

54. Trebilcock, *Industrialization of the Continental Powers*, pp. 40–43; McKeown, "Hegemonic Stability Theory," p. 85.

55. Fritz Fischer, *Germany's Aims in the First World War* (New York: Norton, 1967), p. 5; Helmut Böhme, *An Introduction to the Social and Economic History of Germany: Politics and Economic Change in the Nineteenth and Twentieth Centuries* (New York: St. Martin's, 1978), p. 56.

56. Maddison, *Phases of Capitalist Development*, p. 54.

57. Trebilcock, *Industrialization of the Continental Powers*, p. 99.

abundance would require a shift in protection toward labor-intensive sectors. This pattern of tariffs is apparent in the United States' movements at roughly the same time. In fact, German tariff protection was given to agriculture, though tariffs were also an integral part of domestic rents favoring capital-intensive sectors before Germany's period of capital accumulation.[58] These policies had been considered necessary to accumulate capital and direct revenues to the state and its supporters when capital was relatively scarce.

As mentioned above, capital accumulation did accelerate. In the period 1816–1859, the level of investment in Prussia had grown by 50 percent or more. In Germany as a whole between 1850 and 1890 the level grew by something approaching 200 percent. Between 1871 and 1911, while the British saved some 12–15 percent of national income, Germans saved 15–20 percent. Between 1891 and 1913, capital formation in Germany has been estimated at almost a quarter of gross national product, higher than in Britain or the United States.[59]

Distortions Resulting from Domestic Rents

Success in German capital formation also meant that the returns to capital should have been declining and wages rising. The gap between actual returns (i.e., with rents sanctioned) and the returns that would have occurred in an open market was widening. This widening gap should have resulted in labor unrest (since growth in the returns to labor should be artificially retarded) and increased problems maintaining growth in capital employment domestically, and it continued to widen because cartels in banking and industry did not give up their rents. In fact, the rents accruing to the cartels expanded after 1880. Free trade was abandoned in 1879 in favor of a strategy of extracting more beneficial bilateral treaties on tariffs. Protection was also expanded after the 1880s, particularly in areas of competition with Britain. For instance, German shipping received favorable treatment in lower tariffs for its required imports, besides subsidies and protection.[60]

The result was a crisis in underconsumption. Production was increasingly in capital-intensive goods, but wages were not allowed to rise to create further demand, so export markets had to be found. German producers had to find

---

58. Ibid., pp. 71, 84.

59. R. H. Tilly, "Capital Formation in Germany in the Nineteenth Century," in *Cambridge Economic History of Europe*, ed. Mathias and Postan, 7.1:427; Trebilcock, *Industrialization of the Continental Powers*, pp. 62, 173.

60. Lake, *Power, Protection, and Free Trade*, p. 122; Hoffman, *Great Britain and the German Trade Rivalry*, p. 64.

new markets for their goods, as the trade offensives of the 1880s illustrate. The code of conduct developed for cartels after 1903 encouraged the subsidization of exporting industries.[61]

The owners of German capital looked to the state for two distinctly different kinds of help. They hoped the state would lead the way in the expansion of trade. They wanted access to British markets, but if rents could be extended in new captive markets, that would be even better. Although David Calleo argues that cartelization and tariff protection were forms of adjustment to the depression of the 1870s, he does note that the desire for markets and self-sufficiency "led both toward the continental policy of *Mitteleuropa* and the imperialist *Weltpolitik* of William II."[62] Yet cartelization and tariffs only lengthened the problem of underconsumption rather than solve it.

Anglo-German relations began to sour as German economic competition with Britain increased. Although this first manifested itself in the Bismarck-Granville quarrel over African colonies in 1884/85, the competition was everywhere, including the markets of Europe. In 1888 the Netherlands had purchased goods worth 20 million guilders more from Britain than from Germany; by 1901 purchases from Germany outstripped those from Britain by 221 million guilders. In the 1880s, German capital had also made a key penetration of the Italian economy.[63]

Britain's relative economic dominance in shares of world trade was waning rapidly. Whereas in 1870 Britain accounted for more than a third of world manufacturing production (and the United States was a distant second with less than a quarter), by 1913 both the United States and Germany accounted for a greater percentage of world manufactures than Britain. In overseas trade, Britain's volume had been twice that of its nearest rival as late as 1880 and, although in 1913 its share of world trade was still the greatest, Germany's share was very close.[64]

Germany had shifted back toward a protective tariff in 1879, which pro-

---

61. Trebilcock, *Industrialization of the Continental Powers*, pp. 73, 78, 393. The term *trade offensive* comes from a discussion of the Anglo-German trade rivalry in W. A. Lewis, *Growth and Fluctuations, 1870–1913* (Boston: Allen & Unwin, 1978).

62. David Calleo, *The German Problem Reconsidered: Germany and the World Order, 1870 to the Present* (New York: Cambridge University Press, 1978), p. 17. Calleo's argument, however, points out that all states suffered in the depression of the 1870s and that most moved to some form of protectionism. Calleo's book assumes that German policies were somewhat unique and indeed an international problem. The depression and closure of the world markets may be the spark that ignited "the German problem," but these factors alone are not enough to explain why Germany turned to conquest.

63. Hoffman, *Great Britain and the German Trade Rivalry*, pp. 73, 116, 125.

64. May, *Economic and Social History*, p. 278.

tected industry more than agriculture. Additional protection was given to agriculture in 1885 and 1887; attempts to lower protection for agriculture in return for access for German industrial exports in the 1890s were opposed by the farming sector. These tensions were resolved only by a 1902 tariff that again protected agriculture, one that raised the number of categories subject to duties and the overall average rate of duty.[65] Germany was not able to make the transition in tariffs America had—shifting protection from industry only, to both industry and agriculture, and then to agriculture only. Instead, it shifted to protection of both industry and agriculture and could not move out of this position; from there, its continued participation in the liberal international subsystem would become increasingly intolerable, both for the leader of the open subsystem, which would not accept Germany's failure to adhere to the principles and norms of the system, and for Germany, since continued participation merely widened the gap between the relative returns capital was gaining through domestic rents and the declining relative returns capital should have been earning in an open system.

As evidence of the different incentives open to German capital at this time, consider the investment patterns of capital from domestically closed and domestically open economies. In closed economies, capital can maintain an above-market return, despite capital abundance, through rents. Growing capital abundance does not alter decisions about where to invest, since the ordering of returns does not shift. The same cannot be said of open economies, in which capital abundance forces capital's relative returns down through the market's operations, thereby giving the holders of capital an incentive to find new areas to employ their capital for higher relative returns. This explains the patterns of investment one finds for this period: British capital became increasingly tied to foreign investment, whereas Germany's remained domestically oriented. This trend in Germany deepened: its ratio of domestic to foreign investment went from 2:1 in 1886–1900 to 9:1 in 1906–1910. In 1911, only some 11 percent of all new securities sold in Germany went to foreign investment (the corresponding figure for France that year is 77 percent).[66]

Economic changes created strong interests within Germany for a change in state policy away from accommodation with Britain and toward policies antagonistic to the open international subsystem. For German capital to main-

65. Ramm, *Europe in the Nineteenth Century*, p. 340; Tracy, "Agriculture in Western Europe," pp. 105–106; Lake, *Power, Protection, and Free Trade*, pp. 129–130.

66. Zara S. Steiner, *Britain and the Origins of the First World War* (New York: Macmillan, 1977), p. 63; Trebilcock, *Industrialization of the Continental Powers*, p. 80; Calleo, *German Problem Reconsidered*, p. 64.

tain its relative returns despite the underlying economic changes, rents would have to be expanded. As late as 1898–1901, there were discussions between the two governments about a possible alliance. Britain needed Germany as an ally to relieve pressures in Europe so it could concentrate on global affairs. As late as 1897, German fleet maneuvers were explicitly based on fighting the combination of France and Russia only. Britain, however, feared the increased German naval strength, and this hurt the chances of forming an alliance. But the negotiations were doomed to fail because the two countries did not have similar interests. The failure to reach an accord put Germany on a path that ultimately led to World War I.[67]

German capitalists also hoped that increased state expenditures would consume more capital-intensive goods and help maintain returns to capital. The construction of the fleet was based on an alliance of state and commercial interests. Much emphasis has been put on the defense expenditures of the German state, which grew more than twice as much as Britain's or France's between 1875 and 1908; but defense expenditures were consistently less than social services before World War I in Germany.[68] Both forms of government expenditure can be seen as efforts by the state to deal with the same problem: (1) higher defense expenditures increased the consumption of capital-intensive goods, thereby supporting the relative returns to capital; (2) defense expenditures increased the state's actual international power, thereby giving the state new options for dealing with the problem of pressure on capital's relative returns; and (3) greater social expenditures were ways to give more to labor, to offset the gap between the relative returns labor would have earned in an open system and that which labor was actually getting as long as the state continued to sanction rents benefiting capital.

Germany's Foreign Policy as an Expansionary Challenger

Whereas economic competition between the United States and Britain did not develop into political confrontation because of a deeper underlying complementarity of interests, the same was not true of Germany and Britain. In the Boer Wars, the threat of German encroachment on the British Empire brought about political confrontation. Eventually, Germany began making

---

67. Ramm, *Europe in the Nineteenth Century*, p. 377; Andreas Hillgruber, *Germany and the Two World Wars* (Cambridge: Harvard University Press, 1981), pp. 4–5, 10–11; Eckart Kehr, *Economic Interest, Militarism, and Foreign Policy: Essays on German History*, ed. Gordon A. Craig (Berkeley: University of California Press, 1977), pp. 8–9; Fischer, *Germany's Aims*, p. 21.

68. Fischer, *Germany's Aims*, pp. 17–18; Trebilcock, *Industrialization of the Continental Powers*, p. 82.

more aggressive acts toward Britain's open subsystem. The decisive shift in Germany's domestic scene occurred in 1897, when a set of aggressive leaders took office: Alfred von Tirpitz became naval secretary, Bernhard von Bülow became foreign secretary, and Johannes Miquel became Prussian minister of finance and vice-president of the Prussian council of ministers. Government policy adopted the concepts of *Weltpolitik*, *Flottenpolitik*, and the "mobilization of the masses." For German conservatives, high tariffs and expansion of the fleet were viewed as means to maintain the closed German economy.[69]

As an example of this group's thinking, Gen. Friedrich von Bernhardi noted three things necessary for Germany's continued advancement: defeat of France, the formation of a closed central European economic system dominated by Germany, and the acquisition of colonies. Contemporary German historians had been continually stressing that a redistribution of world power was occurring and that German supremacy would succeed British. Theobald Bethmann-Hollweg is quoted as saying, in 1903, "It is the Kaiser's first and basic idea to break England's hegemony to Germany's advantage." Even earlier, in 1895, German political groups were speaking of a closed central European economic area under German influence.[70]

Weltpolitik and *Flottenpolitik* combined to give impetus to the creation of a strong battlefleet, which could press Britain but also give Germany a global military presence. As one German put it, "It would be unthinkable to engage on a national basis in world trade or world industry or even, up to a point, in deep-sea fishing, international transport, and colonization, without the backing of an offensive fleet."[71] The state accepted these arguments. To give the fleet a global reach, the number of cruisers to be built for overseas service was doubled (to twenty-six) with the Naval Bill of 1900.

The theme of German foreign policy was to claim "a place in the sun." In Morocco (1906 and 1911), Samoa, and elsewhere, Germany tried to upset the existing situation in order to split off part of the open system. The implications of these policies were not lost on Britain. A British newspaper, the *Spectator*, noted on 20 May 1911, "There is an inevitable conflict of ideals between Germany and Great Britain, between the satisfied nation and the unsatisfied nation, between the nation which desires to maintain the status quo and the

69. Kennedy, *Samoan Tangle*, pp. 122–123; Kehr, *Economic Interest, Militarism, and Foreign Policy*, pp. 32–33.

70. Fischer, *Germany's Aims*, pp. 34–35; and also from his *War of Illusions: German Policies from 1911 to 1914* (London: Chatto & Windus, 1975), pp. 1, 7, 31.

71. Hillgruber, *Germany and the Two World Wars*, p. 9. Quotation from Kehr, *Economic Interest, Militarism, and Foreign Policy*, pp. 9–10.

nation which desires to alter it."[72] Just as Britain had feared Russian expansion earlier, it now perceived Germany as a threat. The Boer Wars were merely the first strong example of British fears of German expansion that might upset the empire and the economically open subsystem.

Britain in Decline

Britain was faced with two major problems in the late 1800s: relative economic decline and military rivalry with Germany. These problems were related, but the first did not cause the second. In Chapters 2 and 3 we have seen how challenge can occur without the liberal leader's relative economic decline. Obviously, economic decline does make responding to challenge difficult.

Relative Economic Decline

First, let us return to the argument on the cause of a liberal leader's relative economic decline. As specialization occurs through the successful implementation of leadership policies, the labor-intensive sectors of the leader's economy lose competitiveness. Initially this can be offset by extensive growth via specialization in capital-intensive sectors. But after the great gains from specialization are made, labor's position worsens; this is particularly true for the labor-intensive sectors. This happened in Britain after the 1860s. As evidence of labor-intensive sectors' problems with uncompetitiveness, consider the impact capital accumulation had on labor's wages. Labor was now the scarce factor, and therefore labor's relative returns increased. In the period 1874–1900, real wages in Britain rose more than a third, at basically the same rate as in the previous twenty-five years; in the period 1890–1914, real wages rose only a tenth.[73]

By the 1870s, the problem developed into the Climacteric, when the capital-intensive sectors also came under increased foreign competition. Other nation-states such as France, Germany, and the United States were now producing capital-intensive goods and exporting some of them into Britain. In 1870, Britain had almost a third of the world's manufacturing capacity, but this had

72. As quoted by Paul Kennedy, *The Realities behind Diplomacy: Background Influences on British External Policy, 1865–1980* (London: Allen & Unwin, 1981), p. 129.

73. Deane and Cole, *British Economic Growth*, pp. 25–26.

fallen to 15 percent in 1910; Britain's share of world trade had been around a quarter in 1870, but by 1913 this had fallen to 14 percent.[74]

Support for free trade in Britain was slowly being eroded. In 1881 the Fair Trade League was formed, with the goal of establishing moderate tariffs on foreign manufactures to be used as a lever to lower other countries' tariffs on British goods. This policy clearly would have hurt the capital-services sector of the British economy, though, which was earning money on invisibles. Joseph Chamberlain's call for a return to mercantilism presented Britain's options before Parliament. Yet few measures were passed to protect manufacturing interests. Liberal and Conservative governments of the 1880s and 1890s remained supportive of free trade. Instead of listening to the labor-intensive sectors, Parliament heeded commercial, financial, and shipping interests. The industrial community itself was divided over support for protective tariffs. This rejection of protectionism was solidified in the Liberals' defeat of the Tories in 1906.[75]

Only the most capital-intensive sectors were still competitive and continued to support liberal leadership. For instance, British shipping actually increased its dominance of the international carrying trade between the 1850s and the 1870s. As late as 1912, British ships carried more than nine-tenths of intraimperial trade, more than half the trade between the empire and foreign countries, and close to a third of interforeign trade. The same could be said about other international services: in 1879 almost one-fourth of all life cover insurance in Canada was by British companies, as was nearly one-fifth of fire coverage in the United States. In particular, the City of London, which provided so many services of capital to the international market, still strongly supported leading the liberal subsystem, perhaps even more so as other countries' economies grew.[76] This process was producing a new balance among the domestic economic interests: more and more sectors were falling out of the coalition

74. Aaron L. Friedberg, *The Weary Titan: Britain and the Experience of Relative Decline, 1895–1905* (Princeton: Princeton University Press, 1988), p. 37; Kennedy, *Realities behind Diplomacy*, p. 22.

75. Peter Gourevitch, *Politics in Hard Times: Comparative Responses to International Economic Crises* (Ithaca: Cornell University Press, 1986), p. 78, describes this split at an earlier stage, although that split continued much the same for a long time thereafter. These changes in this period are also seen in Steiner, *Britain and the Origins of the First World War*, p. 15. Calleo and Rowland, *America and the World Political Economy*, pp. 30–31, describe the City of London's continued interest in free trade. Also see Friedberg, *Weary Titan*, pp. 38–39; Hoffman, *Great Britain and the German Trade Rivalry*, pp. 98, 288; and Checkland, *British Public Policy*, pp. 170–171.

76. Hoffman, *Great Britain and the German Trade Rivalry*, pp. 4–5; May, *Economic and Social History*, p. 187; Kennedy, *Realities behind Diplomacy*, p. 24.

that supported Britain's liberal international leadership. Only the most capital-intensive sectors (particularly capital services, which catered to the international market) were still benefiting from liberal international policies.

Invisibles became an ever greater proportion of Britain's positive balance of payments, running at an average level of 35–40 percent of total receipts from abroad in the years just before World War I. This growing reliance on capital-intensive international services meant that the pound became overvalued, which probably slowed domestic industrial investment.[77] Continual overvaluation of the currency also prevented the possibility of changing the competitiveness of Britain's other sectors through currency manipulation.

At the same time, British capital was now flowing overseas at a prodigious rate. Between 1870 and 1913, 40 percent of total capital accumulation in the United Kingdom was invested overseas. In 1900, Britain accounted for three-fourths of all international capital movements. By the decade before 1914, the amount of investment in other countries matched that invested domestically, and foreign investments had grown to one and a half times gross domestic product. Investment in other countries was a direct substitute for investment at home; these two always moved in opposite directions.[78]

The British state could not have improved its situation by ending liberal policies. Reverting to mercantilism within the empire and dominions would have kept wages high and employment up, but it would not have maintained the same returns to capital. The British would likely have lost the only sectors that were still economically competitive, since other states would retaliate and close access to their markets for British capital services. Even if this did not occur, but some protective measures were taken and overall trade levels fell, Britain's international service sectors could be hurt.

Changes in tariffs in the various countries of the international system between the 1880s and 1914 therefore conform to the pattern expected by the model: Germany (as an emerging expansionist political challenger) had a high level of protection for both industry and agriculture; the United States (as an economic challenger only) had begun with high tariffs for industry and some protection for agriculture but eventually lowered all tariffs; France (as a supporter) had protection for industry; Russia (as an ambivalent power) had

77. Deane and Cole, *British Economic Growth*, p. 35; Maddison, *Phases of Capitalist Development*, p. 38.
78. Buckley and Roberts, *European Direct Investment*, pp. 12–14; Maddison, *Phases of Capitalist Development*, pp. 37–38; Deane and Cole, *British Economic Growth*, p. 267.

protection for industry; and Britain (as leader of the liberal subsystem) had continual low tariffs for both industry and agriculture.[79]

Relating Economic Decline to Political Crises and Challenge

The decades after 1900 placed Britain in a poor position. The British state was faced with declining returns from its continued role as leader of the liberal subsystem, while at the same time it had to face the German political challenge, which was raising the costs of providing protection and order to the subsystem. And it was clear that Britain now perceived Germany as the true political challenger. In 1895, the *Times*' Berlin correspondent would argue in a dispatch that "Germany is by far the most dangerous of our industrial competitors at the present moment all the world over, and one cannot but regret that the influence of German competition upon British industry has not yet received the full amount of official attention which the magnitude of the interests at stake deserve." Some British politicans, such as Ramsay Macdonald, still hoped to separate economic and political competition. In a speech to the House of Commons in 1911, Macdonald argued: "Germany is going to be a more and more effective competitor with us in world markets. We had better in a scientific and calm frame of mind regard that, than constantly lose our tempers, and very often throw common sense behind us and engage in foolish, windy and cant phrases about Germany being the enemy."[80] But it was Germany's relentless pushing and the inability to find some sort of common ground which dictated the inevitability of confrontation.

One obvious problem was the naval challenge Germany was mounting. Britain could respond by redeploying its existing forces, which in fact happened after 1902. Redeployment signaled where the threat was perceived. But the realization of the British position is best seen in the abandonment of the Two-Power Standard as a guide for British naval requirements. The Admiralty had realized as early as 1909 that to build against both the German and American fleets was foolish in terms of strategy and cost; Winston Churchill was the first to tell Parliament that Britain was racing to keep ahead of Germany only. This change in policy was to deal with the convergence of the different trends at work at this time: Britain's declining ability to spend for defense, America's rise as a likely ally, and the growing German threat. By explicitly dropping the U.S. Navy from the Two-Power Standard, the Admiralty and the British government conceded hemispheric supremacy to the United States. This allowed

79. For some of the relative positions on tariffs, see Gourevitch, *Politics in Hard Times*, p. 76.
80. Hoffman, *Great Britain and the German Trade Rivalry*, pp. 230, 262–263.

the latter to play a greater role in international affairs, which in turn eased British efforts to prevent Germany from gaining sway in international relations.

The obvious way for Britain to reduce these rising costs was to find allies. Although the United States was no longer considered a military rival, this did not aid in countering the German threat. Indeed, attempts by Britain to create an alliance with the United States in the late 1890s got nothing more than the concession of U.S. dominance in the Americas. As the arguments in Chapter 1 predict, the United States tried to free ride on British liberal leadership. This was true not only of the United States but also of the dominions inside the British Empire.[81]

The British began to search out allies actively. The French did not have to be convinced of the danger of Germany. As a supporter, France made a good ally for Britain. Among the ambivalent powers, Russia and Japan were both willing by 1914, the first because it feared Germany, the second because it saw an alliance with Britain as the best way to achieve its own expansionary goals.

World War I

The Serbian crisis in 1914 became the excuse for a war of challenge. By this time, the European countries had been divided into two camps, along the lines the model would predict. Although this model can suggest nothing about the specific incident that started the war of challenge, it does explain much about why both alliances were looking for a reason to begin a major war.

Alliances in the International System

Germany had found two major allies, Austria-Hungary and Turkey. Both countries were capital-poor major powers with autocratic states (i.e., they were ambivalent powers) which had come to rely on German sources of capital. The German-Austro-Hungarian alliance had been agreed to in 1879. Italy was added as a partner in 1882. Turkey and Austria-Hungary saw the war as an opportunity to take more territory and thereby increase the area in which rents could be sanctioned.

The alliance confronting the Germans was rooted in France, a country with

---

81. Robert Huttenback and Lance Davis provide evidence of the resistance the dominions put up in refusing to pay even for their own defense; see *Mammon and the Pursuit of Empire: The Political Economy of British Imperialism, 1860–1912* (Cambridge: Cambridge University Press, 1986).

international power, republican institutions, and near capital abundance. France supported British leadership. France and Russia had allied in 1894; Britain and France had allied in 1904, an alliance augmented by the direct linkage of Britain and Russia in 1907. Russia was a capital-poor internationally powerful country with an autocratic state (i.e., it was ambivalent) which hoped to improve its position territorially by allying with the liberal leader. Japan's position mirrored Russia's, and it was also allied with Britain.

Two other major powers, Italy and the United States, avoided participation once war broke out. Italy, a capital-poor, internationally powerful country with a republican state, should have been a supporter of British liberal leadership. In fact, the Italians were linked through alliances to both sides. Italy's true interests were clarified when that country refused to side with the Central Powers and instead joined the Allies in 1915—not when the Allies seemed to be winning (as we would expect a bandwagoning power to do) but when they were struggling (as we would expect from supporters).

By 1914 the United States was capital-rich, with a republican state, and was potentially quite powerful. But as an economic challenger only it had avoided building up military power. America's interests coincided with Britain's in that both countries strongly supported the open international economic subsystem, although these two countries were economic competitors within that subsystem. The United States' late entry into the war is explained by its willingness to defend the subsystem—but not to defend Britain. It entered the war because the freedom of the seas and the viability of the open subsystem were challenged. The threat to Britain's position was at first treated as an opportunity for even greater assumption of Britain's economic role. But after Germany was more successful in closing the international economy (as with submarine warfare), American interests were challenged.

In 1914, Germany, Austria-Hungary, and Turkey faced Britain, France, Russia, and Japan. Eventually the United States, Italy, and several other countries would join the Allies against the Central Powers. The greater resources of the Allied maximum-winning coalition would then be brought to bear against the challenger's coalition.

Strategies of World War I

Germany's war aims in World War I have been the subject of great debate. Fritz Fischer maintains that Germany developed the aims for a closed central European economic system it could dominate (*Mitteleuropa*) before the war. He shows that this was expressed in the views of German politicians and industrialists at the heart of the group forming Germany's prewar foreign policy. What clearly developed *during* the war was the goal of establishing a closed, German-dominated economic area in central and eastern Europe. *Mitteleuropa* was even expanded into the broader concept of *Ostraum*: Germany would now extend all the way through the Ukraine to the Caucasus and Georgia. Although such a scheme seems to involve smaller gains than the loss of markets in the Allied countries and empires, this was in fact the policy chosen.[82] Presumably, the returns to capital would be higher in these conquered areas than German investors could have gotten from free trade in the international economy.

Eventually, German attempts to create an economic bloc they would dominate even created friction with their erstwhile allies, Austria-Hungary and Turkey.[83] This case once again underlines the difficulties challengers have in constructing durable alliances, given the different interests of challengers and their allies.

As the weaker alliance in 1914, the Central Powers (and in particular, Germany) knew that a bold offensive strategy had to be employed to win and achieve German war aims. This bold gamble was embodied in the Schlieffen Plan, which concentrated Germany's forces in the west, where they could be swung through Belgium to outflank France's armies; after defeating France, Germany's armies could be reconcentrated on the eastern front against Russia.

The Schlieffen Plan's violation of Belgian neutrality forced Britain to the side of Germany's enemies, which the Germans certainly expected, as the army planner's (Helmuth von Moltke) own writings clearly show. The boldness of the German plan is also a great example of why the model identifies Germany as the challenger, since it clearly shows Germany's intent to make any war it was involved in a major war; only the German plan called for attacks on neutrals, and only the German plan automatically assumed that full mobilization meant war.[84]

Whereas Germany's strategy relied on surprise and speed, the Allies hoped to use their power and numerical advantage to win through attrition. This logic underpinned the Anglo-French alliance with Russia. As Paul Kennedy notes, "The alliance system itself virtually guaranteed that the war would *not*

---

82. Fritz Fischer, *World Power or Decline: The Controversy over Germany's Aims in the First World War* (New York: Norton, 1974), pp. 33–34, 46; Calleo, *German Problem Reconsidered*, p. 48; Hillgruber, *Germany and the Two World Wars*, pp. 38, 45.

83. Calleo, *German Problem Reconsidered*, p. 48.

84. Moltke's 1913 memorandum "Germany's Posture in a War of the Triple Alliance," as quoted in Hillgruber, *Germany and the Two World Wars*, pp. 28–29; also see Paul Kennedy, "Editor's Introduction," in *The War Plans of the Great Powers, 1880–1914* (London: Allen & Unwin, 1979), pp. 15–16.

be swiftly decided, and meant in turn that victory in this lengthy duel would finally go to the side whose combination of financial, industrial, and technological resources was the greatest."[85] Originally, the Allies' plan was envisioned as winning through overwhelming numbers attacking on several fronts. Germany's success in repelling the Russians at Tannenberg, and then sweeping through Belgium, upset that plan.

Still, the early German offensives failed to achieve all their objectives. The devolution of the war into trench warfare and defensive struggle worked to the Allies' advantage. With the time accorded the Allies, their greater economic resources could be brought to bear.

Germany's navy had developed an offensive strategy as well. This was the aim of Admiral Tirpitz's Risiko fleet, which had been constructed with one enemy in mind—Britain. The initial impetus for the construction of this fleet had been the Boer Wars. The fleet's raison d'etre was to counter the British fleet, and its failure to do so at the Battle of Jutland showed the flaw in the German plan as long as the Germans had fewer ships than the British: the Royal Navy could lose one ship for every German ship sunk and still come out ahead. For Britain, a stalemate between the fleets in the North Sea was as good as a victory. As in the earlier wars of challenge with France, the task for the British navy was to play a decisive part in the war after the enemy had abandoned full fleet operations.

The failure to challenge Britain's surface fleet forced the German navy to shift to commerce raiding in its modern form. Surface raiders were used with some success in the beginning of the war. Later, submarines would take over this role. This shift in naval strategy brought Germany into conflict with America. Because the German plan involved restricting Britain's maritime ties, American interests were placed at risk. German attacks not only damaged American economic interests but also helped shift American public opinion against Germany.

After the United States officially entered the hostilities, the conclusion of the war still depended on the successful implementation of the attrition strategy. American men and materiel ensured the strategy's success. Russia dropped out of the alliance in 1917, but the addition of the United States

85. Kennedy, "First World War," p. 11. Although Kennedy's point that the alliance system made a long war more likely is certainly true, it is also quite true that there have been wars in which several great powers participate but which do not develop into long wars of attrition. Notable examples before World War I include the Crimean War, the French revolutionary wars, and the Seven Years' War. To fault the logic of Germany's instigation of a war that would be difficult to win if it lasted beyond a couple of years, without considering the unique problems and possibilities confronting Germany, seems a bit out of place. Germany gambled and lost.

more than compensated for Russia's withdrawal. With the balance of resources tilted decisively against Germany, it was only a matter of time before the challenger's coalition collapsed.

The Outcome of World War I

Germany was battered and worn out, and it eventually gave up without having been decisively routed on the battlefield. The German military was falling apart by the autumn of 1918, but this was because the support system and morale were run down. When the German economy collapsed, the war effort had to end. Austria-Hungary and Turkey were also suffering from severe stress economically and politically by this time. Yet the Allies' victory, as in other successful defenses of liberal international subsystems, had been costly. The attrition strategy succeeded, but the cost was enormous, in terms of both men and materiel. Profound political and economic changes occurred among all the major powers, on both winning and losing sides.

In Germany the imperial government, discredited by failure, was replaced by a democracy. Germany's economy was in shambles, and capital was scarcer than before the war. The victors imposed the Peace Treaty of Versailles, which called for Germany to pay reparations to France and Britain, which would further consume Germany's capital. The treaty also reduced the levels of armaments Germany was allowed, including an outright prohibition of aircraft, tanks, and submarines. Defeat therefore moved Germany from the category of expansive challenger into one of supporter or follower. Germany entered the 1920s as a rather different country than a decade before. In 1910 it had been capital-rich, powerful, and autocratic; in 1920 it was poorer in capital, weaker, and had a representative state.

Austria-Hungary was less fortunate than Germany. Not only was the government replaced by a democracy, the country was divided into several self-determining nation-states. Where once the Dual Monarchy had stood, there was now Austria, an independent Hungary, and Czechoslovakia. New states were also created from Austria-Hungary's and other countries' territories. From parts of Germany and Russia, Poland was created; Yugoslavia was formed out of independent Balkan states and parts of Austria-Hungary. Romania received territory from Austria-Hungary. Finland, Estonia, Latvia, and Lithuania received their independence from Russia. These smaller states were weak and still essentially capital-poor. They would either be followers of a liberal leader or ambivalent toward liberal leadership. The range of possibilities depended on domestic political systems; some, but not all, had representative governments.

The war had sparked revolution in Russia and forced that country out of the war in 1917. The tsar's rule was replaced by that of the Communist party, which then consolidated its position through civil war and domestic terror. The emergent leadership concentrated and centralized its power. As in Germany, the Russian economy collapsed under the war effort. After the revolution, Russia was still capital-poor. Civil war temporarily removed Russia from the ranks of the most powerful states: it emerged from the civil war as a capital-scarce, weak country with a nonrepresentative state—ambivalent toward any liberal leader.

Although France was victorious in World War I, it made a high military sacrifice. French capital accumulation rates had been climbing just before the war, but these trends were reversed by the war as capital was consumed at a prodigious rate. France had to borrow heavily from the United States. But it stayed a major power and, as a major power with a republican state, remained a supporter of a liberal leader.

Britain remained one of the major military powers, and the British state remained republican.[86] What had radically changed was Britain's relative abundance in capital. Before 1914 the United States had passed Britain in terms of fixed nonresidential capital stock per employee. During the war, Britain was forced to look abroad for loans, accumulating some £2,062,000,000 of debt by 1919. Britain also cashed in much of the overseas investment built up in the previous century. During the war, some 15 percent of British-owned foreign assets were sold off.[87] As a result, Britain's interests and capabilities in continued liberal leadership were called into question. During the war, Britain passed the McKenna Duties, which established a 33.5 percent levy on low-priority goods in an effort to limit Britain's trade imbalance.[88]

At the same time, the United States shifted from international debtor to international banker, as it was the only country capable of mobilizing new sources of liquid capital. In 1914 the United States had been a net debtor by some $2–2.5 million; by 1928 it was a net creditor, exclusive of political loans,

---

86. Actually, Britain would become more democratic with the reforms of 1918, which opened political participation to all male adults.

87. C. H. Lee, *The British Economy since 1700: A Macroeconomic Perspective* (New York: Cambridge University Press, 1986), pp. 228, 232.

88. Checkland, *British Public Policy*, p. 265.

by $8–11 million.[89] The war hastened this change because Britain's purchases of war materiel stimulated American industry, but these purchases were made with loans from New York, which stimulated American financial ascendance as well.

Because the German challenge occurred after Britain had lost its economic dominance rather than during the liberal leader's economic ascendance or peak, as in the previous two challenges to a liberal leader, capital had to be pulled back into the leader's domestic economy. In the previous two cases of challenge, capital had flowed from the liberal international leader to its allies. This time, since challenge occurred after relative economic decline had more than begun, the flow of capital was reversed.

Since the United States came through the war with relatively little damage, increased capital abundance, democratic institutions intact, and a newly mobilized military machine, it seemed poised to become the new liberal leader. Moreover, several major countries were potential supporters (France, Italy, Germany) or at least followers (Belgium, the Netherlands, Czechoslovakia, Austria, and several others) of a new leader. It seemed that the war would effect a transition to a new leadership of the open international subsystem.

89. Williams, *Economic Foreign Policy*, pp. 18–19. Kennedy, *Realities behind Diplomacy*, pp. 148–149.

FIVE

A Stumbling Start to
American Liberal Leadership,
and Challenge Renewed,
1918–1945

The breakdown of the open international economy after that same subsystem was successfully defended in World War I is a troubling case for traditional models of hegemonic stability theory. Since most theories of hegemony are based on purely structural explanations, they have a difficult time accounting for American foreign policy: the international position of the United States changed dramatically between 1910 and 1929, but American foreign policy did not. The United States did not act hegemonically but instead returned to the role of a peaceful economic challenger, content to follow Britain's lead politically. Alone, Britain failed to reconstruct and stabilize the international economy in the 1920s.

The breakdown of the open international economy raises numerous questions about hegemonic transitions and the problems therein. Since this phenomenon is the most intensively studied change of hegemonic leadership, scholars have concluded that smooth transitions from one country's liberal leadership to that of another are unlikely. By analyzing American interwar foreign policy in terms of this book's model, we may be able to determine if the problems of this period are inherent to all liberal leadership transitions or specific to this case.

Choices for the United States after World War I

After World War I, most major powers had republican states (the United States, Britain, France, and Germany), making them amenable to a liberal leader's activities, and two major powers were ruled by autocratic states (the

Soviet Union and Japan). Among the former group, the United States was now the country most abundant in capital. Britain, having survived the war with many of its assets intact, was still relatively capital-abundant compared to most other countries, though not to the same degree. According to the expectations of the model presented here, the United States should have tried to recreate the open subsystem *only after British leadership failed*, and it should have had several supporters. There were willing supporters. But, as the historical record shows, support for leadership was not the problem; the problem was over which country would provide leadership. Britain finished the war with continued economic interest in performing this role but with diminished capability to do so; the United States had similar interests *and* a state capable of international leadership, but the state sought a return to its previous, low-cost position as an economic rival to Britain.

As David Lake describes the interplay of American and British foreign economic policies, the years immediately following World War I were characterized by competition as Britain tried to rebuild its financial system and reintegrate the United States in a subordinate position, while the United States strove to improve and consolidate its own position in the liberal international economic subsystem. From the early 1920s to the middle of that decade, there were elements of cooperation in stabilization attempts, such as the London Conference, the Dawes Plan, and the Locarno Treaty.[1] The pattern Lake describes for the period between 1918 and 1929 fits an explanation in which the American state attempts to return to a position as economic challenger and Britain's state tries to resume international economic and political leadership.

The United States had the economic interests of a prospective liberal leader in 1918. It emerged from the war as the greatest international creditor and the most capital-abundant country in the system. Before American entry in the war, America's trade surplus was five times prewar levels; private loans to Britain and France were around $2.6 billion, and Britain and France were eventually forced to sell off around $2 billion of their investments in the United States. Conversely, total American direct investment in Europe went from a prewar total of $200 million to $1.4 billion in 1929. In 1913, American banks had only some 26 foreign branch offices, compared to 2,279 for Britain, 175 for France, 70 for Germany, and 68 for the Netherlands. By 1918, National City Bank of New York (later Citibank) had 18 foreign branches itself,

---

1. David A. Lake, *Power, Protection, and Free Trade: International Sources of U.S. Commercial Strategy, 1887–1939* (Ithaca: Cornell University Press, 1988), p. 178. Lake misses the point that most of these attempts were undertaken by the United States as private missions: the state was still trying to avoid the costs of hegemony. Then, at the end of the 1920s, this cooperation unraveled, and it did so strongly after the Crash of 1929.

and by 1926 this number had grown to 84, while American Express Bank had 47 foreign offices of its own by 1926. Between 1914 and 1920, the overseas sales of American manufactured goods increased some 500 percent.[2]

The war had afforded other capital-intensive sectors in the United States the opportunity to encroach on markets and activities traditionally held by British firms. During the war, the United States had tried to expand its involvement in the carrying trade, particularly with Latin America. After the war, the financial community desired greater trade liberalization, American aid for European reconstruction, and American international monetary and financial leadership.[3] These are all policies consistent with liberal leadership—but they were not employed.

Privatization of American Foreign Policy

The Harding administration was clearly aware that, as a creditor nation and major exporter, the United States had a responsibility to make foreign loans in support of other countries' currencies and American exports. But during the late 1920s, American diplomacy became increasingly decentralized and increasingly left up to private actors and private resources. The administration included many men (such as Secretary of State Charles Evans Hughes, Secretary of the Treasury Andrew Mellon, and Secretary of Commerce Herbert Hoover) who felt that, although the United States should be more prominent in world economic affairs, it should be so through private business and finance. The goals of American foreign economic policies of this period could still be characterized as the creation of a stable and peaceful international order conducive to the United States playing a greater economic role in the world, but the state was not willing to bear a greater burden in this effort.[4]

As evidence of this split between the state and private interests, consider some crucial examples. The League of Nations, as a forum for improved international relations, was formed after American initiatives during the war, with most of the major powers participating. Yet the United States, fearing the obligations possible, refused to become a member. Even though the interna-

---

2. Jeffry A. Frieden, *Banking on the World: The Politics of American International Finance* (New York: Harper & Row, 1987), pp. 25–28, 33; also see his "The Internationalization of United States Finance and the Transformation of United States Foreign Policy, 1890–1940," paper presented at the 1984 APSA meeting, Washington, D.C., August 30–September 2, 1984, p. 33; Melvyn P. Leffler, "1921–1932: Expansionist Impulses and Domestic Constraints," in *Economics and World Power*, ed. William H. Becker and Samuel F. Wells, Jr. (New York: Columbia University Press, 1984), p. 228.

3. D. Cameron Watt, *Succeeding John Bull: America in Britain's Place, 1900–1975* (New York: Cambridge University Press, 1984), p. 32; Frieden, *Banking on the World*, p. 35.

4. Watt, *Succeeding John Bull*, p. 40; Leffler, "1921–1932: Expansionist Impulses," pp. 226, 232.

tional institution to coordinate policies among the members of an open international system was created, the United States balked at the possible costs involved with membership. Private American actors attempted to fill the stabilizing function in international affairs which the state was unwilling to underwrite. Collaboratively arranged private loans to first Austria and then Belgium, Italy, Poland, and Romania helped stabilize the European economy in 1923.

The issue of reparations created some of the major problems of returning to normal economic relations after the war. Britain and France owed the United States money for its war loans but could pay these back comfortably only if Germany paid reparations. Germany had been hit hard economically by the war and could only pay reparations with great difficulty. To stimulate the economic process to generate the money for reparations, foreign capital had to be invested in Germany.

In the Dawes Plan of April 1924, American banks privately extended a $200 million stabilization loan to Germany. In the six years that followed, private American sources loaned another $1.2 billion to Germany and $1.4 billion to other European countries.[5] This same mechanism of private aid was extended in the Young Plan of 1929, which also negotiated a cap on German reparations. The Bank of International Settlements, set up to smooth out problems in the realm of international payments, was supposed to be a central bankers' association—but the American chair was filled by a representative of the New York banks, not by the Federal Reserve. During the 1920s, American stabilization efforts were all private.

In the merry-go-round of funds, Britain and France paid interest on war debts to the United States, Germany paid reparations to Britain and France, but these could be paid only as long as the United States loaned new money to Germany. This flow of funds was weakened at its source by speculation in real estate and stocks in America in 1928 and finally disrupted by the Crash in 1929, the tightening of American investments, and the increased closure of the United States to foreign trade with the Smoot-Hawley Tariff in 1930.[6]

In some ways, the state did move to protect the new international interests. Earlier, in China, the Wilson administration's policy emphasizing the sovereign rights of debtor countries had been reversed into an emphasis on the security of foreign loans to the detriment of the rights of borrowers.[7] This clearly shows how policy changed as the United States moved from debtor to

---

5. Frieden, *Banking on the World*, pp. 32–33.
6. Ibid., pp. 41–42.
7. Benjamin H. Williams, *Economic Foreign Policy of the United States* (New York: McGraw-Hill, 1929), p. 50.

creditor. At the same time, the United States declined to act as a liberal leader in other areas. America avoided protection of the open international system by refusing to join the League of Nations and scaled back its military. It tried to leave protection to the British.

Importance of Size in the American Refusal to Lead

The United States was an economic challenger until 1929. The Crash of 1929 was a blow to America's economic position and lessened pressures from capital-intensive sectors to locate new avenues of investment. Strangely, America's great size was relevant to its rejection of leadership of the liberal subsystem. Whereas traditional arguments on hegemony relate large size to the motivation for undertaking leadership, size is not a factor in the model presented here. In fact, in the first case of prospective liberal leadership, the small size of the Netherlands (and hence poor resource base) made the gains to that country from trade high, and therefore smallness stimulated the pressures for the state to pursue leadership of a liberal subsystem. In the same way, America's large size and abundant resources made the costs of turning its back on trade easier to bear. Rather than being an incentive to pursue hegemony, largeness gave the United States the opportunity to pursue optimal tariff policies and move in directions other than liberal leadership after 1929. Tactics to solve the economic problems of the depression were often viewed in a purely domestic scenario, without full consideration of the international ramifications. In a smaller country, this would not have been possible.

At this time, the international interests were still too small a part of the national economy to win when foreign economic policy clashed with domestic economic policy. The model presented here argues that growing capital abundance in the United States made the capital-intensive sectors of the economy ally to support policies of liberal leadership. The international interests that emerged during the war had to unite with other capital-intensive sectors to get control of the foreign economic policy. This alliance fell apart after the stock market crash, when some capital-intensive sectors lost interest in pursuing new international activities. Moreover, economic growth in the 1920s in the United States had not been in the foreign trade sectors: exports as a proportion of total production fell, the percentage of farm income derived from exports fell, and the book value of American foreign direct investment was unchanged. Although manufactures as a percentage of all exports was growing, the domestic market was growing even faster, and in specific industries such as chemicals, textiles, radios, and cast iron pipe exports were very small percentages of total production; exports were a significantly declining part of petroleum production. Given these conditions, the business community was split on the importance of foreign trade considerations, so that when the Crash came, both the State and Commerce departments were somewhat limited by the lack of support for any great international policy response.[8] In terms of the model presented here, the Crash temporarily relieved any coordinated domestic pressures building for the United States to expand its leadership in the international system.

In fact, in the critical period of 1931–1932, the U.S. government exacerbated international economic problems by refusing to cancel war debts, scale down tariffs, or extend loans to the hard-pressed countries of Latin America. At the same time, the government rejected political support for an open international subsystem by refusing to assume strategic commitments in Europe or intervene in affairs in East Asia. Clearly, after World War I the United States hoped to remain an economic challenger while some other country bore the brunt of the costs of leading the open subsystem.

Britain's Choices in the 1920s

After World War I, Britain still had strong international interests located in London. American politicians saw Britain trying to continue to lead the liberal subsystem, so they allowed Britain to carry all the burdens. Britain was trapped in its leadership role, because the most competitive parts of Britain's economy were in capital-intensive international services. The declining competitiveness of the rest of the economy continued as it had before the war. The inability to respond adequately to these economic problems, which had become apparent before the war, was exacerbated by Britain's declining relative capital abundance: it was now losing competitiveness in the capital-services sectors to the United States.

Because of the declining relative capital richness, restrictions on economic activities were put in place during the war. After the war, Britain tried to return to its earlier economic role. The McKenna Duties (also established during the war) were dropped in 1924, and the embargo on foreign lending was ended in 1925.[9] The return to the gold standard at a high valuation of the pound also trapped Britain in a difficult position, if the goals of reducing unemployment, expanding foreign lending, and stabilizing the international

---

8. Leffler, "1921–1932: Expansionist Impulses," pp. 258–260.

9. D. E. Moggridge, "British Controls on Long Term Capital Movements, 1924–1931," in *Essays on a Mature Economy: Britain after 1840*, ed. Donald N. McCloskey (Princeton: Princeton University Press, 1971), p. 117; Sydney Checkland, *British Public Policy, 1776–1939: An Economic, Social, and Political Perspective* (New York: Cambridge University Press, 1983), p. 276.

economy were all to be achieved. A high valuation of the pound ensured that foreigners would continue to hold pounds, which in turn gave a competitive edge to Britain's international service sectors. For this reason the high valuation of the pound was accepted. Returning to the prewar valuation of sterling to gold left the prices of British goods about 10 percent above their real value. To cut prices, either industrial rationalization would have to occur or wages would have to be pushed down; since the first required capital that was not to be found, and interest rates were kept high to maintain the gold standard, the second solution was adopted. The General Strike of 1926 resulted. That same year, the McKenna Duties had to be reimposed.[10]

The failure of Britain to regain its prewar economic position brought about great economic problems. The issue of high unemployment led directly to the Labour government taking office in 1929. This government tried to deal with unemployment by raising government expenditures, just as the New York stock market crashed and world trade entered a tailspin. The stock market crash led to the withdrawal of short-term credits from Europe and an agreement for a moratorium on debt repayments, but even with this pressure removed Britain was in trouble, for funds could not be drawn in from overseas; in fact, gold was flowing out of Britain as foreigners sold off sterling. The decision to borrow from foreign sources split the government, and even after loans were received the gold standard could not be maintained. Sterling had to be taken off the gold standard in September 1931. By abandoning the international services sectors, the government was finally free to help other sectors of the economy. Between 1931 and 1939, Britain's economic policies were more malleable, since currency stability could be achieved through means that did not sacrifice manufacturing interests for maintenance of an overvalued pound. Policies such as devaluation could now be executed in order to stimulate the export of manufactures.

Britain's position in the 1920s was not an enviable one. As the Dutch had been unable to fight economic decline in the eighteenth century, Britain could not stop its own economic slide in the 1920s. This situation worsened when the United States dropped efforts to support and stabilize the international system after 1929. At the heart of this decline was the change in Britain's capital abundance. Exports of goods and services failed to increase at the same pace as imports. As part of this dynamic, exports of capital decreased in the 1920s, and Britain actually began to import capital in the 1930s. Before World War I, Britain exported one-fourth of its total production; by 1939 only one-

---

10. Moggridge, "British Controls," p. 113; Trevor May, *An Economic and Social History of Britain, 1760–1970* (New York: Longman, 1987), p. 350; Checkland, *British Public Policy*, pp. 302–307.

eighth of total production was exported. Even when production totals rebounded from the drop experienced in the Great Depression, Britain's share of world trade declined.[11]

After the war, and even with the great debts incurred, Britain would have been able to pay off war debts if its other overseas assets had kept performing as they did in the 1920s.[12] But after the Crash of 1929, the open subsystem was not maintained. Britain's overseas investments and international service sectors could no longer counterbalance the traditional deficit from imports plus the new burden of international debts.

British Decline and the Great Depression

What the German challenge and World War I had failed to do—knock Britain out of the dominant position in the international economy—the Great Depression did with a vengence. The depression created problems for all sectors of the British economy. Britain's visible trade had always been balanced by invisibles earned by the international service sectors. The depression reduced world trade in manufactures by a third and in primary products by over a half. These reductions dropped the demand for British shipping: earnings from that sector fell from £143 million in 1924 to £68 million in 1933. Likewise, earnings from financial services fell from £80 million in 1913 to £40 million in the years 1934–1938. As Paul Kennedy describes this fall in income from invisibles, "Britain's most important 'cushion' fell away."[13] Britain could no longer pay for expensive labor, because it no longer had the cheapest capital; the capital it did have could no longer find employment internationally on as wide a scale as before.

One way Britain did respond, though, was for the state to lessen its provision of protection and order for the open international subsystem. It no longer accepted the responsibility for protecting a system that no longer provided reasonable returns. As John Ferris notes, though, Britain's military establishment was already too weak to undertake this old mission, even though it still cost too much. Military redeployment was only one obvious facet of this change in policy. British military power was increasingly focused in Eu-

11. Phyllis Deane and W. A. Cole, *British Economic Growth, 1688–1959: Trends and Structure* (Cambridge: Cambridge University Press, 1962), p. 37; Paul Kennedy, *The Rise and Fall of British Naval Mastery* (London: Lane, 1976), p. 269.

12. C. H. Lee, *The British Economy since 1700: A Macroeconomic Perspective* (New York: Cambridge University Press, 1986), p. 228.

13. Kennedy, *Rise and Fall of British Naval Mastery*, p. 269.

rope, even as the Japanese were building large fleets in the Pacific.[14] In economic affairs, Britain also stopped playing a stabilizing role. Instabilities in
exchange rates and currencies of the 1930s were no longer met by British
intervention. Problems of international liquidity, which would have been resolved by British practices in previous decades, resulted.[15]

Britain Turns Inward

British capital, which had once pressed for new employment through extension of the international market, was now in greater demand at home. The
investment patterns of the 1930s are further evidence of Britain's relative decline in capital richness and the changing interests of British capital. Except
for some opportunities in precious metals, the domestic market was now
more attractive to investors. Realizing that it was no longer so capital-rich,
Britain moved to protect capital-intensive sectors from foreign competition by
closing off the empire and dominions in the Imperial Preference System, in
1931.[16]

Britain also pulled back foreign investments. In 1913 some 20 percent of
Britain's total foreign investment had been in the United States, but this fell to
5 percent in 1930, with much more now invested in the empire. By going off
the gold standard, the Bank of England and the treasury could exert influence
to direct the flow of investment toward the empire: in the 1930s loans to the
empire were six times greater than foreign loans (although the absolute sizes
of the loans were less than in the previous decade, as all nondomestic investment fell off). The turn toward the empire worked in that the United Kingdom sent some 47 percent of exports there in 1938 compared to only 22
percent in 1913; imports from foreign countries fell from 80 percent in 1913
to only 61 percent in 1938.[17]

14. On the theoretical level, Arthur A. Stein, "The Hegemon's Dilemma: Great Britain, the
United States, and the International Economic Order," *International Organization* 38 (Spring
1984): 376, makes much the same argument. For some of the specifics in this case, see John
Robert Ferris, *Men, Money, and Diplomacy: The Evolution of British Strategic Policy, 1919–1926*
(Ithaca: Cornell University Press, 1989), p. 53; Kennedy, *Rise and Fall of British Naval Mastery*, p.
262.

15. J. D. Gould, *Economic Growth in History: Survey and Analysis* (London: Methuen, 1972), p.
193.

16. Ian M. Drummond, *British Economic Policy and the Empire, 1919–1939* (London: Allen &
Unwin, 1972), p. 120; David P. Calleo and Benjamin M. Rowland, *America and the World Political Economy* (Bloomington: Indiana University Press, 1973), p. 32.

17. Peter J. Buckley and Brian R. Roberts, *European Direct Investment in the U.S.A. before
World War I* (New York: St. Martin's, 1982), p. 125; Drummond, *British Economic Policy*, pp. 18,

Britain's changes in policy reflect the movement from the position of liberal leader to that of supporter, and the United States continued to act as an economic challenger after the Crash of 1929. In fact, the Crash had temporarily reduced American interests in economic expansion. Thus both countries had abandoned efforts to lead the open subsystem; instead, each was trying to close itself off from some international competition.

The Collapse of the Open International Subsystem

Since the United States did much the same with the Smoot-Hawley Tariff of 1930 as Britain later tried with the Imperial Preference System, each state's efforts to cheat on an open subsystem run by the other failed. In 1922 the Fordney-McCumber Tariff had raised the overall U.S. rate to 13.9 percent by raising the average rate on dutiable goods and decreasing the number of free items. The United States had managed to negotiate several unconditional most-favored-nation treaties with many countries, but not with Britain or France. The Smoot-Hawley Tariff of 1930 established some of the highest rates of duty in American history, but at the same time the free list was expanded, resulting in a rise of the overall average rate of duties from 13.9 percent to 19 percent.[18]

When Franklin Roosevelt took office in 1933, he continued this trend toward closure and refusal to lead the open subsystem. Roosevelt refused to help stabilize the international economy by not allowing a moratorium on Britain's war debts. He created new instabilities by taking the United States off the gold standard. He failed to provide international leadership by refusing to commit the United States to international cooperation at the World Monetary and Economic Conference in London in June 1933.

Because America's incentives to act as an international liberal leader were preempted by Britain's willingness to return to that role in the years before 1928, the American state had refused to take responsibility. The crash of the stock market in 1929 then reduced any domestic pressures for such policies. For a few short years, the capital-intensive sectors of the United States looked to improve their business domestically rather than internationally. Instead of

---

21, 118–119. Drummond explains the government preference for imperial loans as based on the greater likelihood of such borrowings remaining in London or being spent on British goods— and therefore of being less of a threat to Britain's exchange rate and reserves of gold and dollars (pp. 119–120).

18. Lake, *Power, Protection, and Free Trade*, pp. 167, 171–172, 184, 194–195. Lake argues the United States exhibited a limited form of leadership in this period.

acting as a liberal leader, the United States began to act as a supporter and moved to protect the domestic market. It took the lead in closing the system, and American trade suffered accordingly. The 1933 level of American volume in world trade was only 70 percent of its level in 1929, and the value of this trade was only 35 percent of that in 1929.[19]

This trend toward closure did not last long. When Cordell Hull was named secretary of state in 1933, the United States was set on the path toward commitment to liberalizing international trade through the most-favored-nation principle. The Reciprocal Trade Agreements Act passed in 1934 authorized the president to reduce tariffs, and America finally took a lead in establishing a more open international economy. At the same time, the United States took a longer view of international problems when it decided to leave foreign debts unchanged. Although Lake's interpretation of this period is correct in that the reciprocal trade act left American tariffs in place, the act's overall impact was to lower the average rate of duty.[20]

Hull argued that economic rivalry and the breakdown of the world into autarchic blocs would eventually lead to political rivalry and war. He therefore saw the issues of trade not only in terms of economic gain, but also in terms of a diplomatic effort for peace. Hull faced opposition from other parts of the government. Attempts to follow foreign policies of liberal leadership were effectively limited by the isolationists in the Democratic party (such as senators LaFollette, Norris, Wheeler, Borah, and Johnson), who continued to eschew international obligations.[21]

Still, in minor ways the United States began to take the lead in opening and stabilizing the system. The dollar was set at $35 per ounce of gold in 1934, and in the spring of 1935 the United States cooperated with France to stabilize the French franc. The United States also pushed for greater cooperation with France and Britain in currency markets, which was achieved in 1936. Other policies of liberal leadership were undertaken, particularly with supporter states. By 1938 the United States, Britain, and Canada were able to sign a treaty lowering tariffs between them. Even with this the most comprehensive

19. Ibid., p. 186. Robert M. Hathaway, "1933–1945: Economic Diplomacy in a Time of Crisis," in *Economics and World Power*, ed. Becker and Wells, p. 278, gives slightly different figures, although the magnitude of the drops are approximately the same.

20. Stein, "Hegemon's Dilemma," pp. 376–377; Hathaway, "1933–1945: Economic Diplomacy," p. 286; Lake, *Power, Protection, and Free Trade*, pp. 204–208.

21. Hathaway, "1933–1945: Economic Diplomacy," pp. 281, 283.

of the interwar trade treaties, levels of protection in both Britain and the United States remained high.[22]

Full-fledged American interest in the international economy would have to wait until either the American market recovered or opportunities in the international market appeared. Many American loans to Latin America, as well as half those to Europe, were in default by 1936, so few attractive opportunities for international investment existed.[23] Because of this situation, little new pressure appeared to encourage the American state to extend its leadership.

There is no reason to believe that in 1930 the system's requirements were too high for the United States to have taken over leadership. In fact, American capital exports in the period after the Crash of 1929 up to World War II saw the absolute volume stay low, but relative to domestic and total capital formation it remained high.[24] Unlike earlier liberal leaders, the United States would have had several supporters. The real problem was that, with two possible leaders in the liberal subsystem, the U.S. government did not have clear incentives to act as leader. Immediately after the war, economic incentives existed for Britain to resume leadership, especially since Britain hoped to thwart American economic competition in capital services by reexerting its political role. When Britain's economic position and international power proved incapable of returning that country to its prewar position, it was willing to be a supporter of American liberal leadership. But when Britain had been trying to regain its leadership, the American state had been more than willing to forfeit that role and return to the position of economic challenger in order to avoid the costs associated with international burdens. When Britain finally relinquished leadership aspirations at the end of the 1920s, the United States continued eschewing international obligations.

Private interests in the United States had provided some international economic leadership in the 1920s, but this declined with the onset of the Great Depression. Ironically, America's large size provided the opportunity to abandon the open system and turn inward in 1930—contrary to the traditional models of hegemony that argue that large size is a predictive factor of hegemonic leadership. Only after the international economy closed following American closure did the United States discover that its interests were more greatly served by maintaining an open international subsystem, even if the

---

22. Lake, *Power, Protection, and Free Trade*, p. 208; Hathaway, "1933–1945: Economic Diplomacy," pp. 297–298.
23. Frieden, *Banking on the World*, p. 51.
24. Simon Kuznets, *Capital in the American Economy: Its Formation and Financing* (Princeton: Princeton University Press, 1961), p. 141.

cost was American leadership. Only after this lesson was learned did the United States act as the liberal leader.

Germany as a Reborn Political Challenger

Germany's position in the international system as a supporter of the liberal leader was established in the 1920s. It had changed from the third largest exporter of capital in 1914 to an importer of capital from the United States after World War I.[25] The German military was still limited by the Versailles treaty, though early on it was apparent that German troop levels were being secretly maintained above allowable amounts.

Germany's economy had been severely affected by war. Government spending during World War I accelerated trends toward the concentration of industry in Germany, since the government preferred to give large wartime contracts to single, large firms when possible. Large firms also lent personnel and expertise to the government. This concentration continued after the war, despite some attempts by the Weimar regime to regulate cartels and trusts. In 1925–1926, for example, I. G. Farben and the United Steel Works were formed.

When the Great Depression came, it hit Germany especially hard. Overall industrial production in 1931 was only about one-third that of 1928; one-fourth of the labor force (more than five million people) was unemployed. Tax revenues fell, so that the government deficit increased, at the same time foreign capital fled and exports rapidly fell off.[26] The deepening economic crisis created a series of political crises. In this sense the failure of the United States and Britain to maintain the open international economic subsystem indirectly led to the end of the Weimar regime. Out of these political-economic crises, the Nazi party emerged as a successful mass movement. Adolf Hitler was asked to lead the cabinet as chancellor in January 1933. After further crises (some instigated by the Nazis), presidential emergency powers were placed with the cabinet. Then, in March 1933, the Reichstag voted Hitler dictatorial powers with the passage of the Enabling Act.[27]

Although many have assumed that big business (i.e., the holders of capital)

25. Gould, *Economic Growth in History*, p. 181.
26. Henry Ashby Turner, Jr., *German Big Business and the Rise of Hitler* (New York: Oxford University Press, 1985), p. 158.
27. Ibid., pp. 23, 111, 332–333. Nazi party gains in terms of seats in the Reichstag went from 12 to 107 in 1930 (the largest jump by a party in the Reichstag since 1871) to 230 in July 1932 (when the Nazis became the single largest party).

supported Hitler's rise and therefore supported the same goals as Hitler, this picture has been disproven. Henry Ashby Turner, Jr., using an interest group argument, and David Abraham, using class analysis, make basically the same point: the Weimar Republic could not ensure the success or stability of the business community, and therefore this regime was undermined. Yet both authors are quick to note that these same domestic actors did not necessarily see the Nazis as a solution to their problems. It is true that business could always conform to the Nazi vision. As Turner points out, the return to profitability made it easier for business to swallow the interventions in market relations the Nazis carried out, even though the regime often ignored them. Abraham raises similar issues in order to argue that the Nazis were in many ways disappointing for industrialists, if not actually perceived as threatening. Both authors portray the Nazi's support of business interests as a means to an end, with the business community accepting this relationship in order to recover profitablity.[28]

My argument here does not predict the fall of specific regimes or the rise of specific political groups. Instead, it simply gives a framework for describing how the failure of the open international economic subsystem and the consequent economic dislocation everywhere created a political climate that allowed parties like the Nazis in Germany or the Fascists in Italy to take power. To understand why the Nazi party took the form it did, and then was successful, would require a long examination of political economic and sociological issues; I am not so much interested in why the Nazis appeared as in the international consequences of their seizure of power. The important point is that a political party based on a modern ideology, using modern propoganda techniques, took control of a democratic state and transformed it into an autocracy.

The Nazi party involved many different groups, and a clear picture of a political-economic program before the Nazis' attainment of power is difficult to form. Some authors note that the Nazi party was not democratic, so no consensus was ever achieved. Nor was it doctrinal, so no coherent theory was necessary. Instead, the party was based around Hitler, so to understand Nazi policies one must understand Hitler's views.[29] In this particular state, then, the rents the state established would be designed to enhance state power for goals

28. Ibid., pp. 337–338; Turner shows that business wanted an end to the social policies of the Social Democrats but were reluctant to support the Nazis. David Abraham, *The Collapse of the Weimar Republic: Political Economy and Crisis*, 2d ed. (New York: Holmes & Meier, 1986), p. xvi.
29. Turner, *German Big Business*, develops this logic in several places in great detail; see p. 70 for an example.

that can only be understood via Nazi ideology. The rhetoric that justified the state's intervention in the economic sphere (as in other facets of society) would also be unique to the Nazi movement.

Hitler, His Ideology, and the Policies of Nazi Germany

Hitler was in control of policymaking. As chancellor, he controlled executive authority. After the Enabling Act, he controlled legislative authority. With the death of President von Hindenburg in August 1934, and the merger of the offices of the president and chancellor, Hitler also held the supreme command of the armed forces. Some efforts to centralize the administration of the country were made, particularly by the Reich Ministry of the Interior, which took on itself the enforcement of Reich laws rather than entrusting that activity to the interior ministries of the various states.[30]

Hitler viewed international relations as a struggle between racial groups for existence (*Lebenskampf*). He adopted this social darwinist point of view by 1924 at the latest and specifically saw Germany's future living space (*Lebensraum*) expanding into eastern Europe. He saw eastern Europe, and especially European Russia, as an area of rich agricultural lands into which the German nation could expand. Thus his goals were in agricultural expansion and did not include taking over the populations in conquered territories: indeed, the indigenous populations of the east would have to be moved or exterminated so as not to mix with Germans. More interesting, expansion was also seen as a way to relieve the tensions inherent in a modern industrial nondemocratic system: as Turner put it, "Industry and trade would be forced out of their unwholesome positions of leadership in the national economy into the framework of a more balanced national life." In the domestic economy, German peasant agriculture was to be protected, though primarily as a source for the "proper" racial stock.[31] The return to a large agricultural base can be seen as an attempt to return to labor-intensive production; the inherent distortions created by the garnering of intensified rents by capital in a closed economy where capital was becoming more abundant would be offset by expansion of the labor-intensive sectors.

30. Norman Rich, *Hitler's War Aims, Ideology, the Nazi State, and the Course of Expansion*, vol. 1 (New York: Norton, 1973), pp. 11–13, 38, 43. Although it should be remembered that underneath Hitler the structure was a mess, since various bureaucratic jurisdictions (such as Reich offices, Prussian state offices, offices of other lesser states and of the Nazi party itself) overlapped.

31. Turner, *German Big Business*, pp. 72–74. Also, Gerhard L. Weinberg, *The Foreign Policy of Hitler's Germany: Diplomatic Revolution in Europe, 1933–1936* (Chicago: University of Chicago Press, 1970), chap. 1. Rich, *Hitler's War Aims*, chap. 1.

To carry out the necessary expansion, the state would need absolute authority over the economy. Moreover, expansion required further development of capital-intensive sectors—most obviously in armaments. It is therefore difficult to imagine an end to the dynamic driving the expansionary tendency within the Nazis' vision of their own system. Expansion could alleviate the inherent tensions, but the military buildup supporting expansion would also exacerbate those tensions.

This need for absolute state control over the economy did not require the end of private ownership of property, since domestic competition fit Hitler's social darwinism.[32] The interesting conclusion about the sources of Nazi Germany's challenge to the liberal subsystem is that the domestic process points to the state itself as the origin of the expansionist policies at the root of challenge. It was the state and not the capital-intensive sectors that initiated the intensification of distortionary rents. The state (or rather the Nazi party) regarded the existing situation as untenable and worked to change it without impetus from capital-intensive sectors (which would have been trying to maintain relative returns) or labor-intensive sectors (which would have been trying to get the higher returns the changing capital-labor ratio brought them).

This point should not be construed to mean that business interests were always ignored or necessarily mistreated by the Nazis. The Nazis followed policies that closely resembled mercantilism and increased capital accumulation. Autarchy was the goal, but ultimately autarchy led to conquest of greater resources.[33] These policies were designed to accumulate capital and build a closed state-directed market, which the state could harness for continual wars of expansion.

Nazi Policies Exacerbate International Tensions

Tensions between the United States and Germany were heightened in the late 1930s, because the closed economic order the Nazis were creating thwarted America's efforts to stimulate economic recovery through exports. Attempts by the United States to work out a compromise on Germany's foreign debts in 1933 failed dismally, as Germany claimed to lack the necessary foreign exchange while simultaneously purchasing goods for rearmament

---

32. Turner, *German Big Business*, p. 76.
33. Kennedy, *Rise and Fall of British Naval Mastery*, p. 308. This point is echoed by Ronald Rogowski, *Commerce and Coalitions* (Princeton: Princeton University Press, 1989), p. 5, n. 11.

from other countries. Likewise, the German tariff program of 1933 discriminated against American goods, thus harming America's trade position but also undercutting the international rules the United States was newly espousing.[34]

These policies of the Reich ran up against America's efforts to create an open subsystem in the late 1930s. Germany used quotas, bilateral trade agreements, and state monopolies to divert Europe's trade from the United States. Severe restrictions on capital flows forced American companies in Germany to reinvest their profits there, aiding Germany's economic recovery and seeming to disprove Hull's theories concerning the benefits of liberal trade. Traditional American markets were penetrated by the Germans, who used leveraging techniques such as barter transactions, state subsidies, and blocked credits to gain a greater market share in Latin America. These techniques worked as German trade with Latin America as a whole increased some 50 percent in 1935; from 1934 to 1937, Germany's share of Brazilian imports rose from 14 to 25 percent, of Mexican imports from 9 to just below 20 percent, and of Chile's from 10 to 25 percent (surpassing the U.S. share of imports).

These actions threatened American attempts to reconstruct the liberal international economy, and they created parallel problems with Britain, which was also concerned about support for the rules of the open system and protection for Britain's international investments.[35] Further attempts to monopolize markets were made in southeastern Europe, where the Nazis agreed to buy agricultural goods and raw materials at prices above world market prices in exchange for purchases of German capital-intensive goods. For instance, in February 1934, Germany signed such a trade diversion agreement with Hungary.[36] Others were signed with Romania and Yugoslavia.

Nazi foreign and domestic policies stimulated the accumulation of capital in Germany, and the movement toward autarchy was largely successful. In fact, by 1936, Germany was approaching self-sufficiency in several areas, including (synthetic) petroleum products, although further economic expansion or war would require more consumption and therefore change this balance.[37] Under autarchy, Germany would prevent the escape of capital, thereby hastening its accumulation. But successful capital accumulation merely brought on the problems the Nazis feared: the changing capital-labor ratio created pres-

---

34. Hathaway, "1933–1945: Economic Diplomacy," p. 300; Weinberg, *Foreign Policy of Hitler's Germany*, pp. 136–140.
35. Hathaway, "1933–1945: Economic Diplomacy," pp. 300–301; Weinberg, *Foreign Policy of Hitler's Germany*, p. 201.
36. Weinberg, *Foreign Policy of Hitler's Germany*, p. 115.
37. Ibid., p. 350.

sures to alter the relative returns to capital and labor, which would upset the state-sanctioned rents so strenuously created and maintained in the first years of Nazi rule.

The buildup of the military encouraged investment and the consumption of capital-intensive goods. By 1936 problems with this arrangement began to emerge. Trade union strength had been broken, so wage levels were not yet growing despite underlying labor tension. Foreign exchange reserves were being run down as the government focused foreign consumption for rearmament purposes; devaluation was blocked by Hitler for political and symbolic reasons. As a result, Germany's ability to import food was greatly lessened, and a harsh winter in 1935/36 brought on a crisis over food imports, followed in the spring and summer by shortages of raw materials imports.[38]

The goal of these domestic and foreign economic policies was the development of Germany in preparation for the military conquest of *Lebensraum* in the east. Hitler first had to secure his position against other possible enemies before moving to attain his ultimate goal, the conquest of land from the Soviet Union. This expansion was to relieve tensions within Germany by creating areas for increased agriculture; but the policies of preparation were raising the very tensions expansion was meant to relieve.

First, lacking strong armed forces, Hitler tried expansion by aiding internal disruption of bordering countries. Efforts to retake Danzig and Memel and to effect the *Anschluss* with Austria in 1933 and 1934 failed. Although Germany made threatening gestures, these were not backed by force, for its military was not yet rebuilt. Rearmament programs were already well under way, though. The navy began building up after 1934, although this was not expanded to cover an arms race with Britain until 1938. The air force, outlawed by the Versailles treaty, not only started to rebuild after 1934 but also began secret aerial reconnaissance of other countries. In fact, General Goering had told Luftwaffe generals in December 1936, "We already find ourselves at war. Only the shooting hasn't started."[39]

Hitler's foreign policy could move from bluff to the actual exercise of force once rearmament had begun. In March 1938, German troops moved into Austria. In October 1938, German forces seized the Sudetenland from Czechoslovakia, and in March 1939, troops moved into the rest of that country. Memel, along the border of eastern Prussia and Lithuania, was seized in March 1939. All these actions were moves to either reclaim parts of the prewar

38. Ibid., pp. 348–349.
39. Ibid., pp. 176–177, 355.

German state or claim bordering German-speaking areas; as such, other states grudgingly accepted these actions. After these latent aggressions however, actual attacks on other countries were undertaken.

To carry out the expansion of Germany, Hitler chose an offensive strategy that was supremely designed for the task he foresaw: the accumulation of territory without placing the true rigors of war on the domestic population. Such a strategy of knocking out opponents before total mobilization of resources could be effected (blitzkrieg, or "lightning war") was developed within the German military. Although some members of the military (most notably Gen. Georg Thomas, of the military-economic planning staff) argued for total economic mobilization and preparation for a war of attrition (similar to the struggle of World War I), Hitler ignored these recommendations.[40] Nazi Germany was now prepared to begin a war of challenge.

The Rise of Japan as an Expansionary Challenger

At the same time Germany was set to begin wars to expand a closed economic system, another political challenger to the liberal subsystem was emerging elsewhere. Japan's experiences since 1900 had pushed that country toward economic closure and territorial expansion.

Japan came out of World War I as a country just beginning to develop a democratic tradition, militarily growing in power, and increasing in capital richness. Although its government had the appearance of a democracy, whether political power was actually invested in republican institutions is an arguable point;[41] given the other factors in this model, Japan was either an ambivalent power (moving toward challenge) or a supporter (moving toward economic challenge). Whereas the nature of Japan's political system can be debated, the direction of economic changes was apparent. Gross domestic capital formation averaged 16.1 percent between 1887 and 1940, and the growth pattern included dramatic spurts during World War I and the 1930s. Capital formation peaked at the end of that decade. By basically sitting out World War I, Japan had been able to make gains in international trade, which were then built on later. The time encompassing the war and several years just afterward

40. Ibid., pp. 349–351.
41. Japan had adopted universal manhood suffrage in 1925, but real executive power remained with the cabinet and bureaucracies; see Edwin O. Reischauer, *Japan: The Story of a Nation* (New York: Knopf, 1981), pp. 170–171.

was the only period before 1930 when Japan exported large amounts of producers' durables.[42]

As evidence of the impact of wars of challenge on countries that are at most peripherally involved, consider World War I and Japan. The war led to a great displacement of normal trading and consumption patterns, which stimulated Japan's nascent capital-intensive industries. In the 1915–1920 period, the fastest growing sectors were machinery and tools, metals, and chemicals. Furthermore, the surge in domestic growth, coupled with a large current account surplus in the balance of payments, resulted in the accumulation of vast foreign reserves, so that Japan went from a position of international indebtedness in 1913 to a period of surplus in 1919.[43]

All these factors meant increasing capital accumulation in Japan. Whereas 74 percent of the capital stock had been in the primary sector in 1868, capital stock in this sector amounted to only 17 percent of the total by 1941. Heavy industry's share of total output by value increased from 16.7 percent in 1885 to 21 percent in 1910, 32.8 percent in 1930, and 58.8 percent in 1940. After World War I, Japan began producing electrical machinery, ships, rayon, and aircraft—all high-technology, capital-intensive industries.[44]

World War I had come unexpectedly, but Japanese producers were quick to increase exports to areas where foreign producers were no longer meeting demand. These increased exports raised domestic income and therefore stimulated domestic demand. When this demand was not met, inflation emerged; since prices grew faster than wages, profits increased, which made for a boom distorted in the favor of capital income, which supported greater investment in heavy industries. This investment ended when wholesale prices collapsed after the war (in 1920), to which the heavy industries responded by forming cartels.[45] In this way, the war and its aftermath led to concentration in many sectors.

The 1920s were difficult times for the Japanese economy, because it was a period of continued deflation; only after devaluing the yen in the 1930s would

---

42. Henry Rosovsky, *Capital Formation in Japan, 1868–1940* (New York: Free Press of Glencoe, 1961), pp. 8, 11.

43. Takafusa Nakamura, *Economic Growth in Prewar Japan* (New Haven: Yale University Press, 1981; Japanese original, 1971), p. 144; Hugh T. Patrick, "The Economic Muddle of the 1920's," in *Dilemmas of Growth in Prewar Japan*, ed. James W. Morley (Princeton: Princeton University Press, 1971), p. 226.

44. Nakamura, *Economic Growth in Prewar Japan*, pp. 11, 23 (tab. 1.15); also see his "The Japanese Economy in the Interwar Period: A Brief Summary," in *Japan and World Depression: Then and Now*, ed. Ronald Dore and Radha Sinha (London: Macmillan, 1987), pp. 58–59.

45. Nakamura, *Economic Growth in Prewar Japan*, pp. 153, 224–231.

Japan rebound. Japan had joined the gold standard in 1897, but the growth in the world gold supply, as well as increases in government spending in the Russo-Japanese War and World War I, meant that Japan had known inflation for more than two decades before the 1920s. The deflation of the 1920s caught all but the most conservatively managed companies unprepared. Furthermore, the ability to finance activity within firms was important in this time of rising real interest rates. These factors combined to give the *zaibatsu* (conglomerates) tremendous advantages over other firms. The *zaibatsu*, or members of *zaibatsu* groups, became central parties to many of the cartels that formed after the 1920s. Cartelization was not pervasive until the Great Depression. Of the major cartels existing in 1932, forty-eight had been formed between 1930 and 1932, twelve between 1927 and 1929, twelve between 1914 and 1926, and only seven before 1914.[46]

The trends of concentration and capital accumulation begun during World War I continued after the war. By the late 1920s, Japan actually caught up with the advanced countries in technology in the capital-intensive sectors.[47] These changes in Japan's capital-labor ratio and product mix should have led to changes in Japanese tariffs. Japan had protected nascent capital-intensive industries with tariffs in 1920. In 1926 this position was changed, in that industries remained protected, but raw materials were now allowed in free of duty, and luxuries had high tariffs placed on them.[48] Capital accumulation did not overturn protection; instead, the gap between capital's relative returns and the relative returns capital would have received in the absence of protection increased.

The Great Depression and Japan's Response

In the face of continued deflation and contracting world markets, the Japanese government took an interesting stand. Some of this was the result of unfortunate timing. The government that came to power in 1929 adopted harsh fiscal and financial policies to get Japan back on the gold standard, thereby setting Japan on a deeper deflationary trajectory *before* the world depression began. When the depression came, it manifested itself in Japan as a collapse of prices rather than a decline in production. Although the depression did shave a few points off the volume of Japanese exports, it was the fall in

46. Nakamura, "Japanese Economy," pp. 55–57; Nakamura, *Economic Growth in Prewar Japan*, p. 202.

47. Nakamura, *Economic Growth in Prewar Japan*, p. 76.

48. Patrick, "Economic Muddle," pp. 237–238.

prices of roughly 40 percent for these exports which hurt the Japanese economy most. The prices of rice, silk, and other agricultural products were especially hard hit.[49]

In response to the Great Depression, Finance Minister Takahashi increased government expenditures (especially in the military's budget and relief for farming villages). Military expenditure between 1929 and 1931 was ¥460 million, went to ¥830 million between 1932 and 1934, and would grow to even higher levels after the military's role in the cabinet became predominant. Compared to the fiscal expansion, private investment was somewhat small, constituting only 8 percent of the gross national product in 1932 and less than 12 percent in 1936.[50]

After abandoning the gold standard, the government used various monetary policies, including a wide range of exchange controls, to follow fiscal expansion at home (insulated from the world economy) and still stimulate exports by depreciating the yen. In fact, Finance Minister Takahashi devalued the yen some 40 percent.[51] Other market interventions followed. Domestic prices of staples such as rice and silk were supported by the government, and price-fixing and output-restricting cartels were not only accepted but made compulsory in several industries between 1931 and 1934.[52] This period clearly shows the increasing employment of state-sanctioned rents in the Japanese economy. Again, as in the case of Nazi Germany, the state was key in intiating the arrangements.

Early attempts at autarchy had mixed results. Between 1929 and 1936, Japan reduced its imports of finished products, substituting raw materials (such as wool and natural rubber) and semifinished goods for intermediate use (such as ginned cotton and steel) instead. But at the same time, Japan's need for metal, machinery, and petroleum imports in the later 1930s was balanced out only by the ability of her shipping sector to earn foreign currency.[53] When the ability of these capital service sectors to earn high returns was threatened by competition, Japan began to look for captive markets. It is indeed ironic that Japan chose autarchy at the very time its international economic perfor-

49. Nakamura, "Japanese Economy," pp. 59–62; Nakamura, *Economic Growth in Prewar Japan*, p. 236.

50. Nakamura, *Economic Growth in Prewar Japan*, pp. 236, 238, 244.

51. Ibid., pp. 232–233. See also Michael A. Barnhart, *Japan Prepares for Total War: The Search for Economic Security, 1919–1941* (Ithaca: Cornell University Press, 1987), p. 66; Nakamura, "Japanese Economy," p. 62.

52. Martin Bronfenbrenner, "Japan and Two World Economic Depressions," in *Japan and World Depression*, ed. Dore and Sinha, p. 36.

53. Nakamura, *Economic Growth in Prewar Japan*, pp. 255–261.

mance was on the rise—which suggests that the move toward autarchy resulted from changes on the domestic political scene.[54]

Political Changes within Japan and the Desire to Expand

In terms of domestic political system, Japan had known true two-party parliamentary government only from 1918 to 1932. Although the constitution of 1889 proclaimed the emperor as sacred and inviolable, his political role was largely symbolic. In fact, Emperor Hirohito criticized the military's early expansionism and appears to have been against the alliance with Germany and against war with the Western countries.[55] His views did not determine policy. Decision-making power did not reside with the emperor, nor in the Diet, but in the cabinet. Cabinet decisions normally could not be blocked by the Diet.

By the early 1930s, assassination and terror were used to manipulate the cabinet. Violent acts became commonplace in Japanese politics. In March 1931 there was an aborted coup. After this failed, sympathetic elements of the army staged the Manchurian incident at Mukden in September, hoping to instigate reforms at home through their actions abroad. In October there was an aborted plot to bomb a cabinet meeting. In early 1932 former finance minister Inoue and general manager of the Mitsui *zaibatsu* Takuma Dan were assassinated; Prime Minister Inukai was assassinated in May that same year.[56] Some scholars mark this period of violence as the end of democracy in Japan.

After this violence, the army's role in politics increased. In February 1936, units of the army instigated a full-scale revolt, killing Finance Minister Takahashi and narrowly failing to assassinate Prime Minister Okada. After this rebellion was successfully put down, the military, under the leadership of a different group, assumed a predominant role in the cabinet. The 1936 coup attempt was made by a faction of radical conservatives; its failure led to the ascendance of a faction that based its power on the central command organs of the army. The dominant position taken by the military in the cabinet in 1936 clearly establishes the end of representative government in Japan.[57] After this

54. Patrick, "Economic Muddle," p. 262, specifically blames the failure of parliamentary democracy.

55. Kentaro Hayashi, "Japan and Germany in the Interwar Period," in *Dilemmas of Growth,* ed. Morley, pp. 462, 465, 478.

56. James B. Crowley, *Japan's Quest for Autonomy, 1930–1938* (Princeton: Princeton University Press, 1966), p. 95; Nakamura, *Economic Growth in Prewar Japan,* p. 232.

57. Nakamura, *Economic Growth in Prewar Japan,* p. 232. Also, Hayashi, "Japan and Germany," p. 476. Reischauer dates the end of Japanese democracy at 1932; see his *Japan: The Story of a Nation.*

change in regime type, Japan embarked on policies of expansion and challenge.

At almost the same time, successful application of deficit-spending policies stimulated an economic recovery from the Great Depression and increased capital accumulation. As further evidence of capital accumulation in the 1930s, average yearly interest rates fell fairly steadily from 10.1 percent in 1920 to 7.8 percent in 1931, climbed back up to 8.1 percent in 1932, then continued to fall smoothly to 6.5 percent in 1937. Annual interest rates on the Bank of Japan's year-end discount rate on commercial bills went from 6.6 percent in 1931 to 3.3 percent from 1935 through 1938. National bond yields fell from 5.0 percent in 1929 to 4.0 percent in 1938.[58]

By 1936 at the latest, these increases in Japan's capital abundance and the end of civilian government suggest, in terms of the model, that Japan should have become an expansive challenger. The tensions in Japan's domestic and international policies mirror those already described for Germany at this time. Capital-intensive sectors' relative returns had to be supported through continued rents, enforced via trade controls. In the late 1930s, Japan had a trade surplus within the yen bloc due to exports of capital-intensive goods but was running a deficit of some ¥200–400 million per year with the rest of the world. By March 1937, the Bank of Japan was forced to export gold to balance out this trade.[59]

Before 1936, friction between Japan and the liberal subsystem had already begun to develop. In December 1934, Japan dropped its obligations on arms limits under the Washington Naval Treaty. In January 1936, Japan withdrew its delegation from the London Naval Conference.[60] Japanese policymakers (and particularly the Japanese military) saw their country's only hopes for continued economic growth in military expansion and were therefore not willing to have limits imposed on the size of the military.

The area initially targeted for Japanese expansion was the Asian mainland. In April 1934, Japan's government announced its China policy in the Amau statement: Japan would be solely responsible for the maintenance of peace and order in East Asia, China should develop itself without the interference of outside powers, and any attempts by outside powers to create spheres of influence would be resisted by the Japanese. These ideas were elaborated further by

---

58. Nakamura, *Economic Growth in Prewar Japan*, pp. 206 (tab. 7.6), 242 (tab. 9.6).

59. Ibid., pp. 257–263.

60. Masamichi Royama, *Foreign Policy of Japan: 1914–1939* (Westport, Conn.: Greenwood Press, 1973; reprint of 1941 original, by the Japanese Council, Institute of Pacific Relations, Tokyo), pp. 136–137.

Prince Konoe's outline for a "New Order in East Asia," in November 1938.[61] In effect, China was to be set aside for Japan's economic domination.

To pursue this continental expansion, the general headquarters of the army had issued a set of conditions for its participation in any new cabinet in January 1937. These demands included "full provision for armaments and equipment," "creation of an aviation industry within five years that will surpass the world standard," and "the creation of a self-sufficient economy in the area of Japan and Manchuria by 1941, to secure a base for the prosecution of war."[62] In the minds of the military, the need for expansion of the Japanese political economy was so apparent that expansion as soon as possible was required to ensure the option to pursue expansion later; frustrations with the collapse of trade earlier made these needs urgent. Later in 1937, Japan began full-scale war against China, and the military's needs grew accordingly. The overall government budget submitted for the fiscal year 1937 was ¥3.0 billion, with ¥1.4 billion allocated for the military (an increase of ¥730 million over the previous year).[63]

Great State Control of the Japanese Economy

The war also justified a dramatic increase in state control of economic activity after 1937. The Cabinet Planning Office, staffed by military personnel, took over much of the Finance Ministry's activities. The Temporary Funds Adjustment Law and Temporary Import-Export Grading Measures Law (both passed in 1937) controlled domestic investment and trade. Implementation of the Military Industrial Mobilization Law of 1918 (first applied in 1937) and the National General Mobilization Law (passed in 1938) allowed the military to take direct control of industries. The earlier Foreign Exchange Control Law (of 1932) and Capital Flight Prevention Law (also of 1932) prevented the free movement of capital out of the country. More direct influence over firms was achieved through a whole series of laws enacted in the Seventy-first and Seventy-second Diets, which gave the government precise control over trade.[64]

The logic of these controls has been presented as a complicated set of six related propositions. (1) Military investment was desired, so funds had to be channeled to select industries. (2) Similarly, military investment required cer-

---

61. Ibid., p. 134; Immanuel C. Hsü, *The Rise of Modern China*, 3d ed. (New York: Oxford University Press, 1983), p. 585.
62. Nakamura, *Economic Growth in Prewar Japan*, p. 272.
63. Ibid., p. 266.
64. Reischauer, *Japan*, p. 198; Nakamura, *Economic Growth in Prewar Japan*, pp. 288–289; Barnhart, *Japan Prepares for Total War*, pp. 94–96.

tain imports, which were also given preference over other imports, which had to be paid for with hard currency earned through exports and services or gold. (3) To operate the light industries that made up exports, further imports of raw materials were required. (4) This placed a squeeze on private consumption of imports, so price controls were required to prevent problems with the balance of payments. (5) This in turn required controls on the distribution of goods, and (6) labor had to be kept in line to secure steady production. This entire set of policies could not be executed simultaneously. In August 1939, Japan began stockpiling strategic resources, but the Bank of Japan ran out of gold reserves in 1940, making payment for further imports extremely difficult. This problem was heightened after Britain, the Netherlands, and the United States froze Japanese assets in July 1941.[65]

In the face of these international problems and growing domestic economic tension, the state further centralized its position versus other domestic actors. Control over wages and the allocation of labor was achieved with the issuance of the National General Mobilization Law in June 1938. Under the same law, companies could be forced into cartels. In the summer of 1939, rice production, mineral extraction, and shipping were unified into cartels by acts of the Diet. In June 1940, Prince Konoe formed a new cabinet, signaling the complete end of party politics, and the army began to rule Japan through the bureaucracy.[66] Through command (and force if necessary) the military would direct Japan's economic growth and political expansion.

The military's viewpoint was consistently that peaceful economic expansion had failed in the 1920s and that, if Japan was to continue growing, force would have to be used to capture trading partners.[67] But a deep split within the military emerged over the direction of expansion. Since the army viewed China and Manuchuria as the main area containing the raw materials necessary to carry out war, it saw the war in China as the central thrust of expansion and the Soviet Union as the main international threat. The navy viewed the resources of Southeast Asia, particularly the oil of the Dutch East Indies, as the necessary ingredients for successful war and perceived its principal enemies as the American and British fleets. To satisfy the desires of both the army and the navy, Japan would attack in both directions and bring on a war it could not win.[68]

65. Nakamura, *Economic Growth in Prewar Japan*, pp. 290–293.
66. Barnhart, *Japan Prepares for Total War*, pp. 105–106, 110–111, 139; Hayashi, "Japan and Germany," pp. 477–478.
67. Akira Iriye, "The Failure of Military Expansionism," in *Dilemmas of Growth*, ed. Morley, p. 107.
68. Ibid., p. 125. Also, Crowley, *Japan's Quest for Autonomy*, p. 391.

As in the case of Nazi Germany, the domestic process argument emphasizes the role of the state in initiating and establishing policies granting rents to the capital-intensive sectors. Although oligopolization of the economy increased after 1931, the *zaibatsu* that had previously exercised a strong political voice actually lost their particular advantages in economics and consequently could no longer make any special political claims. In its exploitation of the resource-rich areas of China under its control, the state actually created "new *zaibatsu*."[69] Instead of the old *zaibatsu* bargaining with the state, the state itself proposed policies of challenge.

World War II as the Most Recent War of Challenge

In the 1930s, after the United States and Britain both failed to provide leadership to the liberal subsystem, two expansionary challengers appeared. In both the German and Japanese cases, capital abundance in a powerful country created the driving impulse behind expansion and challenge. Each had begun similar expansionary policies in the 1930s: Germany had taken Austria and Czechoslovakia before the wider war broke out in 1939, and Japan had taken Manchuria and been involved in armed conflict with China since 1937.

Alliances in World War II

Likewise, Italy had embarked on expansionary policies in the early 1930s in Africa. Italy was an ambivalent power—capital-poor with an autocratic state and growing in power. As an ambivalent power, it sought expansion by aligning with Germany. Italy and Germany had signed a pact recognizing their common political and economic interests in October 1936. This relationship was expanded into a formal military alliance in May 1938 with the Pact of Steel. Germany and Japan moved together with the signing of the Anti-Comintern Pact of 1935. This relationship was extended to cover a defensive alliance against non-European powers with the Tripartite Pact of September 1940. The three major powers of Germany, Japan, and Italy comprised the challenging coalition.

One other autocratic major power existed. The Soviet Union was an ambivalent power—capital-poor, with an autocratic state and growing international power. The Soviet Union had closed itself off from the world's economy during the 1920s. As an ambivalent power, it had no interest in supporting the

69. Nakamura, *Economic Growth in Prewar Japan*, pp. 251–252; Reischauer, *Japan*, p. 199.

open subsystem; since it was also cut off from trade, it saw little to gain from alliance with a liberal leader. Transformation of the domestic society plus the hope of autarchy based on a continental economy were more attractive than liberal international links. On the other hand, alliance with the challengers might provide the opportunity for expansion.

The real danger for the Soviets in such a plan was that both Japan and Germany had none too secret designs on expanding at the Soviet Union's expense. All the same, the USSR signed a nonaggression pact with Germany and, though not acting in direct alliance, took the opportunity provided by Germany's invasion of Poland to seize parts of that country as well as the Baltic republics and part of Romania and later attacked Finland. All these acts are consistent with the Soviet Union's position as a bandwagoning ambivalent power.

Only the major powers with republican states stood against the challengers. Britain, the recently dethroned liberal leader, and the United States, the ascending leader, were the two most powerful countries in this group. France was democratic but not as capital-abundant as before. It still had a large military establishment, so France would have been a supporter of a liberal leader had one clearly stepped forward and acted responsibly. In the face of the rising expansionary powers, France and Britain maintained an alliance, but the United States could not be induced into joining this coalition.

When Germany attacked Poland in 1939, the most recent war of challenge began. By this attack, Germany went to war against Britain and France. After seizing Poland, Germany assaulted Denmark and Norway so as to preempt possible flanking movements by the USSR and to ensure the continued supply of Swedish iron ore, which was delivered to Germany via Norwegian ports.[70]

Following a true bandwagoning strategy, the Soviet Union tried to stay out of the war until a favorite appeared. After taking part in the division of Poland, the Soviet Union hoped that Germany would be satisfied with its conquests. British leaders, unsure of Soviet aims and seeing German expansion eastward, thought it best to wait to see if the Germans would attack the USSR. Britain did little to engage the Soviets in a defensive alliance.

Hitler knew that a two-front war, and especially a war of attrition, would be difficult for Germany to win. He therefore hoped to settle his defensive arrangements in the north, south, and west before attacking east. Hitler realized the advantages for the British and French in fighting a war of attrition. He also knew that these opponents would maintain a defensive posture in pursuit

70. Rich, *Hitler's War Aims*, chap. 13.

of this strategy, thus allowing him to concentrate German offensive forces in the east. To lull the British and French leaders into the belief that their estimations of the situation were correct, Hitler had not only the army but also the air force and navy take unoffensive positions versus the western powers in the first months of the war. In this way, German forces did not provoke the Allies out of their defensive posture.

After successfully moving into Poland and securing the Scandinavian flank, Hitler launched a blitzkrieg through the Netherlands and Belgium, decisively defeating the armies of France and Britain in 1940. Germany was now dominant on the continent of Europe. For a time, as in the Napoleonic Wars, Britain stood alone against the challenger. But without a strong navy to carry out an invasion, Hitler was unable to defeat Britain. Instead, German energies were refocused in the east, where they launched a massive assault on the Soviet Union in June 1941.

The only other major power not involved in the war by this time was the United States. As in World War I, the United States had interests in preserving an open international subsystem, but it was not bent on coming to the rescue of its prime economic competitors. As in World War I, the expansionary challenger's actions began to damage the international economy. Even before the attack on Pearl Harbor, the threat to the subsystem and American interests became clear.

Germany's submarine warfare threatened international trade. As this threat grew, the United States began to pick up the slack in Britain's leadership duties in defense of liberal trade. First, forms of aid were given to Britain, such as the bases-for-destroyers deal of 1940: Britain got desperately needed war materiel and at the same time relieved itself of defense obligations in parts of the Western Hemisphere. The United States also agreed to finance much of Britain's war effort with the Lend-Lease Act of March 1941. Soon after, the United States agreed to allow British warships and merchantmen to seek repairs in American ports, whereas all Axis (and even Danish) ships would be seized. On April 4, 1941, the United States extended its Pan American security zone to cover the east coast of Greenland. In June, Axis assets in the United States were frozen. In July, the United States took over the defense of Iceland.

With the Atlantic Charter, signed by Winston Churchill and Franklin Roosevelt in August 1941, joint war aims were discussed. One major issue was the creation of a free-trade system after the war.[71] Clearly the United States would come into the war on the British side; it was only a matter of time before an

---

71. Frieden, *Banking on the World*, p. 61. Also, Rich, *Hitler's War Aims*, p. 244.

acceptably egregious incident occurred to justify entry. Steps leading toward involvement were already being taken. After the *Greer* incident (when an American destroyer and German U-boat fired on each other), Roosevelt issued orders for the U.S. Navy to shoot on sight any Axis ships in the American neutrality zone.[72]

In the Pacific, the United States also took on greater responsibilities. It began supplying weapons and ammunition to China, the British, and the Dutch in the Pacific. New airfields and bases were constructed. Joint staff talks were held between the Americans, British, and Dutch to discuss the defense of Southeast Asia. The American, British, and Dutch East Indies governments acted in concert on July 26, 1941, to announce economic reprisals for the Japanese seizure of southern Indochina. All these actions convinced the Japanese military commanders that any further military expansion in the Pacific would provoke war with the United States.[73] Japan's calculations on this subject led to America's entry into the war when the Japanese tried to strike a knockout blow against the U.S. Navy at Pearl Harbor. America's late entry into the war is ironic, since World War II should have been a challenge to American liberal leadership. It is less ironic considering the efforts the United States had made to bring about a confrontation with the Axis powers.

Attrition and Blitzkrieg: The Strategies of World War II

As the expansionary challengers, the Axis powers adopted bold offensive strategies. The early German plan was to defeat Britain and France in the west, consolidate this area as a strategic base, and then conquer lands in the east.[74] For Germany, the bold offensive strategy for territorial conquest was the blitzkrieg, which used highly mobile forces, concentrated for local advantages in numbers, to break through enemy defenses. Breakthroughs were exploited by spreading havoc behind enemy lines. This strategy required the development of new weapons and tactics for the use of armor, paratroops, and aerial support.

The Japanese used their navy, air forces, and highly mobile troops in a similar manner. The similarity between German and Japanese military strategies is often missed by those authors who argue that technology drives the choice of military strategy. Troops on bicycles (such as the Japanese used in Malaya) are not usually considered an example of a blitzkrieg, even though

72. Rich, *Hitler's War Aims*, pp. 244–245.
73. See Bruce M. Russett, "Pearl Harbor: Deterrence Theory and Decision Theory," *Journal of Peace Research* 4 (1967): 80–106.
74. Andreas Hillgruber, *Germany and the Two World Wars* (Cambridge: Harvard University Press, 1981), p. 82.

conceptually these troops were carrying out the same missions as German panzer divisions. I would argue that the choice of an offensive strategy was based on the goals of military action—and not driven by technological innovation.

The challengers used an offensive, bold strategy to conquer large areas. At the high point of expansion, Germany held Austria, Czechoslovakia, Poland, Denmark, Norway, the Netherlands, Belgium, France, Yugoslavia, Greece, and vast parts of Russia and was allied with Finland, Hungary, Bulgaria, Romania, and Italy (which held Albania and parts of North Africa). Japan held Korea, parts of China, Indochina, Malaya, the Philippines, Borneo, Sumatra, Burma, much of New Guinea, plus many of the South Pacific islands and was allied with Thailand.

The Allies hoped to achieve victory through attrition, as in World War I. Since Germany and Italy would probably attack simultaneously—and would probably have an advantage in troops and air power but be weaker in economic potential and seapower—the Allies' initial response to war was to assume a defensive posture out of which they could later shift as their economies were mobilized.[75] In the opening phase of the European war, these plans resulted in the "Sitzkrieg": neither side moved against the other until May 1940. After France fell to an attack around the flank of the Maginot line, Britain's attrition strategy reverted to naval blockade. It appears doubtful that such a blockade could actually have defeated Germany. German gains in eastern and southern Europe offset attempts to strangle its imports of raw materials. Once the Soviet Union and the United States entered the war, though, the attrition strategy took on new forms.

Instead of emphasizing economic strangulation, or defeating the enemy's forces decisively in the field, destruction of the enemy's ability to prosecute war became the Anglo-American goal. Air power was used to destroy the economies of the Axis powers. At the same time, larger forces were brought to bear against Germany on the eastern front as Soviet armies engaged German forces, and resistance groups in occupied Europe tied down ever more German troops. Germany's military was slowly ground down. Anglo-American contributions were made in the forms of materiel, money, and guidance.

In European naval operations, Germany never had much of a chance to prosecute the war with surface ships. The only episodes were isolated runs by raiders such as the battleships *Graf Spee* and *Bismarck*. As in World War I, Germany's navy focused its efforts on submarine warfare.

The Japanese made their gamble for control of the Pacific with the attack

75. Ibid., p. 71.

on Pearl Harbor. The Japanese naval command had decided that America would not stand by if Japan attacked British possessions in the Far East; British and American military and economic interests there were seen as inseparable.[76] Fighting one would require fighting both. The attack on Pearl Harbor was intended to tip the balance of naval power in Japan's favor. After gaining the initial advantage, Japan could then expand into Southwest Asia.

The Battle of Midway was Japan's attempt to force a showdown between the naval surface fleets in which the temporary advantage gained from the Pearl Harbor attack could be solidified. In fact, the Pearl Harbor attack had failed to destroy any U.S. aircraft carriers, so the fleets that met at Midway were fairly evenly matched. The American victory, combined with the earlier defense of Australia in the Battle of the Coral Sea, stemmed the tide of Japanese expansion.

As the economic base for the attrition strategy, the United States was pivotal in arming the other powers in the liberal leader's coalition. Between March 1941 and June 1945, the United States extended $42 billion in goods and services to its allies through the Lend-Lease program.[77] As an indication of the importance of the American economy in the war effort, American-made weapons could be found around the world.

Despite some obvious exceptions such as Germany's eastern front, American troops were moving into many parts of the globe. War by attrition was used on land, on sea, and through the air. This strategy required the establishment of airbases, ports, and transport and storage facilities ringing the globe. The Americans' ability to deliver vast quantities of war materiel great distances and to arm not only themselves but also the Chinese, Soviet, and Commonwealth forces allowed the Allies to overwhelm Germany and Japan. Despite the Axis powers' early victories, the Allies pushed them back. Challenge by expansionary powers had once again been turned away.

The International System Emerges from World War II

When the war ended, the United States was in a position of unparalleled military strength. It had the largest and strongest navy and air force and also the single greatest weapon—the atomic bomb. Alone among the major powers, America's political institutions and domestic economy were intact. Economically, the early challenge to American liberal leadership concentrated capital in the United States, not least by destroying capital elsewhere.

For Britain, the war effort required more liquidation of international assets

76. Ibid., p. 91.
77. Hathaway, "1933–1945: Economic Diplomacy," p. 314.

and further imports of capital in the form of war loans. Whereas in World War I 15 percent of Britain's total foreign assets were sold off, in World War II the figure was almost twice as high, at 28 percent.[78] The British state could no longer justify defending the liberal international subsystem, or even defending its empire for that matter. The postwar period became one of withdrawal, except for some minor gasps as in the Suez in 1956. Likewise, France, though on the winning side, ended the war a broken military power and less capital-rich than before. Both countries remained democratic and would be supporters of or peaceful economic challengers to American liberal leadership in the postwar period.

Germany's military establishment was destroyed, and that country was divided to prevent it from recovering military strength. It was split into democratic and nondemocratic zones—the former a supporter of, the latter ambivalent to, American liberal leadership. The German economy was virtually destroyed too. In many ways, the Japanese situation paralleled that of Germany, except that the United States alone rebuilt Japan. The war destroyed Japan's military forces and economy, and its government was refashioned by the occupation forces. As in the Western zone in Germany, a democratic government was established. Postwar Japan was weak, capital-poor, and democratic—another supporter of American leadership.

Of the major powers to survive the war, only the Soviet Union was still a autocratic state, and therefore it was not a supporter of the American-led liberal subsystem. Only the Soviet Union could possibly rival the United States militarily, although the Americans were much stronger on the seas and in the air. The Soviet Union was far behind the United States economically, especially in relative capital abundance. Therefore in the immediate postwar period, it should have been ambivalent to American leadership of a liberal subsystem.

In the new liberal international system after World War II, the United States was willing to accept leadership. No other country could have possibly led, so when problems emerged in the postwar reconstruction there was no doubt about undertaking responsibilities. Moreover, there were several supporters of American leadership, with only one major ambivalent power in the system. The obstacles to liberal leadership were especially low, and the incentives high—one reason the American assumption of liberal leadership in the postwar period was so definite.

78. Deane and Cole, *British Economic Growth*, p. 37; Lee, *British Economy since 1700*, p. 232.

SIX

American International Liberal Leadership, 1945–1990s, and Beyond?

In 1945 the United States had both the domestic interests and the international capabilities to act as a liberal leader. It was far and away the most capital-abundant country in the international system. Political competition in democratic institutions allowed these economic interests to be heard. My important task in this chapter is not to argue that America was a liberal leader after World War II; that is well documented elsewhere. Instead, in this chapter I provide a brief overview of the establishment of American leadership in order to locate the United States in its present situation and identify the sorts of problems and opportunities that country now faces.

The Early Years of American Liberal Leadership

The domestic process argument for a prospective liberal leader has the capital-intensive sectors appealing to the state for help in expanding their activities internationally. After World War II, this appeal did not have to be made: on the one hand, the economic penetration took place as part of the war effort; on the other hand, the state had already made a great military commitment to defend the open international subsystem and had this military force in position around the globe. Unlike the post–World War I period, there were no other possible liberal leaders, so American decision makers realized that they alone would have to bear the burden of leadership. Domestically, the shift to liberal leadership was not opposed in its initial phase because labor could still be moved out of the labor-intensive sectors and into capital-intensive sectors. In the short run, labor in the United States would benefit from leading an economically liberal international subsystem, since the United States would be able to export more.

There was also little international opposition to American leadership. Other nation-states in the system were mostly supporters and therefore willing to follow American leadership, as illlustrated by their membership in international institutions such as the United Nations. The only exceptional major power, the Soviet Union, was ambivalent; it joined some but not all the international economic bodies constructed as part of America's open subsystem. Friction did arise between the United States and supporters of American liberal leadership because the United States took steps to break up their empires, but this friction did not override the fact that these states shared much more important interests with the United States.

Having learned from the mistakes of the 1920s, the United States took its leadership role seriously after international problems emerged. The U.S. government made massive loans to help rebuild and stabilize Europe, the most famous example being the Marshall Plan. Passed in 1948, the Marshall Plan sent $17 billion to Europe over a five-year period. This was only one of the steps taken to create a liberal subsystem. During the war, the United States and Britain had laid the foundations for international institutions to govern the open international economy the United States wished to create. The United Nations was perhaps the grandest of these institutions. Other specialized institutions were designed to provide technical expertise in certain areas of international intercourse.

To help provide for a stable international monetary system in the postwar world, the United States (again, after close negotiations with Britain) developed the International Monetary Fund (IMF) and the World Bank. The rules of the Bretton Woods System established fixed, stable exchange rates with currency convertible into gold. Stable currencies facilitated greater amounts of international trade. The Bretton Woods System also established the dollar as the key currency of international exchange and reserve. International liquidity was provided by the United States' balance of payments deficit. The Bretton Woods System facilitated the flow of American capital abroad.

The United States could now more directly stabilize the international economy. American capital, made available either directly from American private actors (such as multinational firms) or the U.S. government or via international institutions such as the IMF, helped stabilize the international economy by stabilizing the economies of other countries and then coordinating macroeconomic policies. Not only could international institutions such as the IMF and World Bank (IBRD) be used to generate stability, but the dollar itself could be manipulated through the U.S. government's domestic policy instruments to ensure international financial stability.

To encourage a free trading system, the United States engineered the General Agreement on Trade and Tariffs (GATT). GATT's rules emphasized non-discrimination in international trade and continual efforts to liberalize trade—that is, to free trade from noneconomic restrictions. GATT's initial rules stressed three points: (1) nondiscrimination and multilateralism, as best indicated by the use of most-favored-nation trade reduction treaties, (2) trade expansion through lower trade barriers, and (3) unconditional reciprocity in trade negotiations. By encouraging many nations to join GATT, the United States successfully lowered tariffs across a broad range of goods in trade between many countries.

The American system of liberal leadership was built on the base of a monetary regime. International trade was liberalized and maintained by the GATT arrangements. American leadership was pivotal in the establishment of this postwar international economy; American threats and American promises were necessary to get the wide international membership actually achieved. At the same time, the exceptions to the rules within the system follow the pattern we would expect: ambivalent powers and supporters worked to get exceptions to the rules to protect their capital-intensive sectors. Later, the United States itself began to bend the rules of the subsystem in order to protect its labor-intensive sectors.

Liberal Leadership and Bipolarity

One of the obvious advantages of the liberal leadership model developed in this book is its ability to deal with the bipolarity of the international system after World War II. Since many models of hegemony are structural and based purely on the systemic distribution of power, they cannot possibly explain hegemony and bipolarity simultaneously. In the model presented here, the United States has been the leader of a liberal economic subsystem. As a very part of this leadership, the United States has defined the Soviet Union as the likely challenger to the liberal international economy and therefore defined the international system in terms of bipolarity.

The bipolar division of the world is an indirect outcome of the distribution of the various types of country in the system, which was reinforced by ideological rivalry. Since almost all other major powers in the postwar system had republican states, all accepted the rules of the American-led system. Only the Soviet Union was not an active supporter of American leadership; but this model depicts the postwar USSR as ambivalent toward the liberal leader and the open subsystem. The same holds true for Soviet satellites and the People's Republic of China.

As ambivalent powers, these states should oppose the rules of the open international political economy, but they should also find economic relations with the United States attractive. Rather than portraying a world divided by deep ideological conflicts, the argument I develop in this book paints a picture of a Soviet Union that could have been accommodated into the American-led liberal trading system.[1] If the Soviet Union was ambivalent to American leadership rather than a challenger, why did the postwar system devolve into the Cold War? The United States quickly perceived the threat the Soviets could potentially pose to the open international subsystem, without realizing the potential of mutually beneficial relations between the two countries.

Just as Britain had perceived Russia as the principal threat in the nineteenth century, the United States focused on the USSR as the potential challenger to its own leadership. Just as Britain had brought together a wide alliance to block a minor Russian advance in the Crimea in 1854, the United States brought together a broad alliance to stop Communist expansion in Korea in 1950. In both cases, the liberal leader treated the attempted expansion as the beginning of a war of challenge. Despite the large number of participating countries in these instances, the wars failed to spread or reach high levels of intensity. Both remained limited affairs, reflecting the lack of intensity of interests at stake. Despite the existing alliances, wars of challenge did not occur. And just as Britain feared possible Russian expansion and domino effects in Asia, and therefore entered a long and bloody war in Afghanistan to save India, the United States fought a bloody war in Indochina to stop dominos from falling in Asia.

Britain's eventual solution to the Russian threat was the creation of several alliances to guard Britain's far-flung interests. Most important of these was the alliance with Japan. Britain supported this ambivalent power with technology and military assistance in order to block Russian expansion in Asia. In the long run, this proved to be a mistake, for it was Japan that became the expansionary challenger in the 1930s, and it was Japan that nearly swept Britain out of the Far East for good.

The United States has made some of the same mistakes. By stressing the potential for political challenge by an ambivalent power, it encouraged the economic and military development of *other* ambivalent powers that over the long run may be just as threatening. The U.S. policy of "containing" the Soviet Union led to a series of alliances ringing the globe. Outside the NATO alliance members, most members of these pacts were countries ambivalent

---

1. This model also fits comfortably with a tripolar model of the international system, with the shifting balancing of power driven by the U.S. ability to attract alternately Russia and China as potential allies through offers of trade or other economic relations.

toward American leadership of the liberal subsystem. These ambivalent powers either genuinely feared possible Soviet aggression or hoped to benefit economically from an alliance with America.

The U.S. policy of aiding authoritarian dictatorships in much of the Third World may prove to have been more dangerous to American interests in the long run, for several of these countries have greater ability to develop economically and accumulate capital at a faster pace than the states that were once the Soviet Union. The collapse of the Soviet Union exposed how weak most of that country's economy was and also illustrated the importance of domestic political institutions for international relations: despite the fact that power remains concentrated in the United States and the Commonwealth of Independent States, the rise of democratic institutions in what was once the USSR eased tensions dramatically and moved the countries' interests closer together.

Perhaps more menacing, by supporting the economic development of the People's Republic of China as a counter to Soviet military power the United States may have made a mistake parallel to Britain's when that country supported the rise of Japan at the end of the nineteenth century. The liberal leader must take care that a policy of active support for the economic development of an ambivalent power is tied to democratization. Otherwise the policy may backfire and create the very expansionary political challenge to liberal leadership that it is intended to prevent. Put bluntly, America's long-term position is best defended by the spread of republican institutions in the world. Developments in China show how far that country must come in order to earn greater economic and military assistance from the United States. The same standards should be applied to America's relations with other major powers.

This linkage between assistance in economic development and democratization should continue to be applied to American relations with the ex-Soviet states. The Soviet Union failed to develop into an expansionary challenger because it failed to develop economically. If these states dramatically alter their relative capital-labor ratio without installing stable representative government, thereby moving into the challenger category, their relations with the United States could change dramatically. Economic accommodation with them would no longer be possible. The United States can gain the most by aiding the economic development of the old Eastern bloc, but it must tie this help to greater democratization domestically.

The International System since World War II

Although the Soviet Union was not able to catch up to the United States economically, several other countries in the international system have been able to change their economic positions since World War II quite impressively. Because America successfully led a liberal subsystem, American capital diffused throughout the open international system, and freer trade extended economic gains to many participating countries. On the one hand, two peaceful, economic challengers have emerged; on the other, ambivalent powers have joined together to challenge the rules and principles of the open international subsystem.

Germany has developed into a capital-rich, potentially internationally powerful country with republican state institutions. Although still catching up in capital abundance through the 1950s and 1960s, West Germany was a strong supporter of American leadership. Once West Germany's capital abundance began to rival American capital abundance (in the 1970s and 1980s), West Germany became a serious economic challenger. The heightened economic competition between the United States and West Germany, combined with the limited efforts by West Germany to help stabilize the international economy, created some difficulties in German-American relations. Now a unified Germany stabilizes and supports the open subsystem as it acts as a regional leader in Europe. Through the European Economic Community and the European Monetary System, Germany stabilizes what may be the most economically significant region in the world. In this way Germany's regional leadership is building a base from which to compete peacefully with America's economic position.

Japan has also developed a stable democratic tradition and has grown capital-rich. Between 1982 and 1986, Japanese foreign assets trebled to $727 billion, and many of the world's largest financial institutions are Japanese.[2] Japan's role as a peaceful economic competitor has created international tensions: the American and European public has become particularly sensitive to Japanese imports and to the latest waves of Japanese foreign investment. The height of these tensions can be seen in the recent spate of books and articles dealing with Japanese investment in the United States and in the manner trade relations with Japan have been handled in American and European election campaigns.

Whereas Germany had to build up its military in response to the nearness of the potential Soviet threat, Japan has been better able to free ride on American defense. This has also played a part in the sensitivity Americans tend to have toward the Japanese economic competition: many Americans feel that

2. "The Moneymen's Pursuit of Money," *The Economist*, March 5, 1988, p. 83, noted that seven of the top ten banks were Japanese, though that figure has dropped to six in a more recent survey by that magazine (May 1992).

Japan's economy can outperform the American economy because the burdens of defending the open international economic system rest too heavily on American shoulders. Japan's slight role in the war against Iraq served to re-emphasize this point in the public's eyes.

Another dramatic shift in the postwar economy involves the less economically developed regions of the world. In the Third World, the end of the French and British empires created a large number of weak, capital-poor non-democracies. These Third World countries fall mostly into the category of weaker countries ambivalent to American liberal leadership. In general, they fit the model's expectations: most of them are political allies of the liberal leader, but they also happen to oppose the rules and principles of the open international economy.

Two illustrations of this ambivalence are the relationship of Third World countries with the IMF and the calls for the formation of the New International Economic Order (NIEO). These ambivalent countries seek capital and economic assistance from the IMF, but they always grumble about their relationship with that organization. Meanwhile, the IMF does its best to impose the international system's liberal rules on these countries. The Third World states argue over the terms of their relationship with the IMF, but they do not often seek to terminate that relationship.

The NIEO is a program for changing the international economy proposed by Third World countries. The NIEO reads like a list of grievances and demands, which includes greater transfers of capital to Third World countries in the form of aid, preferential treatment in trade negotiations, greater regulation of investment and technology transfers, and easier credit facilities through monetary reform. These demands underscore the goal of many Third World countries: to alter the open international subsystem radically. At the same time, many of the same countries have quite extensive and cordial relations with the United States, exactly as ambivalent countries would.[3]

A few Third World countries have successfully developed by integrating themselves in the liberal trading system led by the United States. The "Gang of Four," also known as the Asian Dragons or Tigers (Singapore, Hong Kong, Taiwan, and South Korea), have begun to accumulate capital and are now

3. One significant exception to this pattern is India, a large, capital-poor country with a state sensitive to domestic political competition. India should, on this model, be a supporter of American democracy; in fact, it has been a leader of the nonaligned movement and has developed strong ties to other countries besides the United States. This exception can be explained by the fact that the Indian economy is more closed, because of India's overall national development strategy, than the model presented here would expect. Thus India acts more like an ambivalent power than a supporter.

increasing their competition in capital-intensive goods and services. They have developed in a pattern similar to the Japanese, effectively grasping opportunities in international trade to their own benefit. Only recently, in 1988, has the United States stripped South Korea, Taiwan, Hong Kong, and Singapore of the concessions and exceptions given in the Generalized System of Preferences of the GATT.[4]

The Consequences of Relative American Economic Decline

After Japan and Europe recovered their economic positions in the 1960s, the first hints of relative American decline could be found. The signs of decline grew in the 1960s and blossomed in the 1970s. But economic and political decline are too often confused. Many people saw the beginning of America's relative economic decline as the end of liberal leadership. By the 1960s, American leadership of the liberal subsystem had successfully leveled out the distribution of capital among the economically advanced countries. Signs of this leveling can be seen in U.S. domestic problems as well as in the first strains on the open international subsystem. The problem of this period was the shift from the dollar shortage of the 1950s to the dollar glut of the 1960s.

As the model presented in this book would expect, labor-intensive sectors of the American economy were the first to fall from among the groups supporting a foreign economic policy of liberal leadership. The textile industries were some of the first to defect from the system. Textiles and the apparel industry were both labor intensive in the 1950s.[5] These groups got voluntary export restraints with Japan on the importation of textiles as early as 1957, and these were broadened in later agreements.

Protectionist appeals by other labor-intensive sectors were to follow. Orderly marketing agreements were established with Taiwan and Korea in 1976 for footwear. Eventually, sectors using a greater ratio of capital in production also cried for protection. Steel had the first voluntary export restraints with the European Economic Community and Japan established in 1969, the television industry received an orderly marketing agreement in 1977, and the automobile industry received protection via voluntary export restraints in 1981. But the picture drawn from evidence from a variety of sectors in the U.S. economy shows precisely the pattern predicted by the liberal leadership

4. *The Economist*, February 6, 1988, p. 61.
5. Vinod K. Aggarwal, Robert O. Keohane, and David B. Yoffie, "The Dynamics of Negotiated Protectionism," *American Political Science Review* 81 (June 1987): 353–354.

model: labor-intensive sectors received institutionalized protection while less labor-intensive sectors received only temporary protection and capital-intensive sectors received only sporadic protection.[6]

The evidence given by Vinod Aggarwal, Robert Keohane, and David Yoffie on these patterns of protection also confirms the expectations of this model concerning the sanctioning of rents when the state is sensitive to domestic political competition. In this case, the state is able to give consistent protection only to those industries clearly unable to compete internationally, so that these sectors do not benefit greatly—they merely survive. Protection that leads to profits creates the political pressures to remove that protection, so only protection that fails is acceptable politically. As they put it, in the United States, "protectionism's economic failures are often its political successes and vice versa."[7]

Internationally, the costs and benefits of America's leadership of the liberal subsystem were shifting to make the pursuit of leadership less attractive. Another major problem of the 1960s upsetting American leadership was the burgeoning defense burden, which was heightened by the war in Vietnam. Confrontations in the Third World, defense of Europe and Japan, as well as the overall arms race with the Soviet Union made the burdens of providing protection and order more expensive. As mentioned above, the successful exportation of capital turned into a problem. Since World War II the United States had exported capital in the form of dollars. Now there were too many dollars in the international system. By exporting so many dollars, international liquidity had been assured but further demand for the dollar was eroded.

By the time of Richard Nixon's administration (1968–1974), three crises had come to a head: (1) labor-intensive sectors of the American economy were increasingly dissatisfied with their situation, and now capital-intensive sectors were coming under foreign competition; (2) the currency was overvalued, which enabled capital services to continue to earn international profits but tied the state's hands in terms of adjusting the currency to encourage greater exports of manufactured goods; and (3) the state was having trouble making ends meet, both in meeting defense costs and in intervening in the international economy.

Nixon responded to each of these problems. With the currency problem, the "Nixon shocks" of August 1971 provided some alleviation by devaluing the dollar. Eventually, the dollar would be taken off the gold standard and the

6. Ibid.
7. Ibid. This clearly states their agreement with some of Robert Ekelund and Robert Tollison's positions on rent-seeking in at least one important republican state.

exchange rate allowed to float. By going off the fixed exchange rate, the United States solved the technical problem of currency valuation and was still able to maintain a form of leadership by being able to intervene (perhaps less effectively) in exchange markets. The labor-intensive sectors' problems were solved in an ad hoc manner, with increased use of voluntary export restraints, orderly market agreements, threats of retaliation, and so forth. The pattern that had already emerged was merely strengthened. By dealing with problems in an ad hoc manner, the United States tried to draw exceptions to the rules of the open international economy without undermining the overall principles.

The problem with the rising costs associated with leadership was confronted with policies such as Vietnamization and attempts to get other countries to pay their "fair share" for the defense and maintenance of order in the subsystem. Not only did the United States withdraw from Vietnam, but NATO countries were asked to contribute more for their own defense. Under the guidance of Secretary of State Henry Kissinger, Third World countries such as Iran and Saudi Arabia were militarily strengthened as regional allies, and overtures were made to China to arrange an alliance to balance Soviet military competition. The United States also began to take a harder look at accepting further international obligations.

None of these actions reversed the trend of relative economic decline in the 1970s. Stagflation, begun in the United States, spread through the international economy and gripped all the economically advanced countries. Inflation was no longer a tradeoff for employment. In the United States, capital was cheap but labor stayed expensive; the labor-intensive sectors remained uncompetitive. Capital accumulation here slowed, as it continued to flow to places where labor was cheap. There was reduced growth in the capital-labor ratio in the United States from 1973 to 1978. As expected, this slowdown in the growth of labor productivity did not affect all sectors. Capital-intensive sectors, and particularly capital services, continued to do well. Communication, finance, insurance, and real estate all improved productivity during the late 1970s.[8]

In the 1980s, Ronald Reagan's presidency marked America's return to a reinvigorated political role as liberal leader. Reagan's avowed goal was to make the United States the leader of the open international political economy again, but this renewed leadership came in a different form. For one thing, the

---

8. R. M. Marshall, "Factors Influencing Changes in Productivity," in *Economics in the Long View: Essays in Honour of W. W. Rostow*, Vol. 3: *Applications and Cases, Pt. 2*, ed. Charles P. Kindleberger and Guido di Tella (New York: New York University Press, 1982), pp. 85, 89–90.

United States was not shy about putting pressure on other states to increase their share of the defense burden for the subsystem. Even with some advances in this area, the Reagan administration still felt compelled to increase America's defense spending. To prevent problems of rising costs to the state yet maintain a large commitment to military might, Reagan cut back the state's domestic spending in other areas.

More specifically, on the domestic front, the Reagan administration stressed "supply-side" economics. What this really amounted to was a cut in real wages, making labor appear less expensive. Along similar lines, labor unions were attacked.

Cutting real wages was a more effective counter to the economic problems of relative economic decline than increased protection from international competition for several reasons. Reagan could squeeze real wages because capital-intensive sectors supported such a policy. Whereas protection for labor-intensive sectors undermined the principles and rules of the open international economy and invited retaliation by other states, squeezing real wages would not incur international repercussions. Reagan's rhetoric and foreign policy also helped undercut domestic opposition. But squeezing real wages can be successful only in the short term; the political backlash cannot be far off. The only real solution for the liberal leader's economic decline is to accept the changes and allow labor-intensive sectors to die but also to work continually to shift resources (both physical and human) into capital-intensive sectors. This continual shift can be achieved only if retraining, education, technological innovation, and research are stressed. Most of these measures for adapting to economic change remain largely ignored in the United States.

For the United States, there may be little to be learned from the earlier examples of liberal leaders in economic decline. The United States is in a very different situation. Only by beginning research with an abstract, deductive model could the differences be identified. A notable factor distinguishing the current situation from the earlier cases is the economic decline *before* an expansionary political challenger emerged. Whereas Britain had to face relative economic decline in a series of drawn out traumas beginning with the Climacteric of the 1870s after enjoying economic dominance for decades, America's economic decline came rather rapidly, primarily because the success of U.S. leadership ensured that American capital was rapidly diffused throughout the world. Britain's relative economic decline was then radically hastened by the German challenge culminating in World War I—a political problem the United States is quite unlikely to face in the near future. The Dutch lost the capability to maintain policies of leadership for the liberal subsystem before capital abundance in other countries matched their own. Because decline in relative power came before relative economic decline, the Netherlands' experience was the reverse of that the United States is now going through.

Yet at the heart of a liberal leader's relative economic decline there remain certain similarities and relevant lessons. The United States is trapped in a political and economic dynamic resulting in relative economic decline. To satisfy the capital-services sectors, the state continues to support high currency valuation, which reduces the international competitiveness of other sectors. Solutions for adapting the American economy to increased foreign competition are still few in number. At the same time, the state continues to bear an enormous defense burden, which is a financial drag on the rest of the economy. The biggest problem in American foreign policy remains how to relinquish the burdens of leadership as the benefits decline; the end of the Soviet Union may ease these costs, but the dangers from Third World problems spilling over into foreign policy remain. Reducing other government expenditure would enable the government to bear this large defense burden for a longer period but would create further domestic political problems.

Long-term plans must include other countries sharing part of the burdens of international leadership. Some movements toward multilateral leadership with the economic rivals within the liberal subsystem have been made. The Germans have partly responded, especially in their actions in the opening of the Eastern bloc. Through European monetary relations, Germany has done more to stabilize the European economy (at least until 1992). The Japanese have continued to free ride, although some changes in the overall trend are apparent, especially in the area of international finance, where Japan has recently asked for more responsibility in managing international affairs. The signals continue to be mixed, however. Prime Minister Noboru Takeshita said in Washington in February 1989, "No nation can substitute for the United States as the leader of the democracies around the world," telling President George Bush, "I look to you . . . for wise and firm leadership."[9] Later that year, in San Francisco, Takeshita's successor Toshiki Kaifu stated, "No country can replace the United States in its position and role as leader of the Free World."[10] But in August 1989, Tomomitsu Oba, a senior official at Japan's Ministry of Finance, queried this: "We had 100 years of Pax Britannica and 50 years of Pax Americana. What comes next? Pax Consortia!"[11] This is a possibility, but the inability or unwillingness of Japan to project political power has

9. Art Pine, "U.S. and Japan in Quiet but Critical Fight over Political and Economic Leadership," *Los Angeles Times*, February 26, 1989, pt. 1, p. 12.

10. Karl Schoenberger, "U.S. Still Global Leader, Japan Prime Minister Says," *Los Angeles Times*, August 31, 1989, pt. 1, p. 8.

11. Art Pine and Tom Redburn, "Clamor Increasing in U.S. for Trade War with Japan," *Los Angeles Times*, August 10, 1989, pt. 1, p. 1.

resurfaced with the long debates about Japanese forces becoming involved in crises such as the Gulf War or other U.N. peace-keeping operations in Asia.

The United States must also consider whether it really wants to relinquish its position of leadership. Leadership entails more than costs: the services that generate those costs were taken on because of the associated benefits. Although the relative gains from having an open international system have declined, they are far from nonexistent. And the United States still has the ability to negotiate over these concerns; as of yet, there are no political challengers. Without an obvious challenger, the chances of the United States maintaining leadership of the *expanding* liberal subsystem, sharing leadership with other powers, or at a minimum effecting a peaceful transition of leadership are high.

Evaluating the Liberal Leadership Model

In Chapter 1, I outlined several questions in the existing research agenda on hegemony and major wars. After presenting an alternative model and applying it to explain changes in the international system over the past three centuries, the time has come to compare the answers derived from this model with the answers given by other arguments and theories.

To begin with, we identify the leader of the liberal subsystem deductively. If liberal leadership is defined as a set of policies undertaken by a state to create, stabilize, and then maintain an open international economic subsystem, this model can predict not only which country will attempt to do this but also when, how, and with what degree of success. The model accounts not only for similarities between periods but also for differences. The combination of domestic interests and international power suggests when countries will attempt policies of liberal leadership; wider knowledge of the other states in the system is required to indicate whether the attempts at liberal leadership will be successful.

The historical record distinguishes three periods of at least partially successful liberal leadership as well as several periods of prospective liberal leadership. First, the Dutch led a liberal subsystem from 1648 until 1713, but this subsystem was limited in size because of the inability of the Dutch to open the economies of the other major powers. Britain failed in an attempt to establish a liberal subsystem in the 1780s but later successfully constructed one beginning in the 1840s and maintained it until 1914. In the 1920s, Britain and the United States acted loosely in concert to reconstruct a liberal subsystem, but the United States abandoned these efforts after the stock market crash in 1929. The United States then made an abortive attempt at liberal leadership in the late 1930s but only succeeded in building a liberal international economic subsystem after 1945.

How is the liberal leader's interest in free trade explained? The model explains this by arguing that capital abundance causes capital-intensive sectors to search for ways to extend the use of capital on the international market—an outcome that is expected only from capital-abundant countries with republican states, since capital in countries with more autocratic states has the option of capturing state-sanctioned rents. Moreover, this liberalizing policy is not truly free trade: low tariffs in all sectors are in place only during a transition between earlier policies that protect scarce capital and later policies that protect scarce labor as a country shifts from labor abundance to capital abundance. Liberal leaders are expected to have open trade in capital-intensive sectors, but to protect their labor-intensive sectors increasingly over time. Overall openness to trade may be prolonged, though, as capital-intensive sectors (and particularly capital-intensive services) remain competitive enough to offset the uncompetitiveness of labor-intensive sectors.

In the Dutch case, the capital-services sectors tried to open international trade, but in the international system of the 1600s the first steps toward freer trade were merely opening the oceans to free passage and ending outright prohibitions on trade. Investment by Dutchmen in other countries was not limited by the Dutch state but in fact encouraged. The Dutch economy was unilaterally opened to foreign economic competition to encourage and aid the entrepôt role of Dutch cities. Imports of raw materials stimulated industrial production; other traditionally labor-intensive sectors such as agriculture adjusted by becoming more capital-intensive.

In the British case, the first attempts at freeing trade were made in the 1780s. The unilateral lowering of British tariffs in the 1780s was an attempt to increase the use of British capital in the promotion of trade. The only real achievement in lowering other countries' duties was with France, in the 1786 Eden treaty. Not only was this limited success disrupted by the French revolutionary wars, but British interests in extending capital services were abated by the capital consumption of the Napoleonic Wars. Finally, Britain moved toward freer trade unilaterally in the 1840s, because protection for capital-intensive sectors was no longer needed (though agriculture retained some of its protection). Britain stuck with relatively free trade because the profits capital-intensive sectors thereby earned outweighed the losses in labor-intensive sectors. The state responded to the interests of capital-intensive sectors over the wishes of labor-intensive sectors. This situation ended when World War I undercut Britain's relative position and accentuated American capital abundance.

In the American case, an open trade stance was first assumed with the Underwood Tariff of 1913, when American capital was beginning to search for international applications. This trend toward freer trade was reversed after the Crash of 1929, as the political pressures developing from capital abundance were temporarily abated. These political developments reappeared in the late 1930s and finally came to the fore after World War II, when American capital would clearly gain from liberalizing trade.

How is the process of international regime creation and maintenance explained? In this model, international regimes are created when capital-intensive sectors of the liberal leader ask the state to provide the services of protection and order to the international economy, and the state then tries to carry out these services. The state works with other states; at the same time, the capital-intensive sectors within the leader make contact with economic actors in other countries.

In the case of the Dutch, the ability of the state to construct regimes depended on its ability to exercise both military and economic force. The Dutch fleet was used to punish pirates, to keep navigation of the oceans open, to impose peace on warring countries that upset Dutch trade, and to pressure other states into lowering economic barriers to trade. In regime creation, the greatest Dutch success was in establishing the basis for modern international law, and specifically in establishing the law of the sea. Dutch capital was pivotal in coordinating international trade; it was the link that allowed specialization in grain production in eastern Europe, that developed raw materials industries in Scandinavia, that integrated labor-intensive English cloth production into the international textiles production, and that provided for long-distance trade with Asia.

In the British case, the state acted to extend the economic reach of British capital by encouraging other states to join Britain's trading system and the gold standard, both by extending the incentives of trading with the large market of Britain's empire but also by using force when necessary. Within Europe, Britain was a key state involved in the spread of freer trade after 1860. British capital gained enormously through its extensive links to other countries via investment and capital services.

In the American case, the state not only acted unilaterally but also created many international institutions to install liberal rules in international economic affairs. The rules stressed freedom for the movement of capital and protection of international investment. At the same time, American capital became a significant economic factor in many countries around the globe in the form of American multinational corporations.

How is the liberal hegemon's relative decline explained? In this model, political (or military) decline is covered under the explanation of challenge. Relative economic decline is explained through the *success* of the liberal leader's capital-intensive sectors in exporting capital-intensive goods and services. The ability to achieve large exports of capital goods and services not only lessens the desire to export such goods over time but also allows capital to be accumulated elsewhere—which means that both absolute and relative capital abundance are eroded over time. The model expects this particular pattern of domestic support for policies of liberal leadership: initially, a consensus between capital-intensive and labor-intensive sectors supports leading international economic liberalization, as capital is made better off and labor makes short-run gains through trade specialization; then labor-intensive sectors fall out of this consensus because they come under international competition that lowers their returns relative to capital-intensive sectors; as capital becomes more diffuse in the international economy, more capital-intensive sectors come under international competition, so that in the long run only the most capital-intensive sectors remain competitive.

In the Dutch case, assets from labor-intensive sectors were moved into more capital-intensive forms of production for quite a long time. The war of challenge by Louis XIV occurred before relative Dutch economic decline had actually set in, and the war affected capital accumulation in other countries more strongly than in the Netherlands. Perversely, the war of challenge slowed Dutch economic decline by ending Dutch attempts at political leadership; the Dutch state could no longer muster the international power to maintain even a small open subsystem. Higher barriers between markets slowed the flow of Dutch capital. This undoubtedly extended the Netherlands' position as most capital-abundant nation in the international system.

In the British case, labor-intensive sectors were able to give up labor for more capital-intensive forms of production, most remarkably in the Industrial Revolution. Capital services were very successful, so that, even after competition in capital-intensive goods began in the last decades of the nineteenth century, capital services still earned enough to offset that competition. Labor-intensive sectors wished to change British policy back toward closure. Only after World War I were Britain's most competitive sectors (capital services) finally challenged by American economic competition.

In the American case, the rapid successful export of capital itself meant that the consensus behind policies of liberal leadership began falling apart less than two decades after that consensus was formed in World War II. The political strength of the United States enabled it to establish a large, relatively open subsystem rapidly, so its edge in capital abundance was short-lived. Labor-intensive sectors such as agriculture were always protected; textiles became one of the first manufacturing sectors to defect from the consensus, followed soon afterward by other labor-intensive sectors. By the 1990s ad hoc protection had been given to other sectors, so that the United States has taken up a somewhat confused stand in international trade talks: even as it seeks to liberalize trade in services, it justifies greater protection of its labor-intensive sectors.

Is this model dynamic? Can it deal with these questions in a consistent manner? Clearly, the model is designed to answer how things change with time, in order to predict how policies change. In the Dutch case, the model explains why interests in the pursuit of liberal leadership emerged and how these interests lasted longer than the state's ability to service them. In the British case, interests in liberalizing international economic relations first emerged in the 1780s, subsided, then reappeared in the 1840s and lasted until the 1930s (although dissipating in strength after World War I). In the American case, similar interests emerged after World War I, gained wide acceptance after World War II, and remain dominant today.

At the same time, the model also shows us much about the interests of other countries in participating in or resisting an international economic subsystem based on liberal principles and how these interests change over time. Although most states have some interests in participating in such an international system, the model can predict changes in interests. The most important question to be answered by detecting these changes is why some countries (and not others) challenge the liberal leader. Some countries can rise economically and militarily within the liberal subsystem without desiring to upset the leader's political position. The most obvious case is rise of the United States before World War I. Growing American military power was viewed by British military leaders almost with relief. If all rising powers have the same interests in leadership, how did the relationship between the United States and Britain emerge—with the United States even coming to Britain's aid in World War I? In the earlier Dutch case, England's position vis-à-vis the Dutch clearly vacillated in a manner that no other argument can explain with the accuracy or persuasiveness of this model.

George Modelski, A. F. K. Organski, Immanuel Wallerstein, and Joshua Goldstein argue that hegemonic decline causes major war. In this book, I argue that challenge causes major war but also that this challenge is only partially linked to economic decline. The relationship between relative economic decline and major war depends on other factors. Indeed, one example from the earlier chapters clearly disrupts this other view of the connection between economic decline and major war. It would be ridiculous to argue that Britain was experiencing a relative economic decline at the end of the eighteenth century, just as the Industrial Revolution was beginning. And, as noted above (and as Goldstein and others recognize), the Dutch did not really relinquish their economic position for more than fifty years after the War of the Spanish Succession. Only in the case of World War I would we find economic decline and challenge occurring simultaneously.

This is not to argue that relative economic decline and major war are completely unrelated. Relative economic decline and major war are sometimes related, but this depends on the nature of the other states competing economically with the liberal leader. This can be confirmed by considering the direction of capital flows in each of the wars of challenge. In the War of the Spanish Succession, the Napoleonic Wars, and World War II, capital flowed out of the liberal leader, for there were no other countries in the leader's alliance with capital abundance rivaling its own. Only in World War I was there another capital-abundant country from which the liberal leader could draw capital.

Does major war create a new liberal leader? Is this the only way liberal leaders can be created? Do all major wars create new liberal leaders? This model's interpretation of history presents a way for major war to create a new liberal leader, if liberal economic relations are disrupted and capital and international power are simultaneously concentrated in a country with a republican state. This situation occurred when the Thirty Years' War concentrated capital and international power in the Netherlands; it also occurred with World War I, when power and capital were concentrated in the United States (although American liberal leadership did not directly result from that war). In contrast, the War of the Spanish Succession ended Dutch leadership of a liberal subsystem without creating a new leader, so all major wars have not led to leadership transitions, and there is no theoretical reason to believe they should. The second question concerning the role of major war in creating hegemony is also challenged by the interpretation presented here. British liberal leadership first began in the 1780s, before the major wars against France. In fact, the Napoleonic Wars retarded British interests in opening international economic relations.

Finally, why do challengers always seem to lose? The interpretation presented here agrees with the consensus that challengers have always lost, but it goes a step farther by giving a reason for that result: challengers are driven by their political objectives to build a minimum-winning coalition, which is not likely to be durable since the challenger is seeking to expand at any other countries' expense. These factors drive challengers to undertake a high-risk, offensive strategy in major wars. In contrast, the liberal leader can construct a maximum-winning coalition, which may be quite durable given the number of other types of countries in the international system. Greater resources amassed through wide-reaching, stable alliances allow the liberal leader's coalition to use time to its own advantage, to marshal its forces, and then to pursue a strategy with a higher probability of success. When pitted against each other, the challenger's offensive strategy usually faces an attrition strategy, so the challenger must win quickly or face the liberal leader's slower, surer attack.

If one includes among the challenger's objectives in undertaking major war the destruction of liberal leadership, success has actually been achieved in two of the four major wars (the War of the Spanish Succession and World War I). The liberal leader's economic ascendance was retarded in another (the Napoleonic Wars). But in each case the expansionary challenger could not exploit the situation to its own advantage.

Finally, what does this model show us about hegemonic transitions? It shows that the transition from British to American leadership has been the only direct transition; the role of major wars has been disruptive to transitions in general rather than functional. In fact, there is no example of a smooth peaceful transition from one leadership of the liberal subsystem to another. This does not mean that such a transition could never occur. In fact, this model would lead us to argue that the United States is presently facing relative economic decline without political challenge—certainly a situation more conducive to peaceful transition or shared leadership than earlier liberal leaders ever faced. The question is whether the United States can relinquish some of its leadership and how much of that leadership role will be willingly accepted by other countries (the peaceful economic competitors). It is interesting to note that America's economic rivals seem to understand the need for responsible leadership and for continuing their own interests in such leadership. Discussions between the Americans and Japanese provide some indication of future relations between the United States as a declining liberal leader and Japan as the rising Pacific rival, but an actual transition to multilateral leadership remains to be worked out.

Investigating the Evolution of the International Political Economy

The arguments of this book underline the fact that our intellectual grasp of international relations can be enhanced by a deeper understanding of the interaction of political and economic factors, both between states and domestically. Although the international distribution of power remains a significant explanatory variable, other variables must also be taken into account. The model presented here explains why major wars are fought by incorporating different types of variable drawn from different levels of analysis. The model not only focuses on international power, as traditional theories such as balance of power models do, but also takes economic interests into account. Those economic interests are determined by countries' economic attributes but also by countries' domestic political systems. The model shows how domestic political institutions influence the sort of role countries play in the international political economy.

At the same time, the cases examined show that powerful countries can alter the environment they find themselves in. In the analysis of certain problems in international relations, it may be more useful to think of major powers as the countries able to transform the international system. Leading states are able to alter relations within subsystems. One country's actions influence the actions of other countries, which in turn lead to new characteristics for the international system. Countries can also transform the system by fighting wars; the major wars examined in this book radically altered the system, and in a variety of ways.

The arguments here suggest that there are many ways to analyze these major wars. For instance, Goldstein and others have uncovered certain patterns to these wars. Perhaps two of the more significant are declining length and growing severity. Obvious possible causes are improvements in technology and advances in states' abilities to mobilize resources. Yet the model presented here suggests that other factors, such as the composition of alliances, may be at play. The wars between the Dutch and Louis XIV's France, as well as the Napoleonic Wars, may have lasted so long because in both cases the liberal leader's alliance was unstable. This instability came from the low number of supporters in the international system in the early cases.

Of course, major wars transform the international system by altering the characteristics of existing states. Governments discredited by defeat are often replaced by new regimes. Because the liberal leader's alliance has defeated the challenger's alliance, and republican states have always sided with the liberal leaders, representative governments tend to survive major wars. Perhaps we could understand the success and spread of representative governments in the past few centuries through an analysis of the role of major wars, guided by arguments on alliance composition and likelihood of victory.

Information derived from this model could provide fresh insights on the evolution of the international political economy. Several authors have linked the evolution of the international system to cycles of price changes. Goldstein and others have attempted, with limited success, to tie long Kondratieff waves to cycles of international leadership. One major weakness is these scholars' inability to provide a testable argument for the process that might link these two cycles. This book's use of international trade theory suggests ways in which stronger links between Kondratieff waves and such leadership cycles might be found. I have argued that countries leading liberal international sub-systems are capital-abundant. Capital abundance drives the liberal leader's interest in expanding its position in the international economy. Changes in the direction of price waves (from inflation to deflation and vice versa) are important because they reverse the terms of trade between borrowers and lenders. When there is inflation, loans are easy to repay; when inflation ends and deflation begins, lenders may suddenly find fewer acceptable borrowers. Since peaks and troughs of price waves occur at slightly different times in different countries, lenders in one country may face incentives to expand their international loans, moving from market to market just ahead of the peaking price wave. Changes in the direction of prices could therefore focus lenders' attention on international markets. To test such an argument, unfortunately, we would need enormous amounts of data, such as the price movements of major commodities in several markets over long periods.

This book was written to address not only existing research agendas, which need to be synthesized and reconstructed as a whole, but also the failures of existing models of hegemony, hegemonic cycles, and major wars to capture and explain similarities without ignoring the richness of history. Previous efforts to identify patterns led to some oversimplifications of the history of the past three and a half centuries. I constructed this model in an effort not only to improve our understanding of the dynamics of liberal hegemony and major war but also to capture and harness the richness of history.

Index

Library of Congress Cataloging-in-Publication Data

Brawley, Mark R. (Mark Randal), 1960–
    Liberal leadership : great powers and their challengers in peace
and war / Mark R. Brawley.
       p.   cm.
    Includes bibliographical reerences and index.
    ISBN-0-8014-2808-4 (alk. paper)
    1. International relations.   2. Balance of power.
3. International economic relations.   I. Title.
JX1391.B663   1993
327′.09—dc20
93-4844